A Good Death

Published in 2019 by Murdoch Books, an imprint of Allen & Unwin

Copyright © 2019 Margaret Rice

Murdoch Books Australia
83 Alexander Street,
Crows Nest NSW 2065
Phone: +61 (0)2 8425 0100
murdochbooks.com.au
info@murdochbooks.com.au

Murdoch Books UK
Ormond House, 26–27 Boswell Street,
London WC1N 3JZ
Phone: +44 (0) 20 8785 5995
murdochbooks.co.uk
info@murdochbooks.co.uk

For corporate orders and custom publishing contact our business development team at salesenquiries@murdochbooks.com.au

ISBN 978 1 76063 777 4 Australia
ISBN 978 1 91163 214 6 UK

A catalogue record for this book is available from the National Library of Australia

A catalogue record for this book is available from the British Library

Cover design by Design By Committee
Printed and bound in Australia by Griffin Press

10 9 8 7 6 5 4 3 2 1

A Good Death

A compassionate and practical guide to prepare for the end of life

MARGARET RICE

MURDOCH BOOKS

SYDNEY · LONDON

Contents

PART 01

BEING THERE FOR SOMEONE WHO IS DYING

PART 02

WHEN YOUR OWN TIME COMES

To Mum, Jeanette Marie Rice,
whose question led to this book.

Introduction

Some years ago, I sat at my mother's bedside as she lay dying. My siblings and I were all well-educated people, but I realised we knew nothing about the experience that we as a family were just about to confront.

We had many questions.

Can we predict when someone is likely to die? (Is that even a fair question?) Is there a process that we'll be able to recognise, a set of events, a particular order of events? And just exactly what will happen?

How do we work with the medical experts? How do we deal with the non-medical issues that will come up? Is morphine used to nudge death along or is this just a myth? How does the idea of assisted death fit in with personal, lived experiences?

These questions, some of them seemingly minor, have a very big impact on the dying person and their family and friends, and how they will manage their fears. Having a little information can help a lot. But as my mother lay dying, such questions felt too simple for the busy experts, too biological for counsellors and too broad for the doctors and nurses grappling with her immediate situation. I wished I'd been a little bit more curious before her life reached this particular phase, this time of ending.

We were typical of many people today, facing the death of someone really close for the first time as adults in their late forties and early fifties, although I was later to meet people who hadn't had a close experience of death until they were even older.

You're reading a gentle, practical guide to dying.

We live in a culture that is often described as 'death denying'. Youthfulness is idolised; the elderly are neglected. But we don't have to be this way. Let's take a step in a different direction, towards understanding what we'll face, so that we can help others around us die a better death. In turn, the knowledge we gain and the experiences we have will help us when our own time comes.

Once upon a time, our involvement with death was much more immediate. When our great-grandmothers were children they watched and listened when a death occurred, little observers of their household's dramas and rituals, an experience that was often repeated. They learned unconsciously.

They grew up knowing what it is to have someone they love die, to grieve them, mourn them, then bury them – all from their own or another family member's house.

But theirs was the last generation to grow up with such a close knowledge of death, before it was outsourced.

Today in a thousand different ways we are lucky this has changed. Infant mortality rates have dropped, death from infectious diseases is low and, at least for affluent people in the West, we are pushing death from old age right back. So now it is reasonable for many people to expect to live beyond 80, and increasing numbers are reaching a century. But of course, death is always present. Some will die early from cancers, accidents and a range of chronic illnesses.

So we have to do two things at once. Prepare as though we will live to be 100, and also prepare as though we won't, since we don't know for sure which of these two ends we will have.

This means changing from denying death ourselves to acknowledging in a more practical way than most of us currently do, that we will die. We don't want to be morbid and obsessed with death, but we need to know how to meet it.

When Mum was dying she asked, 'Why?' And that catapulted me into interviews and reflections, in an attempt to learn more. So after Mum's death I started listening to and gathering the everyday stories of people who had experienced the death of someone they love. I'm a journalist and a grandmother. I like to mix sleuthing to find answers to difficult questions with enjoying the company of people – including little ones – and a good cup of tea.

Shortly after I started work on this task, my brother Julian's sudden and unexpected death in a motorcycle accident drew me further into an exploration of grief and how we manage this terrible thing called death. Interviews soothed me, kept me going, as I struggled with my double load of grief.

The stories I heard were profoundly moving – but also full of clues to what people need today. After further research, I realised that themes were emerging. I talked to experts and did a lot of reading, which I then distilled. But I noticed that some of the most helpful information came from those who were giving simple support to their own communities. This tells us something important – what we learn from experts and outsiders, we can feel confident about adapting and changing to suit ourselves and our own people. As you use this guide, keep that in mind.

We can regain the sense generations of our ancestors had, that they could help each other, those close by, to make a good death, at least in those circumstances where death didn't occur suddenly and violently, say as the result of an accident. And even in those circumstances, we can learn to be more effective.

Death is awful. We should never get used to it. We should keep looking for cures for cancers and defying other diseases. We should keep making our drivers safer and challenging the acceptability of war. We should keep doggedly searching for ways to lead people into a rich life, so that suicidal ideas are never shaped. We don't have to romanticise death – and I certainly don't want to.

I've distilled my experiences and thoughts into eleven practical steps, corresponding to the eleven chapters in this book. You can work with these steps, then build on them to make the experience of death better.

A guide to death in eleven ancient woodcuts

It was summer in London and an unseasonably hot one. I was far away from home, but the grass in Kew Gardens had an Aussie-brown tinge to it, suggesting Melbourne in a heatwave, not England. And then a Sydney-style storm raged, so I slept to the familiar sound of the intense pounding of rain.

I was here for a wedding but I allowed myself to be diverted. I was eager to see an etching of the *ars moriendi* – the treatise on the art of dying well that had captured my imagination, so I popped in to see them at the British Museum.

The *ars moriendi* consists of eleven woodcut pictures. It first became popular in Europe in the fourteenth century, the woodcuts copied onto fabrics. At a time when most people couldn't read or write, these images, not words, carried the weight of meaning.

By the fifteenth century, following a period of religious chaos and plague, *ars moriendi* were extremely popular. From Ireland to the Persian Gulf, the plague had devastated the land, killing 60 per cent of some towns' populations. Priests were particularly vulnerable because they performed funeral rites, and as the plague progressed, many died, while others fled, too terrified to attend deathbeds.

Until that point in Christian European civilisation, priests would guide the dying, supervising the acknowledgement of sins and penance that were considered essential to gain entry into Heaven. But because of plague they weren't there. Desperate times called for desperate action. Inspired by earlier ideas of teaching with woodcuts, churchmen came up with the *ars moriendi*. These could be handed from person to person without a priest's involvement, a way of spreading a message quickly and accurately but keeping safe the clerics and lay people who passed these messages along.

I'd first read about the *ars moriendi* in the Nursing Library of Sydney University. This is a place I spent quite a bit of time in, reading to find out whether Mum's death could have been handled differently – and better. Now, at the British Museum, having been directed by the librarians up the stairs and through the door behind 'the Michelangelo cartoon', I was struck by a few things about those etchings.

They were short and sharp; there were no words. Each woodcut's vivid communication is like an Instagram post. (Everything old is new again!)

Five woodcuts illustrate what their medieval makers saw as sins relevant to death: loss of faith, despair, impatience, arrogance and avarice. Another five illustrate the strengths and inspirations we need to overcome these negatives: reaffirmation of faith, hope, patience, humility and unselfishness. The eleventh woodcut illustrates the triumph of the dying sinner, using these.

On one level, these pictures and their medieval worldview are simply not appropriate for our time. But I felt there was something about them that would be worth returning to today.

It struck me that in medieval times, the person holding the *ars moriendi* was not the carer, but the dying person themselves. The dying person handled each picture and looked closely at it. They were doing it for themselves, authors of their own destiny.

It seems to me that in gaining something as powerful and far-reaching as the printed word, we have lost simple, helpful tools like the *ars moriendi* – little prompts of wisdom to help us as we die. But we can get them back.

It's time to make a new set of woodcuts – a set that doesn't quake in fear of offending a hard and punitive God, but instead can set us free to have a better death, with all the assets and resources that are available to us today.

Here's today's set:

First, we learn how to accompany someone who is dying, rather than being afraid of them and their death.

Second, we learn about the non-physical side to death, including spiritual (but not necessarily religious) experiences that transform a human life into something extraordinary.

Third, we learn how to eliminate pain, because pain can prevent a good death.

Fourth, we learn what death looks like, so we are able to face the death of those we love without being afraid of what we do not know.

Fifth, we learn the 'housework' required after death – what's needed and what's not, so we can let go of the person honourably.

Sixth, we develop the skills, particularly the social ones, to help when a death is unexpected.

Seventh, we learn how to say goodbye. We strip away dross, to say our own authentic goodbye – so we discard and recycle, sometimes going back to the ancient, sometimes moving away from it.

Eighth, we find new ways to reach out when grief strikes – for the sake of others and also for ourselves.

Ninth, we plan ahead, taking what we've learnt and applying practical steps, to help ourselves and to help others.

Tenth, we visualise, well before we need to, where we want to die so that this becomes reality.

Eleventh, we learn to talk about how we will die, because using words will show others what we want and also dispel fear – our fear and that of others.

PART **01**

BEING THERE FOR SOMEONE WHO IS DYING

CHAPTER 01

Companioning the dying

We learn how to companion someone who is dying, rather than being afraid of them and their death.

Companioning is an old-fashioned word. For me it conjures someone quietly supporting another. It comes from the Latin for bread and was used in old French to mean 'breaking bread together'. There was a time when it was used to describe a person, usually a woman, either connected through family or paid, who was well bred but retained as the subordinate of a wealthier, usually older person. There is strong evidence that most of us are comforted and our fears quelled by having someone with us as we die. We're talking about someone who could be family, but not necessarily, whose role it is to be with the person until they die. To be the person who holds their hand, metaphorically and literally. This is a place at the deathbed that's been devalued, but it's time to restore its value.

Lighting lanterns for each other

Over the six months from the diagnosis of my mother's cancer until her death, there was plenty of time to think about – and dread – what was coming. I was working as a local newspaper reporter and despite my increasingly eccentric story ideas, my editor, David, remained supportive and a good listener. I wondered out loud to him how we were going to send Mum off in a way that she deserved.

'I'm nervous we won't be able to keep it together for Mum's sake,' I mused.

I expected him to be dismissive, the way I would have been until now, before I had any concept of parental loss.

'It's strange but you'll know what to do, somehow you'll pull together,' he said.

His comment clearly came from deep knowledge.

'My Mum died a few years ago. She was 62. She was planting seedlings in her front garden in Adelaide when she collapsed. The doctor told us she was probably dead by the time her head hit the ground, it was so quick. A neighbour discovered her.'

Her death was later attributed to a sudden and acute mitral valve rupture.

David talked about how he and his two brothers gathered at their mother's home in a shocked and dream-like state. I saw a vivid picture; three bewildered, until now carefree young men in their early thirties struggling with the news that their vibrant and youthful mother was dead.

'We're all so different, and we were all so young and self-absorbed. But instinct kicked in. We all came together and stayed in her house and we all did different jobs. We seemed to naturally gravitate towards different tasks, each doing things that suited our personality. There wasn't a moment of ill-will in the whole of the time we were there. The house was in total chaos and it was a mess but towards the end we all got in and cleaned it up, without having to say a word to each other.'

As Mum's death drew closer my childhood friend Catherine, who now lived on a farming property in country New South Wales, started making regular phone calls.

Her father had died a year before. Catherine is one of ten children, nine still living.

'We all came together at Dad's bedside. There's a strange way in which we pulled together.'

She was echoing what David had said.

A little later I caught up for lunch with my friend Susan W, who had trained with me as a young journalist. Our lives had taken very different courses and then had pulled back into alignment. We both had elderly mothers who were not well and fathers who, although frail, were still alive. We found ourselves confronting the same experience.

We agreed no one had told us about this part of the life script – that the stories about parents dying (not the fact of, but the 'how') hadn't been shared with us, weren't in the public domain.

Only three months after that lunch, I got a phone call from Susan saying her mother, Shirley, had died. I was stunned. My mother was the one with the terminal illness.

After Shirley's funeral Susan and I spoke frequently, particularly as Mum's death edged closer. Susan wasn't ready to tuck her grief away into a secret space and get on with living. We were a good fit for each other.

She sent me a link to a Buddhist guide to the stages of dying. By way of warning, she shared a painful truth: 'I didn't quite realise Mum was dying or maybe I couldn't admit it and so, at the end, I felt as though she just suddenly slipped away.'

Susan also shared the details of the sequence of Shirley's death, something unusual for people to discuss.

I had lunch with another friend, Sheila, about the same time.

'We didn't realise the significance of the morphine, when it was prescribed for my dying mother,' she warned.

'That was the beginning of the end,' Sheila said. 'If we'd known that, we might have reacted a bit differently, might have been a bit more focused.'

Another friend, Virginia, was an only child and, like Susan, had to do the vigil beside her mother's bed alone.

Virginia and I were both raised as Catholics. She used a religious simile to help me understand the emotional impact of the vigil our family would soon face: 'It will be the garden of Gethsemane, both yours and your mother's.'

She added: 'There's something no one told me when I sat with my mum while she was dying. There will come a point where she won't be able to swallow and her mouth and lips will get very dry. Ask the nurses to show you how to dampen your mother's mouth and keep it moist. No one told me about that.'

There was a lot of regret in Virginia's painfully acquired wisdom. Like Susan, she was upset by what she hadn't done, and overwhelmed by what she hadn't been able to achieve.

Their pain was so similar that I wondered whether there is an extra dimension to the burden when the deathbed vigil happens alone. Although Virginia did qualify this: 'I was alone for some of the time but my children joined me one by one. They were wonderful, but she was not their mother, she was no one else's mother but mine. So I was in essence alone.'

As my friends shared the painful experiences of their parents' deaths, they were building the platform from which I would walk to my mother's. It was as if each friend who opened up about their experience was initiating me into a stoical, usually silent and secret society.

I felt I was standing at the bottom of a hill in complete darkness and little lanterns were beginning to light my way.

So here's something worth considering when you are in the same situation. People are largely reluctant to talk about death in our culture, so they don't tend to share their experiences very much unless asked. This means you could be surrounded by more people than you realise, who can support you by sharing stories of their experiences.

If you are supporting someone you love who is dying, don't be afraid to tell people at least this simple fact. Many will merely share a friendly gesture or concerned look in response. But there will be those who will go further, and share a personal experience.

This could be the beginning of a very helpful and powerful conversation.

Putting family at the centre

Companions can make death better, for a number of reasons, not least because they care, bear witness and can act as advocates. Although there will be circumstances where someone will be paid to do the work of deathbed companions, as a general principle, family are the ones who will do this best.

Of the many definitions and descriptions of family, this one feels like the best: 'Those who are closest to the patient in knowledge, care and affection. This may include the biological family, the family of acquisition – related by marriage or contract – and the family and friends of choice.' This is the definition used by the Australian Commission on Safety and Quality in Health Care, in its National Consensus Statement of 2015.

These important people can make death better and here's why.

'Because I'm a midwife as well, I basically see both ends of the spectrum,' explained homecare and palliative care nurse, Sue Pullar.

'I don't see death as a negative. If I can help somebody have a beautiful death I find that just as rewarding as bringing a baby into the world, so I'm not frightened of death,' she explained.

I could see what she meant, although it would never have occurred to me before now. Sitting with Mum as she died I had learnt so much.

Like Sue, I'd been struck by parallels between birth and death. For example even at a trivial level, there are two double-barrelled expressions used – Braxton Hicks contractions, which can fake a real labour, and Cheyne-Stokes breathing, the uneven breathing at the end of life.

And then there's the waiting, the coming together of family, the fact that both birth and death can be short or long, the fact that even though the medical system plays a major role, these rites of passage long predate theory and learning, the fact that each birth or death can be utterly different from the other, that each is so completely unique.

'So what's a bad death?'

'It's instantly recognisable,' Sue pointed out. 'It's a long, protracted uncomfortable one, which is distressing for the patient and for the family. I mean obviously death is distressing but it's additionally distressing because of the agony and the discomfort he or she is in.'

Does it happen much? Sometimes, it's difficult to judge objectively. Sadly, it happens too often.

So what's a good death?

Sue conceded no one's ever come back from the grave to tell us. But she said there are indicators that death can be made 'good'.

'Difficult as death is, it can be a positive experience for everyone concerned, if it is managed with care, skill and sensitivity – even for the person who is dying. From a nursing point of view, it's all about comfort and it's also, to some extent, about balancing the needs of the family as well as the patient's, making that person feel comfortable and the people around them feel comfortable. I believe all deaths can be managed well,' she said.

Was Sue too close to death? When I later put her proposition to other friends, they were doubtful.

'How could there possibly be anything good about it? Surely that's just the point of view of professionals,' said Marilyn.

It was as though she was speaking for the Everyman, the person outside the 'death' fraternity.

But there were others, not just professionals like Sue, who also described a death they had experienced in a positive way, people who had no connection to the medical or caring professions at all. Others noted that the focus is not on 'death' when pain and suffering are over, but on 'dying' and as good a dying as possible.

Ann-Mari was with her husband Jos as he died of liver cancer some years ago. With the support of a hospice and its home-based palliative care service in Canberra, she and their children were able to nurse him at home, with the palliative care team members calling in frequently to advise and support them.

When Jos was dying, the period from diagnosis to death occurred with lightning speed: three months. Ann-Mari lost him very quickly.

'Every time the palliative care service told me about something I might need I said, "Oh we don't need that yet," and sure enough, the next day we did. They gave me a prescription for morphine as it was too dangerous for them to travel with it. I hid it in a high cupboard and felt relieved by their assurance that they could come quickly to my home to administer it any time of the day or night as my main fear was that Jos would be in pain. In the end, we only needed to use morphine in the 48 hours before he died. He never regained consciousness after it was administered.

'Our four children came home the week before he died to be with him. Each one contributed to his care and the planning of his funeral in their own special way. This made these days very special for us and helped us cope with the grief that followed. I am so grateful to the wonderful nurses who enabled him to die in the home he loved with his family around him.

'His death was wonderful. It's an experience I wouldn't have missed for the world. I was so glad we had the opportunity to be part of it,' she said.

What do other professionals think? I went to the Sacred Heart Health Services hospice in inner-city Sydney. The Nurse Manager at the time, Adam Whitby, who now works in palliative care in Darwin, sat talking in his busy office, while he juggled the day-to-day demands of rostering staff and coordinating care. He described what he thought a good death was.

'A good death, from my point of view, is one where the person who's dying is pain free and is at peace with their life,' Adam said.

'Overall they are comfortable and have some dignity. Unfortunately, it doesn't always happen,' he said.

He believes this is largely because the benefits of the specialty 'palliative care' are still poorly understood.

(In this book I will talk about two things that are quite different but might sound the same – 'palliative care', which occurs over a long period after diagnosis, sometimes many years, and 'end-of-life care', which happens at the very end, when death is very close.)

The modern palliative care movement has its origins in Britain, where it was pioneered by Dame Cicely Saunders. A nurse, social worker and doctor, Dame Cicely observed that in the modern hospital, a disease can be cured while the person is overlooked.

This is not much of an issue when everything goes to plan and the patient walks out the door to resume their life where they had left it. But it's a disaster when the hospital 'fails', the disease is not conquered and death is the outcome.

Dame Cicely lobbied and advocated for the preservation of a certain style of hospital care to focus solely on dealing with the needs and suffering of the dying, in fact a return to an ancient one. As a result, the modern hospice movement spread throughout the world, designed to fulfil the centuries-old tradition of offering comfort and solace to the dying. It has continued to evolve and expand ever since.

I went to see the Chair of Cancer Nursing at the University of Sydney's Nursing School, Professor Kate White, based at Royal Prince Alfred Hospital. Just as Adam had been, she was eager to shed light on the realities of palliative care and all it can offer.

I was now beginning to notice a pattern in the attitudes and compassion of those working in palliative care. Kate, like others working in the field, had a remarkable lightness of touch, a softness and preparedness to listen. In addition they each had a paradoxical cheerfulness and joy about them. I now believe this comes from their profound connection to the life cycle.

Kate's responses to questions about a good death were slightly more ethereal than Adam's.

'It's when you walk into a room and someone's dying or has just died and there's a sense of peace and warmth around them, and it feels good,' she said. 'When it feels cold, lonely and sterile, you kind of think of it as bad.'

She agreed with Adam's and Sue's assessments that a death can be made good by those working with the person dying, and explained how.

'I think it's first of all, about asking the patient what they want. How do they want to die and what's important to them at that time, who do they want to have around them, do they want people around them at all? Most people do, but you can't assume that, I think you have to ask. So it's what they want,' she said.

'Obviously the relief of physical symptoms is paramount, but there's more to it. Because if the dying person is suffering physical pain or some other physical symptom it's a distraction from being able to do the things that are important to them, which is, to be with family at some level.

'So to me it's making sure we put certain things in place. From a health professional's point of view and from a nurse's point of view, I see it very much around dignity, in its broadest terms.

'So there are obviously the physical aspects of this, that someone is always cared for in a very appropriate way, that their privacy, and the family's right to privacy, are maintained. But there's also that dignity of soul, which to me is where we provide care that's cognisant with the values of the individual.'

'Dignity of the soul' – what a beautiful expression.

'For someone from the country and a bit of a bloke what gives him dignity may be very different to what gives dignity to a 65-year-old city woman of Jewish background. The things that are important to her are quite different to the things that are important to him. So it's about finding those things out, those core elements.

'I remember one of the patients I looked after, she'd say to me, "Just make sure my lipstick's on, Kate."'

When I told her Marilyn's reaction she said she could see why people ask how any death could be good. Professionals working in the area need to be careful about using the term too glibly, she agreed.

'So I think a good death is possible but I think we've got to be careful what we mean by it. Actually I think it's really about "as good a dying as possible",' she said.

Kate told a story that acknowledged that no matter how good an experience of death can be made by nurses and palliative carers, stepping beyond the person dying, into the world of those who they leave behind can be tragic.

Her story involved looking after a young mother, who was dying of cancer. Kate had been determined to dignify her dying wish, which was to die at home.

'She was young, she died six weeks after the birth of her fourth child and as I looked at that family and I looked at her I remember thinking to myself, "How incredibly arrogant of us to say we've maintained her quality of life."'

That 'quality of life' was a hospital-based metric, ticking a lot of professional boxes. But the reality was, she would soon die.

'All we've done is made her physically comfortable and hopefully we've given some emotional support to her and her family. But the reality is she died a young mum and she had to say goodbye to her husband and four children and incredibly loving extended families on both sides. And they had to say goodbye to their mum.

'For all that, her death was a good death.

'In amongst all this tragedy, this openly grieving family, there was so much love. She died surrounded by her family including her new baby. Her children were in and out of the room and sometimes you could hear their voices in the front yard playing. Her extended families on both sides were there, her husband was lying beside her and it was incredibly peaceful and incredibly dignified.'

People, companions, family, life. The haunting yet soothing image of children playing while this terrible scene played out.

Nothing consoles us. Nothing in this circumstance makes it okay that she died. But at least having the right people around her softened it and made it better, not just for her, but hopefully for the adults and those little people left behind.

How to be there for someone who is dying

The two things the dying fear most are pain and abandonment, according to US palliative care nurse Joy Ufema when she was reflecting on what she had learnt over a long career with the dying. Since we are social beings, this makes perfect sense.

Today there has been a revolution in the attitude towards people at the bedside of the dying, taking us right back to centuries of life experience that pre-dated modern hospitals.

Before the medical science and technology we have today, if people didn't die in the field where they worked, they went home. Once upon a time the cause of disease couldn't be differentiated.

No one focused too much on trying to diagnose what was going on – people would simply gather and pray.

Men died at war, women died in childbirth. The two most common groups to die at home were the elderly and babies. The women of the household, no matter how small or humble their abode was, attended to the familiar experiences and the rituals of dying and preparation for burial, practices they had observed and learnt themselves from the time they were small children and watched as others died around them.

Hospices were originally places in medieval Europe where pilgrims (often terminally ill) rested. These were located close to holy places, such as shrines and churches. The pilgrims received spiritual succour and hospitality from the nuns and other holy people who ran them, in close proximity to the deities they revered. The pilgrims often died there.

At Canterbury in England today, you can still see the doorway to one of the early hospices, in the shadows of that city's great cathedral, where pilgrims travelled from all over England to receive religious grace, something they were often keen to do when they were ill because they knew death was approaching.

I've been describing the Christian experience, but hospices existed all over the world. In China, the hospices of the old days, with the care house above and the animals housed below, are depicted in ancient art, which still survives.

The challenges to old notions about how we should die keep coming – and this is a good thing.

Are you the only one who is supporting the dying person? Maybe, for example, you are an only child who is supporting a dying parent? Make sure you have people you can trust who you can talk to.

Supporters can come from outside the family and this role is expanding. Many palliative care teams welcome volunteers who are prepared to give their time to sit at the bedside of the dying. This is because it is widely acknowledged that the volunteers can give something that the professionals can't: time.

More on the role of family and friends at the bedside

Michael Barbato is a palliative care specialist who has written extensively about the end of life. He runs workshops to teach people how to 'midwife the dying'.

I'd heard that expression before. In Mum's nursing home the leisure officer was particularly attuned to the needs of the dying and had developed what appeared to be an uncanny sense of when a person in the home would die. Unofficially, she supported those who were dying but had no family or friends to sit with them as they died.

'I'm a midwife to the dying. There are very few people who don't want someone with them when they are dying. I sit with them when they've got no one and I see it as a sacred privilege,' she said.

Michael nodded when I told him about this. 'The role is also called the *amicus mortis*, the friend of the dying,' he said. 'The *amicus mortis* doesn't have to be a professional palliative carer.

'In fact, it's a role we should reclaim from professionals. Back in 1969 when Elisabeth Kübler-Ross published *On Death and Dying*, she told a story against herself about a tea lady.

'Kübler-Ross often spoke of how she got very upset at a time early in her career because when people were dying under her care, the families didn't call her. Instead they wanted the tea lady there. So she confronted this woman one day and said: "Why do they call you when I'm the expert?"' The woman replied, "Death is an old friend,"' Michael said.

The tea lady had seen many people die and was able to *be present* to those who sought her out. The privileged role of being present for the dying doesn't need to be delegated to someone who has special skills.

Someone who knows and loves the dying person trumps the presence of others, irrespective of how skilled that other person may be.

'If the person dies pain-free, surrounded by family who see their loved one die in a way compatible with what the dying person wanted, then you couldn't ask for anything more,' said Michael.

Shelley was the person in her family who companioned her mother Rita as she died. It was a task that evolved naturally because when Shelley's mother and father moved to Queensland, Shelley lived closest to them. In the last years of her life, Rita lived quite close by.

Shelley wonders whether there were other inner forces at play, besides just proximity. When she was fifteen, she overheard her father say to her mother after Shelley had argued with her mother: 'Let it go. She's only here under sufferance anyway.'

'I sometimes wonder whether hearing that made me think, at some unconscious level I had to be there for them, especially Mum, for the rest of her life, maybe to prove that I *could* be caring. It's a comment I still remember and I wonder whether somehow it's shaped who I am.

'Being with Mum on that journey to her death was a hard road to walk, but I'm glad I did it.'

Shelley companioned her mother, but others are taking an even more active role at the deathbeds of those they love.

This means reclaiming dormant skills: managing the death of someone we love ourselves, reversing the usual psychology and inviting professionals to take part, rather than the other way around, where the palliative care expert invites the family member in.

Although we have to acknowledge this is complex, as in the case of Rita. At the end of her life, Rita was fed through a tube, had lost her mobility and depended on others for her showering and toileting.

'While she did not say it in a clearly constructed sentence, which would voice a good and clear train of thought, I knew, and the doctor and care staff knew, what she wanted,' said Shelley.

This was, that Rita did not want to live totally dependent and in psychological pain. Shelley knows the outcome was inevitable, but she still wonders about the decision to remove Rita's feeding tube through the abdominal wall into the stomach (percutaneous endoscopic gastrostomy, shortened to PEG).

'While Mum didn't have dementia, her brain was in a fog caused by pain, anxiety, medication for the pain and anxiety, exhaustion, et cetera, so I wonder how that clouded her thinking and whether

her mind was all that clear after all when she agreed to the ceasing of the PEG feed.'

This said, Shelley believes stopping the PEG feeding was the right decision, since Rita had communicated her physical discomfort and anxiety about this earlier.

'Mum had indicated so often that she did not want to live like this any more but I suspect that moral and religious beliefs may have interfered with Mum asking outright and sooner for the PEG to be ceased, along with other more obvious things like ceasing medications,' Shelley said.

'Mum didn't have diagnosed dementia and she still was able to make meaning and to speak with meaning when she did speak – less and less – or was spoken with, as she did in this case a month or so before she died. Mum had the ability and power to make her own decision here and she was "empowered" by the doctor to have the last word, so to speak.'

Obviously, we have to respect the safeguards that have built up over time to ensure there is no suspicious cause for a death, even when the reporting and certification involved seems intrusive.

Irrespective of where the death takes place, you can take an even more active role than simply being present. If a companion is someone to 'be with', a midwife is actively involved. You can be the person who does this.

You don't need to have all the knowledge, but you can access the knowledge, explained Michael Barbato. Taking more control ourselves has centuries of precedent, since people midwifed death until as recently as 100 years ago, when most people died at home, without the involvement of professionals.

If you want to, it is worthwhile for families to rearrange their schedules, no matter how busy, to be with the dying. Not only is this recommended for the sake of the dying person but also for those doing the sitting. There is a role for everyone, the companion, the professional doula, the palliative care professionals such as nurses and doctors – and the family.

To be present for the death of someone you love is an extraordinary experience and it will teach you more about life, something Shelley's experience reveals: 'It had a profound spiritual impact on me.'

And no professional associated with dying would discourage your presence, since, as common sense suggests, no matter how many professionals can be gathered together, the most important people at the bedside, in the end, are the family.

However, a word of caution here: We have the romantic notion that the family is the unit that nurtures us and protects us the most. In reality, it is the unit that can also cause us the greatest suffering. This needs to be acknowledged.

If someone is dying in a place other than a private home, despite the nursing staff's best intentions, they have commitments to many patients not just one and this makes it difficult to focus on one individual, so family being present can be important.

You are also entitled to create an environment of peace and support for someone who is dying. This involves, for example, collecting around them the music the dying person wants to listen to, having their favourite style of pot plants around them and wall hangings, photos or pictures they love.

Family and close friends will recognise what the patient would like to have around them more than professionals will, so this alone makes them important.

The role of family when someone close to them is dying is to be imaginative. What does this person need, what do they want to hear, and who do they want to see? What's going to help them to be able to let go of life?

Is there a right or wrong size of family groups who want to say goodbye at a death bed? Unlike an acute care hospital setting, the patient does not need rest and quiet time so they can recover. They need the opportunity to be with those they love.

In respectful environments, judgements will not be made about whether your family group is too large or too small and how your family is constructed. Professional staff recognise that this is not their concern, particularly if it provides comfort to the dying person and as long as it is not having an impact on other patients.

Why shouldn't many family members say goodbye at the same time, if that's the way your family wants to do it?

'Sometimes you walk in and you see this family around the dying person and you can just feel the love holding the person there,' Kate White said.

Kate said she has no proof for it, but nonetheless, has a strong feeling that these patients often take longer to die.

'When the family asks, "Why are they still here, we can't believe it", I often say to them, "Look, you've all got to say goodbye to that one person. He's got to let go of all of you. It's a much bigger job, it'll take a bit longer."

'We don't know what's going on inside the heads of the dying person. But I do think sometimes it's hard to die when all that love is in the room holding you there, I really do.'

How to be a more effective companion

These are some simple things you can do when you are sitting at the bedside of someone who is dying. None of these suggestions requires any particular skill. None will interfere with the care being given by professionals and none will cause any risk to the dying patient.

- Talk to the patient, read their favourite works to them, sing to them. The sense of hearing is the last sense the dying lose.

- At other times be prepared to sit in silence. It's a time when we reverse the idea 'don't just sit there, do something' to 'don't do something, just sit there'.

- Listen. The dying person may say things that appear not to make any sense, but they may be speaking in metaphors. For the dying person the place of dreams and reality, the present and the past are merging. They may be seeing and want to talk about friends, relatives who are long dead. Listen and support them while they do this.

Encourage life review, if this is what the dying person wants. Life review is a verbal reflection by the dying patient, sometimes quite long. While some dying people have resolved the question, 'What meaning did my life have?', others have not – until now.

Talk among yourselves. Don't whisper, but talk to your family member in a normal voice. Even though the patient may not be able to understand what you are saying, they will recognise your voices and then feel that they're not alone. They will enjoy listening to their family and friends around them, just as they did when they were conscious but too ill to be part of the conversation.

   🍃 Moisten the mouth. At the very end, dying people have no thirst or appetite because they have lost the need to eat and drink as their bodies begin to shut down. But they might be bothered by having a dry mouth. It is common for the dying to have long strings of saliva forming in their mouth, at the end stage, caused by not drinking. Use cotton wool swabs dipped in water to clean their mouth. Get underneath the tongue, and to the back of the cheeks to freshen the mouth up. This can be done every fifteen minutes. You might also want to apply soothing mouth gels with a fresh mint taste. This is done not just for the comfort of the dying but for your comfort, since it gives you permission to touch and have physical contact with the dying.

   🍃 Comb their hair. Do this especially if they were fond of this when they were conscious.

   🍃 If the patient is in a nursing home or hospital, make way for nurses to move the dying person at least every four hours, until unconscious, to avoid the development of pressure sores. This condition can cause unnecessary pain to a patient who is no longer able to explain the source of their pain, and can be mistaken for agitation. If you are looking after the dying person at home, ensure this lifting and movement occurs at least every four hours.

By being involved with the dying patient's comfort, your family can feel you have provided real care and this will help you with your bereavement.

People often don't realise that as someone gets closer to death they stop being able to digest food and don't actually need it. This can be distressing for relatives and friends who worry that the dying person could be hungry or thirsty, when in fact they are not.

Yet the impulse of the family to provide the dying person with food is often very powerful. They want to see Mum or Dad eating because food is one of the basic things of life. But giving somebody at the end stage of life food, even a small amount, isn't actually going to be effective.

The same applies to liquids. A dying person will reach the stage when they are no longer able to absorb any more fluids as their organs are beginning to shut down. At this point, death is closer, since a person can only live up to a week without water.

Once the dying person stops taking fluids, their skin will start to become waxy and lose its suppleness.

Close to death, the dying person will be unable to regulate their body temperature, so can become very hot or very cold, regardless of the weather. Circulation to hands and feet begins to shut down, while blood supply is diverted to major organs, so hands and feet can develop a bluish hue.

Frequently people experience agitation close to death. Hopefully this will be brief, if it is experienced at all. Managing the patient's anxieties about death in the early stages of dying can help reduce agitation, and medications can help too.

Often families want to be with the person as they die, so they want to be called for that moment. But since the exact timing of the death is difficult to predict, staff will be reluctant to attempt any predictions at all.

Staff are often asked, 'What are the signs we should be looking for?' Most of them are not precise indicators, and they are really only present in the last few weeks or days of life.

If the dying patient has a really strong pulse, it's probably okay to go and have a cup of tea, or go home to have a shower.

But when someone's pulse is really thready and irregular, their heart is starting to struggle and is likely to stop. That said, staff will rarely rely on just one sign.

When a death rattle occurs, this can be very frightening for family and friends sitting with the patient, but the dying person is not aware of it. It is caused as air passes secretions in the throat as the dying person breathes in and out. Normally, a person would cough these secretions away but this is not possible because the cough reflex is lost as death approaches. Changing the patient's position may occasionally stop this noise.

Cheyne-Stokes breathing may be experienced, even a few days before death, when the breathing patterns become unusual and breathing appears to stop for short periods of time.

Doctors now believe that as death nears, the dying person will lose their perception of taste and smell early, then the sense of pain and tactile sensation and then the last sense to go will be hearing.

The good news is that even though those patients dying in these ways are often still aware until the end – even if they are unconscious – specialists who have spent most of their professional lives nursing and administering to the dying believe that, although some will, a large number of the dying will not suffer very much physical pain in this late stage. However, the qualifier has to be added that unconsciousness is still poorly understood.

Conflict management

Tensions can arise over issues that appear small to others but are important to the family. To expect everything to be joy and light as you are with someone who is dying is not realistic.

Denise is one of three sisters. Her sisters wanted to restrict access to their mother as she was dying, to immediate family only. But Denise did not agree.

'I spent more time with Mum than the others. I noticed that if a person arrived who Mum hadn't particularly liked, Mum would stay asleep. But if she loved them she would become alert.

'I realised Mum was actually completely in control of her relationships and how she was dealing with them, even though she was dying. If someone asked my sisters if they could visit, often they'd discourage them but if they asked me, because of this awareness, I encouraged everyone. It created enormous tension between my sisters and me, but the nursing staff agreed that even though Mum was barely conscious, she was managing the situation herself and they saw that as her right.'

The death of a parent often results in a change in the relationship between the children. Sometimes siblings no longer feel as close to each other, or experience the death of a parent as an opportunity to redefine themselves in relation to the family. This process can be felt intensely at the time of the death, even in (especially in) those adult children who are of advanced age themselves. Tensions can also be exacerbated if one of the siblings has been given a role in end-of-life decision-making and others have not.

Tensions can also surface because of resentments over what is likely to be in a parent's will.

The realistic goal isn't to eliminate conflict but to find a way of managing it. For most of us, we can apply workplace conflict management skills, since the workplace is a more familiar environment than the deathbed. The same capacity to think objectively is required. For example, you could think about this list by Lee Jay Berman, which he has published at www.mediationtools. com/articles/conflictres.html:

- Stay calm.

- Listen to understand.

- Accentuate the positive.

- State your case tactfully.

- Attack the problem, not the person.

- Avoid the blame game.

- Focus on the future, not the past.

In the case of the dying person themselves, when the first *ars moriendi* were created, eliminating conflict and making peace with others was an important part of the contrition for sins, which was considered essential for the repentance needed for the soul to be pure enough to enter Heaven. And those gremlins and goblins that were always sketched under the bed in these drawings: aren't they recognisable as our own negativity, fatigue and fear as we're struggling in this most demanding of spaces – the vigil for the dying?

Today, whether the patient believes in the concept of Heaven or not, the goal of resolving conflict with others is seen as equally important but not for religious reasons.

Inevitably, unresolved conflicts can feed into the psychological issues of many of those suffering at death, particularly in the many people whose foundation for inner peace depends upon being in harmony with those around them, especially their family and friends.

Barriers can continue at death, despite romantic notions that somehow an impending death will make people behave in a more 'heavenly' way.

If you know someone who has a terminal illness, and you want to have a personal connection with them before they die, try to resolve outstanding conflicts with them as much as possible, particularly before they arrive in any institution.

There's a couple of reasons for this. For a start, it's going to be easier and better managed by all involved if the person is less rather than more unwell. To arrive late in the disease process, very near the end, risks raising the idea, both in yourself and the dying person, that you are there for your benefit, your desire for absolution, rather than for any benefit to them, since they will be struggling with the business of dying.

Families do report getting annoyed over the person who arrives to see the dying patient in order to clear their own conscience over a wrong-doing from the past, and not for the benefit of the patient.

Another reason to resolve conflicts early is that if the patient is already in hospital, they may have given a list of people who they do not want to see – a surprisingly common scenario. The staff will respect this, and will turn you away if this is the patient's documented preference, even if the patient had a later change of heart.

Sometimes the patient is happy to see a particular visitor, but because of the history between that visitor and the family, access to the dying person is denied.

Relatives sometimes impose such restrictions for the sake of their family member without realising it is they themselves who have the issue and not the dying patient. If you are enforcing a restriction of visitors for your dying relative, ask yourself if this is your agenda or the dying patient's and discuss this with the staff, who may be aware that the dying patient had a different view to yours.

Social workers and clinical psychologists do everything they can to try to help dying patients resolve conflicts with close family members if there is an opportunity in a palliative care context, since it is well recognised that in the dying, holding on to conflict will increase anxiety and agitation and commonly aggravates pain.

Conflict between those visiting the dying person is quite common. In fact, the professional staff working with a dying patient accept that conflict between the family at the bedside of the dying patient is normal.

Sibling rivalries and ingrained tensions can have long histories in families, sometimes beginning at birth. Considering that the death of a family member, particularly a parent, will be one of the most distressing events most people will confront – and that they will have to do this with siblings – tensions and conflict, rather than being surprising, are almost expected.

Often, conflict is heightened when family members disagree about end-of-life care – one of a number of reasons why it's a good idea for everyone to set out their own plans and ideas unambiguously in advance.

In a typical example, two daughters argued over whether their mother would want to be resuscitated, both making compelling cases for and against. Their conflict had lasting consequences, well beyond their mother's death. Their mother said she was glad she was revived and the daughter who genuinely believed she wouldn't want to be, suffered enormous anguish, and the relationships in the family were damaged.

In a palliative care environment, nurses will usually consider their most important objective is to shield the patient from any obvious impacts of conflict, since this can destroy the peace and sense of comfort that professional staff are trying to achieve for their patient.

Palliative care specialists believe that even when a patient is unconscious, exposure to bickering or fighting at the bedside still creates problems, because the dying are still aware. So staff will want to shield the patient from conflict at that point too.

Let's face it, even among those we are still close to, parents, siblings and children can be very supportive – or they can be the source of problems.

Reasons for conflict can include:

- historical factors, from mild disagreements to sexual abuse and severely dysfunctional family relationships

- mental health issues

- unresolved problems between family members

- guilt over the dying, sometimes expressed as anger or over-compensating

- an authoritarian approach to birth order, especially in families or cultures where the decision-making is assumed to be done by the eldest

- gender bias: sons and daughters given different decision-making roles, for example a family where the sons are given power of attorney and decision-making and the daughters responsibility for intimate issues, such as purchasing clothes

- tension over who should be the decision-maker, especially if this is a substitute decision-maker. This can be over major issues, such as a decision to stop artificial ventilation, or very little ones, such as opinions on how to give comfort, such as when to give ice-blocks

- differences in attitudes towards siblings and the ways affection is expressed to them, from the dying parent.

Brisbane social worker Anne Hardy said that after twenty years working in palliative care, she still finds the death of someone in a family can bring out the best in a family – or just as easily the worst.

'Even a normally really well-functioning family can be pushed past their stress point and not cope,' she said. 'You can be a family that thought you would manage really well, but there can be a trigger that surprises you, and then things can go quite badly compared to what you had expected.'

Anne has learnt not to make judgements or to attempt to predict how families will manage.

'A family can do really well where you least expected it to. For example, I worked with a family recently in which both parents were drug addicts. I was seeing the mother and helping her to manage her emotional issues for about four weeks before she died. We were doing a lot of work to prepare the children for her death. My expectations of the father were pretty low – but we found he really stepped up.

'Everyone was making judgements about the family, and the father just moved in to support those children. He did a remarkable job with them, so it reminded me once again that you can't judge a book by its cover.

'For the sake of the dying patient, often social workers are asked to intervene, usually in the ward at the bedside. Our goals are, first, to establish a rapport with the patient. The patient is always our priority, so we need to ask first, is this going to be of benefit to the patient?'

If meetings and discussions will only benefit the family, not the person dying, then maybe the meeting needs to be conducted somewhere outside the palliative care setting, so that the patient is not part of them.

'The second goal – working with an invitation issued by the dying person themselves, rather than just simply with their consent – is to organise and run family meetings, family conferencing and family mediation. These will usually involve the medical team.

'This is done so the patient can express their wishes. So it's all about who the dying person wants to be there.'

Anne once worked with a very large family. Nearly twenty family members were in conflict – and all were invited into the room of the dying person for a meeting that had taken a great deal of planning.

'There was a lot of preparation leading up to our meeting. But it was actually about being able to advocate to give the patient a voice in the last few days of her life. It was about the family hearing what her wishes were. The argument was over what would happen to her children, in circumstances where their father had died many years earlier.

'Grandparents and aunts and uncles wanted a say in what would happen to them. But we set up a meeting which gave her an opportunity to express what she really wanted – in a public forum, which was a bit of a surprise for some.

'She was able to state – in front of all her family, so there were several witnesses – that she wanted her children to go to live with a particular aunt of theirs, her sister. This choice was a surprise to some of the family.

'Her parents had assumed the people the children would go to would be them. But she had had many issues with her parents which they had not recognised and these had had an impact on her childhood, something she was really only coming to terms with now.

'Her decision was unexpected and there were lots of people involved who thought they had a say. But she knew the people her children ended up with would have a big impact on their lives, and this was affecting her more and more, as she was dying, so we knew it would be good for her for this to be resolved.

'There were lots of tears involved, but the result was a fantastic outcome for the patient, the children and even the wider family.'

'But we also see many situations where there isn't nearly so much at stake. The emotions are high and there's tension mainly because of what is happening – simply the fact that there is an impending death.'

Any discord among family and friends tends to come to the fore, creating extra problems for the person dying.

Be aware that 'Who's allowed to visit?' is a conversation worth having up front. Consider outlining principles very early.

You can ask the staff to manage this. Most wards will manage it with a sign that says something like: 'All visitors are to report to the nurses' station.'

CHAPTER 02

Spiritual experiences at death

We learn about the non-physical side to death,
including spiritual (but not necessarily religious) experiences
that transform a human life into something extraordinary.

'Soul' pain

There are two distinct aspects to the pain suffered by the dying. One is their physical pain, the other is their 'soul' pain – the fear and distress associated with facing the finality of death. It is this second component that makes the pain of dying different to any other pain experienced through life.

Soul pain is often a major issue to be managed. Hospices and palliative care units put a great deal of effort into managing it – one of the noticeable features distinguishing them from acute care hospitals. (Although attention to psycho-social issues at the end of life is also gradually growing and expanding in these hospitals.)

Some people never come to terms with the fact that they are dying, even though they have been admitted to a hospital, palliative care unit or hospice. This can increase a person's fear and anxiety as death nears. The fear and anxiety, in turn, can increase physical pain.

The importance of soul pain is recognised in hospices and palliative care units. Adam Whitby shared the story of Eileen.

'She was a young woman whose daughters were eleven and twelve. She had horrific pain, to the point where we had to put a spinal infusion into her back and we were giving her enormous doses of drugs to try and help her get on top of this pain.

'And then it transpired she hadn't told her daughters she was dying. So she was going through intense emotional pain because she didn't want to tell them. So a counsellor spent a lot of time with this woman and got her to a stage where we planned that she would go home for the weekend and she would tell her daughters, and then come back.

'Well when she came back she had told her daughters and it all went quite well. Her daughters were obviously upset but they already knew their mum was really sick.

'And when she came back we realised her pain levels had dropped so much we had to cut her opiates right back. She'd got rid of all of that anxiety about telling her daughters and it had had such a marked effect on her pain, we had to really bring back all the drugs. I'll never forget that, I'll just never forget how it showed how powerful emotional pain can be. And the effect that it has on your body. It's quite extraordinary.'

When someone is dying in a hospice or under the care of a palliative team, social workers and psychologists are part of the team caring for the patient, helping them to come to terms with and manage their death. Both physical and soul pain will be managed by them. This follows the tradition established by Dame Cicely Saunders that considers pain to be a multi-dimensional experience, with physical, spiritual and psycho-social elements to it.

Many people and special groups can help to support someone companioning a dying person. One of these groups is the Groundswell Project's Compassionate Communities, which promotes an 'approach to end-of-life care where caring for one another at times of need, loss and/or crisis becomes the task and responsibility of everyone'.

The spiritual dimension to dying

Birth, death, love: they are life's biggest experiences, the sources of all our joy and our pain too. Love and grief are intertwined. Some say you can't have grief without first having love. So maybe the more we love someone, the more we grieve when they die. We lament, we implore fate, the gods, God just to pass us by when death comes. We fight the grim reaper. We survive the inevitable prospect of our death by blocking it out. We live audaciously so we can be filled with thoughts of life, not death.

But by the time we leave our childhood we know what death is. No one has to tell us about it. And so, there is more to death than the physical, no matter who we are.

It's not surprising then that atheists and believers alike report being present at a death is a remarkable, powerful and life-changing experience – so the ideas of transcendence it evokes can be claimed for all of us. But what about the experience for the one who is actually dying? Over the years, so many stories of the spiritual and emotional power exhibited by the dying have emerged.

The dead have not come back to tell us – even people who have had 'near death' experiences can't genuinely claim this. But there is so much for us to learn. The stories are striking. Like the dying woman who stays alive long enough to say goodbye to her son, although deeply unconscious. Or like the man who 'waited' until his birthday and then died. Or even the two great-grandparents in my family who died two days after the birth of another great-grandchild: almost as if, as a new generation is seen in, souls pass each other in the night.

Doctors can be uncomfortable talking about spiritual issues with their patients or feel as though it's not their role. Yet some patients hope a spiritual dimension to the discussion will be forthcoming.

But palliative care is changing and many doctors are now more open to acknowledging the spiritual aspects of death, ready to listen to the patients' concerns and if necessary bring in a chaplain or pastoral care worker.

'One situation most families struggle with is the unconsciousness that heralds death. They believe it is a meaningless time of pain and suffering when in fact the person they love is usually more at peace than ever before. They themselves feel helpless, unsure of what to say or do. We now know that connecting with their loved one verbally or by touch can be healing for both the person dying and the family. It may even create the space in which the dying person can let go of life,' Michael Barbato said.

The dying person can be very intuitive, responding to changes of mood and social nuances in those around them, even when they appear to be unconscious.

Dreams and deathbed visions

When people are dying, dreams and reality, the present and the past often merge. It's likely the dying may see – and want to talk about – friends and relatives who are long dead. Try to listen and be supportive if this occurs. Your belief (or not) in an afterlife is not really relevant. What matters is the dying person's needs. It is the dying person's sense of closeness to these people that will help draw them more comfortably forward and help dissipate their fear.

'Oh, I've just been talking to Mother and I just played a lovely game of tennis,' Mum said one day, not long before she died.

It was as though she had just put down her racquet, then chucked her little pet rabbit, Scuts, under the chin before sitting down to a cup of tea. As I looked into her eyes I could see 'Milano', her childhood home on the other side of Strathfield, named after that great Italian city where her grandfather was born. That Sydney house was where three generations of her family had lived and where the same grandfather and his brothers had played bocce.

There was something idyllic about this, but I soon realised such special moments at this time didn't just happen to Mum. If you ask people, they will report similar stories from a dying person's bedside.

Jenny C said her mother Margaret was looking towards a crack in the wall and smiling in the weeks before she died. Though they are not a family who would normally say they believe in an afterlife, they liked to think there was a chink in the 'veil' between the life on earth and the journey beyond and she could see her mother Caroline waiting for her.

When Joan, aged in her late 80s, lay dying, I asked her if she was frightened. She smiled and said, 'No.' What was helping her?

'Mum and Karan come to me every morning. I see their golden ringlets in the sunshine,' Joan said.

Joan's mother had died 50 years before. Her daughter 30 years before. Yet their presence was helping Joan cope with her own imminent death. They were giving her a sense of security and contentment.

There are many theories surrounding the cause of deathbed visions. Until recently they weren't talked about in the scientific literature, but maybe all this means is that we don't yet understand them. In the past, doctors outside of palliative care tended to be very dismissive of deathbed visions, but that is slowly changing.

'Some suggest the vision may be a side effect of medication, especially morphine; others propose a shortage of oxygen reaching the brain, or other chemical changes in the brain. Another theory is that it's a psychological defence, a way we cope with death and the third one is that it's a transcendental experience, in other words, a mystery that's beyond our understanding,' said Michael Barbato.

The dying often also speak gibberish, which is usually interpreted as delirium. But some say we shouldn't be hasty in our assessments because they could also be speaking in metaphors. The message may be more profound than it seems and could be a gentle way of alerting the family – who until then may have avoided any conversation around death – that they know they are dying.

'When people are dying their intuition is highly tuned and I believe their dreams are very significant, profound and powerful,' said Michael Barbato. 'It's their subconscious speaking and it communicates by way of metaphors, symbolism and myths. The meaning may be oblique, but if the dream is vivid or recurrent, the message is usually significant. This is why dreams are so important.

'People can occasionally misinterpret what the dying person says and mistakenly believe they're delirious. But when they listen with a much greater openness to what is being said, then they may understand the very powerful message that is being communicated.'

Michael told the story of a patient.

'Marina was dying of cancer. She had a deep spiritual life and followed a yogic tradition. The most important thing for her was to maintain consciousness or awareness right up to the time of death. On my second-last visit her family said to me, "We've failed," and I asked, "Why?" "Marina is now hallucinating," they said.

'Marina's words were, "I'm climbing to the top of a mountain and when I get there I have to do an appendix operation and I've never done one before."' Marina was a GP and her family had concluded she was hallucinating and feared the morphine, apart from relieving her pain, was now responsible for the delirium.

Michael told them, 'No, she's telling you she's climbing to the top of the mountain, which for her is the work of dying. What she wants is to die in a conscious state. She's telling you she's doing that. But in speaking about the operation, she's saying she's scared, and needs reassurance she can do it right to the very end because she's never done this before. I suggest you speak to her and say, "You're doing this beautifully."'

The family did that and Marina remained conscious and settled until her death the following day.

Unconscious awareness

Unconsciousness and unconscious awareness are still mysteries. I don't mean in the spiritual sense but in a scientific sense. What exactly is unconsciousness? The more you probe this, the more questions you have, not answers. Despite much writing and discussion about consciousness and unconsciousness in recent years, these states of being are, as yet, poorly understood. Investigation continues.

This topic reminds me of another mystery of the natural world that is still in the process of being revealed to us mere humans; that of some migratory birds who travel thousands of kilometres to breed, then return home. They leave their fledglings behind to grow and strengthen. Later, that new generation makes their first long migratory flight, something they have never done before. They journey thousands of kilometres away, to land exactly where their parents grew, never having made that trip before.

Experts in the area used to talk about unconsciousness, but now they talk of unresponsiveness and note that unresponsiveness does not equal unawareness. This is because there is now evidence that large numbers of patients, up to 40 per cent, who have unresponsive syndromes (what used to be called a vegetative state) have degrees of consciousness not previously understood.

In addition, large numbers of anaesthetised patients have now been found to have 'connected consciousness' – that is, awareness of the outside world.

There is also strong evidence that many unresponsive patients who go on to return to an active life have a range of experiences, from simple sensation to a complex dream-like state.

As an example of this, one man I know who was in a semi-coma in an intensive care unit went on to fully recover. He dreamed that he was fighting enemy soldiers who had tied his arms. Later he found out his arms had been tied – by the nursing staff who were trying to stop him removing tubes connected to him while he was unconscious.

It's now realised similar levels of awareness can exist in those who are unresponsive because they are dying. This leads to numerous stories of people who can be unresponsive for days, apparently deeply unconscious, and then communicate intensely or directly, usually just before they die.

'I've seen it I don't know how many times,' said Adam Whitby, who has attended many hundreds of deaths.

'An unconscious patient waiting for a significant other to arrive from interstate or a long distance before they die, and soon after that significant other has arrived the patient will then die. All palliative care nurses will have experienced that,' he said.

'Some people die on their birthday. It's extraordinary. You can understand the dying responding to the touch and the sound of another person's voice when they're deeply unconscious but if you've been unconscious for days, how do you know it's your birthday tomorrow?' he said.

'It can be where you see patients open their eyes and appear to be looking meaningfully into their loved ones' eyes and smiling and then they die and they haven't opened their eyes for three days,' said Kate White.

'I see it in people who wait for those they love, wait for them to be with them before they die,' said Marie, an intensive care nurse.

'Just last week I nursed an old woman who was dying. She had told me earlier, when she was conscious, she was waiting for her son. All her other children had been to visit and he had to come from Melbourne. He was the last to arrive and the plane was delayed. By now she was unconscious but she was waiting. Just after he visited she died.'

Be aware of the possibility of this experience when you are companioning someone who is dying, even if it challenges your belief system.

Palliative care workers often see this as a valuable opportunity for both the patient and those who love them to be in each other's presence, even if nothing is said. And they note that it is often most obvious in one of the last communications – when someone gives the unconscious, dying person permission to go.

'It seemed that our family friend Margaret was lingering and hanging on, almost as though she needed permission to go,' said Catharine.

'She had always struggled with respiratory problems and had been very much needed by her family when she was younger. So she used to fight her ill health very hard. My uncle sat with her one afternoon and told her, "You can go now, you don't need to be brave any more, you're allowed to go", and shortly after that she died.'

Dying alone

While no one can come back to tell us what was going through their minds at the moment of death, nurses believe that, just as some dying people wait to say goodbye, some people wait to be alone to die, dying when family members have left the room or gone to have a cup of tea.

Jenny T had this experience when her father died.

He had reached the terrible terminal stage of Parkinson's Disease. He was no longer able to swallow and his organs were shutting down. The dying was long and protracted: after many days of being at his hospital bedside pretty much around the clock, Jenny T, her mother and brother were almost hysterical from emotion and exhaustion.

Jenny T recalls: 'I insisted that Mum come out for tea at the cafe. When we returned, about twenty minutes later, Dad was dead. I was struck by guilt, but my mother said she was sure he had chosen that exact moment to spare her the distress of seeing him die.'

Sadly, there will be people dying who had no visitors and no one with them at all, at any time. Sometimes, there are no next of kin nominated. But despite this, palliative care staff will try to ensure the person does not die alone.

Being engaged with people in this situation is sometimes a task handed to a palliative care volunteer, due to the pressures on the time of the professional staff. While these volunteers can't be with the dying person all the time and may not be with them at the moment they die, their goal is to provide companionship and human contact where possible. Volunteers say this is one of their most rewarding experiences.

In rare cases, the dying person will give explicit advance instructions about not having family members with them. Even so, they might ask a nurse to be with them.

Retired palliative care nurse Fran remembered one case when a woman living by herself in her own home sent all her family members away, leaving Fran alone with her as she died. She didn't want her family and friends with her but she wanted Fran, who she saw as objective, neutral about her family relationships, non-judgemental and compassionate.

'They all left and I was the only one there with her when she died. All her family and friends were told not to come by so it was just me and her. I felt sad that I was the only one there with her. It was an experience I will never forget,' Fran said.

Where am I going?

A profound sense of the spiritual nature of death cuts across religious boundaries.

Ensuring the dying person has the right to express their spiritual and religious beliefs is an important aspect of choosing an institution to care for them at their time of death.

As death becomes imminent, for many people, one of the biggest questions will be, Is there life after death? At this time, not everyone will confidently hold the position on this that they've maintained in the past, or even over a lifetime.

Palliative care social worker Anne Hardy said: 'I do find that people who have meaning or some sort of belief, whatever that belief is, if it's in a spiritual or a higher being, often cope better than the ones who are very frightened of death because they don't know what will happen to them.'

But Anne stressed we need to be cautious about generalising from one person's experience to the next.

Previously staunch atheists might ask about God, and the apparently religious can become doubters.

'There's the person who very clearly says, "I want the priest." And among the people who say they're atheists, there are varying degrees of belief about what happens to the soul,' said Adam Whitby.

'I've had patients who believe in an afterlife, who really do start to question it at the end of their life. And the ones who believe there is a Heaven and a Hell sometimes become frightened to die because they don't know which of these they're going to. And that's just awful. They're not reassured when I say, "You're such a good person."

'I've had conversations with people who have always had a faith and then they're at the end of their life and they'll say, "Adam, what do you believe? What do you think happens after death?"

'And I've had a couple of, particularly older women, say, "I don't really know what I believe in any more." And that's a bit sad. All their lives they've had this faith and then at the very end of their lives they're really not very sure about it.'

Allowing each person to express their own religious values in relation to what happens to their body or spirit after they die is important.

In our multicultural, pluralist society, people with different viewpoints will be involved with each other's deaths. A deeply religious person may nurse an atheist and vice versa. Today's medical staff are trained to be respectful of their patient's spiritual beliefs and not to attempt to impose their own beliefs upon them.

Just as they are trained to respect the religious practices of different cultures after death, they are expected to respect the religious values of their patients before death.

Nuanced differences, even between people who appear to have the same religious values, need to be explored.

For example, there are differences between Christian churches, sometimes so subtle that they are not obvious even to those who are a part of them. It is a respectable theological position for a Catholic to doubt their worthiness before God. Through the lens of their theology it's appropriate to ask, in a state of deep spiritual humility, whether they've been good enough – to God and to their neighbour – to be worthy enough to have earned a place in Heaven. This is the incantation a practising Catholic says every time they go to Mass and utter the words, 'Lord, I am not worthy that you should enter under my roof, but only say the word and my soul shall be healed.'

A believing Anglican seeing such doubt will be horrified. The Protestant has 'assurance', the confidence that because they believe in Jesus and His resurrection, they will be saved. What they did during the course of a life to express this, through their relationships with other people, is irrelevant spiritually even if they were good and kind. They are sure of Heaven, and joyously feel entitled to their place there, because they believe.

These differences may seem esoteric to others. But if you are a dying Catholic or Protestant, they might be very important to you.

Life review

Reflecting on our lives at the end is so much a part of what it is to be human that it crosses cultural and religious divides and barriers imposed by time.

For many centuries in Christian cultures the dying person was encouraged to reflect and conduct a formal verbal review of their life, to repent in order to enter the gates of Heaven. Life review is part of the Buddhist tradition, too, done to secure mindfulness at the end, and ensure a higher level of reincarnation in the next life.

Today, whatever the traditions behind it, the urge is still there and life review, in one form or another, is still recommended to help people face their death.

Although attitudes to religion have changed, people still have the need for review, philosophers and palliative care specialists point out. Doctors involved with the dying see a diagnosis of terminal illness as an opportunity for clarity, forgiveness and thoughtful, meaningful goodbyes.

There will be some people who want to tell people things they haven't expressed very much before, to share troubles from the past, or to 'confess' to incidents, regardless of their approach to a formal review.

'I hear people's innermost secrets when they're dying. It's amazing what they tell you,' said Barbara, who works as a carer for the elderly.

'One woman told me about all the affairs her husband had had and how much she hated him for it. He was a respectable member of the community and everyone thought they were the perfect couple. But she needed to talk about what her life was really like. She told me she had never told her daughter. "You're the only person I've ever told," she said.'

There will be those who will not want to talk but just want companionship while they reflect back on their long lives. Share the long silences with them. For people with this personality or in this reflective state, this approach is equally comforting. Ask first if you can just sit with them, gently indicating you will not talk if this is what they would prefer.

There is a tendancy to hope for the transformation of the dying person into someone better, all-seeing or all-wise, which we need to resist. Some will want those we love to reveal special insights on life, or pearls of wisdom to help make their own lives better or to help them cope with the loss of the person about to die. Romanticising the death of someone in this way helps some to come to terms with their loss. But those who work with the dying tend to be very cautious about this. Are we just projecting our own emotional or spiritual needs onto the dying, whose own preference might be for something different?

Those who work with the dying often say, instead, that the way people die can match the way they lived. The person who wants to die alone, might have wanted to live alone; the person who died angry was angry in life. Impending death will not bring heroic transformation to all, although it might to some. A person who lived well and with kindness might become very afraid.

Alternatively, the way they die might only be an approximate reflection of who they really are, because of the limitations placed on their lives, especially closer to death.

So despite the best of intentions, life review doesn't always end well. There are people who won't like what they see when they look back honestly. Professionals are aware that for some, reflecting on their lives will not provide any comfort but only heighten disappointment, so they are careful about encouraging life review. It will not be for everyone.

But life review can be interpreted in new and more contemporary ways, that provide an opportunity to summarise and make meaning of experiences, rather than to make critical self-judgements.

Today, this is done in many institutions with recordings and documents prepared as a legacy for families.

'This is not just about the need to see something written down, it's an opportunity for people to make sense of their lives and give meaning to the experience they are going through now,' said one legacy-writing volunteer.

In response to the expression of life review as a written biography, many hospitals now run biography programs as part of their volunteer programs. Businesses will also take commissions to complete such works; for example, Louise Darmody of Sound Memories prepares podcasts, videos or other media.

Managing fears and anxieties

One of the greatest fears of those who've had cancer is that it will come again. The same is true of those who have had a stroke. New psychological therapies have been developed and enormous amounts invested by health authorities to help people cope with these scenarios, because the fear is very real and the suffering it causes is respected.

If you find yourself in this situation, remember that positive developments are occurring all the time, so try to think optimistically – but at the same time, plan as realistically as you can bear to do. For help to do this, call on others if you need to. For example, rather than ruminating on the very real fear of having a second stroke, if you have had a first, or if you are spooked because it has happened to so many people that you can name, you can actively follow the latest developments in stroke prevention by regularly visiting the pages of the Stroke Foundation and reading its news updates. Follow the good news, implement the changes to lifestyle that you can manage. And get involved with stroke awareness. Committed people are ready to talk to you, and they can offer you ways to become involved if this is helpful for you.

You can apply this same way of thinking to those other conditions that emerge as potentially life-threatening problems.

Networks that offer information and support for those wanting to improve their quality of life while living with a potentially life-threatening illness in Australia include: Dementia Australia, the Heart Foundation, the Lung Foundation and the Cancer Council. Similar organisations and foundations can be found in the United Kingdom and New Zealand.

When Elisabeth Kübler-Ross introduced her then ground-breaking research into understanding death in the 1970s, she posited five stages or emotional states that terminally ill people progressed through. 'Acceptance' was defined as the stage people would, maybe should, reach when they knew they were going to die. Today it's recognised that acceptance is not inevitable, that emotions are not that straightforward. And acceptance may not even be the person's goal, or part of their psychological development. Yet despite this, some say acceptance inevitably often comes, even if at the very end.

Emotional logic suggests it is better to embrace the idea of acceptance – after all, this suggests comfort and some form of peace. So when the time comes that you have to accept that death is likely to be the outcome of the next serious bout of illness, be reassured, you can call on high levels of emotional support from people trained to deliver this.

For the person who is dying, denial – denial of the terminal condition – will be a big factor in how you manage your death. 'Functional denial', in which you block out the prospect that you are dying in order to keep going – an extreme form of positive thinking that works for some people – will serve you less effectively the closer you come to the end. Staff working with the dying say being able to talk about it when death is close, gives the patient an opportunity to talk to others and receive a high level of verbal and non-verbal support.

Remember that whatever you want at your death – dignity, peace, peace among your family, a connection with nature – ultimately, achieving this is up to you. No one can take your dignity, your sense of control, away from you – and no one can give it to you. It is not something that is bestowed by the actions of others. It is not something that comes from being in the most modern, well-equipped palliative care unit.

It is something that comes from you. This means there may be some spiritual work you have to do, and a bit of psychological stretching, too, so that you can achieve the level of dignity you want, as your life comes to an end.

Only you can know what this is. Therefore, only you can do the spiritual work required, whatever that means to you. But once again, it's a good idea to turn to others for help in getting there.

If you have terminal cancer, you can seek out the services of a psychologist. These services might be available at your hospital, so if they have not been discussed, ask about them. You can also ask your general practitioner for help with organising this support.

The services of oncology psychologists, trained to help cancer patients with their emotional and psychological needs, are also now available through some major hospitals, although not all.

If you are the person dying, you are not alone. Do not be afraid to ask your palliative care team for help with this. They can quickly get you in touch with the professionals who can help you.

Medications to manage psychological issues at the end of life can be requested but studies and lived experience show time and again that psychological symptoms will be better managed if the person has been able to deal with relationships in a way that leaves them feeling reassured they have tied up emotional loose ends as well as they can.

But be mindful of certain realities. Many palliative care specialists say they see more difficult deaths in those who have not resolved conflict with others in their lives. Similar observations are made about people who have held on to big secrets that have shaped their lives – for example, the secret lover, the secret child, the secret sexual abuse either as victim or perpetrator.

Palliative care units are very well resourced with allied health professionals, for instance social workers and psychologists, to help you work through the way problems in your life could have an impact on the way you die.

What if someone you were estranged from for decades turns up at your deathbed? How will you respond? You may not want to see them, even if they want to see you. You can ask for people to be vetted by the nursing team before they visit. If you think you will need support with this, you can ask the psychologists, social workers and even the nurses involved in your care, for help with this.

If you are dying at home, managing this might need extra thought and early planning, since vetting the unwelcome visitor is something that will need to be managed by your family, and they may have less skill or detachment in managing this situation than a trained professional, who is essentially a stranger, at the hospital bedside – or they may bring their own judgements to bear on your situation.

We have a fantasy that emotional maturity, if not purity, comes to the dying person because we believe in the idea of 'closure'. We might even be looking for a 'happy' ending, something that will help make the emotional experience of the loss worthwhile. But the reality is that the dying person may not want to see the person they were estranged from at death, any more than they did in life.

It's understandable to be afraid of pain. This is common and occurs in most healthy people. Some types of pain before death can be especially bad, such as bone pain. Some dying people won't experience much pain at all. But your team of carers can usually predict whether this will happen or not. If you are afraid of pain, don't hide it, talk to your treating team. In the ideal setting, they will be able to refer you to the pain management experts you need, who will be on staff. But this is not always the case. If for some reason the staff can't help you with your fears, persist or ask your family to help in finding the professional support that you need.

The modern goal, although still not achieved everywhere, is for every healthcare team and every hospital to know how to access people and resources who can help you manage both the pain itself and your fears of pain.

As mentioned before, we don't fully understand consciousness. By implication, this means we can't be totally sure that an unconscious person does not experience pain. However, most experts studying this currently believe that unconscious awareness often doesn't involve sensory awareness of pain.

CHAPTER 03

Managing pain and other physical problems

We learn how to eliminate pain, since this is an unnecessary burden and can prevent a good death.

Bed ache and bed sores

Even if there has been little obvious pain related to the disease that is causing death, morphine is usually given in the final days but before the very end of life, often to treat back pain and the discomfort caused by not being able to move and change position, referred to by some professionals informally as 'bed ache'. This discomfort is an early sign that pressure sores, also known as bed sores, are developing. Good management of bed sores is a big factor in ensuring a comfortable death.

A healthy person lying down is never completely still, even when they sleep heavily. But as life draws to an end, movement ceases and the stillness can cause skin to break down and sores to form, particularly in places where bones protrude, such as the coccyx (the bone at the base of the spine), the bone at the back of the heel, the hips, the elbows and the shoulders.

The risk of sores and lesions on the skin caused by pressure will increase as the person moves less, is unable to change their position and general muscle weakness increases. Some people will be more vulnerable to developing bed sores than others. To guard against this, the person should be moved regularly. In a palliative care institution, hospital or nursing home, this will usually be done by a nursing assistant. If the patient is dying at home, those caring for the patient need to do this. Ideally, the patient is turned at least every four hours, sometimes more frequently, to ensure those points where the skin rubs or presses on sheets do not break down and develop into sores. Poorly managed skin ruptures can prompt the dying person to shift and try to move away from the sore spot, and this can be misinterpreted as restlessness. Bed sores are usually treated with dressings and cleaning, and can be managed with undulating mattresses.

This intervention is balanced against treating bed sores that develop too close to death to be able to achieve anything, since disturbing the dying person to try to solve the problem won't lead to any improvement. This is a time when morphine could be prescribed for pain management, and it can be applied topically.

Confusion

Was there confusion in the patient before they entered this terminal stage? Confusion is often a symptom of dementia in the elderly. Can the strategies to support and manage this that were applied in life be adapted for this person's experience of dying? As a general rule, drugs administered in the patient's past for dementia will have been stopped, since these have a small role in improving 'sharpness' but little role in helping manage behaviour.

The family companioning the patient can make a contribution here, discussing certain things with hospital staff. Is an 85-year-old woman who is talkative, alert and active behaving in a way that is completely consistent with her normal behaviour, or is this out of character? A nurse or a doctor wouldn't be expected to know. Her family will know immediately and can alert the staff to a potential diagnosis of hyperactive delirium. Then again, she could be like that normally, but now be responding slowly to questions, behaving lethargically and not moving very spontaneously, again, behaviours that are entirely normal in the woman the same age in the bed next to hers, but not in her.

In that case, the family can report that her behaviour is unusual, leading to a diagnosis of hypoactive delirium.

If you have conversations about this with the medical staff managing the dying patient, then they can investigate causes and plan changes to medications.

Agitation

Terminal agitation (the old-fashioned term is 'death throes') occurs in many people when death approaches. Modern medical professionals hate the expression 'death throes' but it rings so true. The expression has echoed through millennia. The old English word 'throwian' means to suffer. But it hints at the modern English 'throw', to propel with force through the air by a movement of the arm and hand – the old English version of which is 'thrawan', to twist and turn.

One of the *ars moriendi* depicts the temptation of impatience: a dying man is shown kicking his physician, with his wife standing by, imploring him to stop. But what is his impatience about? Impatience to die? Impatience with those around him? Through a modern lens, I see a person kicking, thrashing about and lashing out without any sense of control. Maybe this is the restlessness – sometimes violent – of terminal agitation.

Some palliative care specialists argue that by discussing this in detail I will make you, the reader, unnecessarily afraid. But I'm hoping that by describing this distinctive agitation accurately, you will be less afraid. Often when it comes to death, especially now that we live in an age when we are shielded from it so much, having such a description helps because what we can imagine is often much worse than reality.

It's estimated that somewhere between 25 and 85 per cent of patients who are dying will experience some form of restlessness before death. It involves agitation, delirium, jerking and irritability, usually after the person has become unresponsive to others. In many cases it is only mild, in others it is more extreme.

The dying person writhes and tosses around in bed. This state may only be fleeting and may also be easily controlled, or it can be quite extended. It is hard to watch. What exactly is going on? Does the person know what's happening? Is the person afraid? Afraid of death? As observers, it's tempting to overlay our own feelings on to it. The person can look as though they are fighting: fighting death, fighting Hell, fighting the grave, fighting others. In very extreme cases they really are fighting others and can be violent, but this is very rare. These responses can create a sense of helplessness in those companioning the dying.

Healthcare professionals try to reassure companions that often, the dying person is not aware or conscious enough to be suffering emotionally. While agitation is a psychological experience, in the dying it can have many physical causes and today it tends to be managed in the way physical problems are, for example, with drug therapies.

As our knowledge improves, this approach could change again.

The wide range of possible causes of terminal agitation has been fully appreciated only recently. Palliative care teams will do all they can to determine what is causing the dying person's agitation at this time, whether it be psychological or physical.

Physical causes include lack of oxygen to the brain, known as hypoxia. If this is the case, oxygen is administered. It can also be a side effect of medication, or caused by pain, drug interactions, fever, excessive levels of calcium in the blood of cancer patients or other physical problems that have not been identified.

It is true that the psychological causes may include a growing sense of dread at the approach of death, loneliness, and spiritual unease, and this is one of the reasons palliative care today involves social, psychological and pastoral teams, working on the basis that if these problems are explored earlier, they will have fewer consequences later in the process of dying, when it is more likely to manifest itself. But some personalities will not benefit from this.

Some people may lose their understanding of what is going on around them, making them frightened. Their next reaction might be to try to run away, climb out of bed, fall, or push others away – all of this at a time when they are unaware of their actions.

If the agitation persists, staff will try to relieve it. To relieve psychological causes, usually talking therapies may be employed if the patient is conscious and aware. But while this can be effective earlier, it is not effective when the person has lost communication skills or is semi-conscious. At this stage, staff may administer one or more sedatives to the patient. Benzodiazepines might be administered, even though the patient never needed such medications in the past. Anti-psychotic medications may also be prescribed to help control any fear or hallucinations being experienced, even though the person may never have had a psychotic episode in the past.

The drugs used to relieve agitation are quite varied. New and improving ones are coming onto the market quite steadily. Many of us, particularly today, like to research, especially through Google, what the drugs on the patient's medical chart are for. Be mindful if you do this. Families report being shocked to see that some drugs administered to ease agitation are the same ones used to treat psychosis, yet their patient didn't suffer from psychotic episodes in life. If you've found out something about the medication that puzzles you, ask the medical staff about it.

Sometimes drugs – including morphine – can cause vivid dreams and nightmares. Ideally, if this problem is going to occur for the patient, it will have been detected by now and the dose of their opioid adapted to take this into account. This needs skilled management, since dreams and visions can be a part of the experience of someone close to dying, as they move closer to unconsciousness anyway. The professionals managing this situation, who focus on the whole person, not just their illness and associated symptoms, can be helped by being aware of the patient's previous fears and reactions to drugs. If, as the companion at the bedside, you have questions or concerns about the drugs being used, ask about them.

Palliative care specialists acknowledge that occasionally, and unfortunately, in rare cases, extreme agitation can't be eliminated.

When breathlessness and pain start to build

As mentioned before, despite our fears, you might be surprised to find that most people won't experience intense pain at the end of their life. However, while pain is less of an issue than most of us realise, breathlessness and respiratory discomfort tend to be more of an issue than we often think they will be.

This is because as someone dies, just as their other organs do, their lungs will deteriorate and so they experience respiratory failure; that is, their lungs fail. They become unable to move and don't take deep breaths. They also become so weak that they can't cough up their sputum, increasing the chance of infection.

It used to be said that opioids shouldn't be prescribed when there is a respiratory issue, for fear of respiratory depression. That thinking, when taking into account the breathlessness experienced at the end of life, has now gone out the window.

The teaching now is that opioids should be avoided in those dying of severe respiratory disease because they could worsen the symptoms, but paradoxically, small doses of morphine are beneficial for respiratory failure at the end of life. The reasons why are not completely clear. But the evidence is that the morphine lessens the dying person's distress, relaxes them, makes them feel more comfortable and less afraid, and therefore helps them to die more easily.

So treating breathlessness is seen in a similar way to treating bed ache. It eases discomfort. But to go back to pain: 'More than 85 per cent of palliative care patients have no severe symptoms by the time they die,' said Australian researchers Kathy Eagar and colleagues, writing on *The Conversation* website.

They argue an excruciating death is extremely rare, and this is encouraging. That said, even though pain management at the end of life is improving all the time, the sad reality is that good pain management strategies aren't put in to place as often as you'd like to think. The encouraging thing is that many institutions are now addressing this very issue.

The 15 per cent mentioned by Eagar is still too high a number of people to be experiencing pain as they die.

Palliative care professionals now believe that 97–98 per cent of the time many of the symptoms encountered at the end of life can be relieved effectively. Unfortunately, this is still seen as an ideal, rather than the expected, outside this specialist area.

Pain management is one of the most written-about areas of hospital and patient care. Yet gaps between pain and pain management still occur, and overcoming this is itself a large part of the academic discussion and, increasingly, a call to action by those working in hospitals.

The most common problems with pain management in the dying happen when death is occurring beyond the reach of a palliative care team. This is often in other specialist units within the hospital that have decided, for whatever reason, not to call in the palliative care team. (Sometimes the reverse happens too. A team might call in the palliative care team, only to face a delay in their response – perhaps because of inadequate staffing.)

Some of the problems in pain management at end of life that have been discussed confidentially with me by staff in these units can be practical. Examples include:

- Some staff are reluctant to give the full level of opioids prescribed and as frequently as prescribed.

- Some nurses identify a problem, either the pain itself or the source of it, but don't document it.

- The early, basic pain relief given, such as paracetamol, is not written in the patient's notes.

- Agitation is not charted.

- Whether the patient can make their own decisions is not documented.

- The patient's wishes are not documented.

These gaps in the knowledge of end-of-life care are now being addressed in many places. For example, in New South Wales the 'Last Days of Life Toolkit' program is being introduced. And throughout Australia, End of Life Coordinators are being employed at hospitals to set up better approaches to end-of-life care in all hospital departments.

The challenge for the dying person's companions is to know when their concerns are justified and when to voice them. You are entitled to start a discussion about your concerns; in fact most of the professionals at a dying person's bedside would welcome your questions. This gives them the opportunity to explain all the things they are doing that you might not be aware of. Companions can expect to be respected.

While we like to think today's students at medical school are now taught to accept nothing less than 97–98 per cent pain free at death as their benchmark, some medical teams still get caught up in the technical aspects of success in treating an illness, rather than controlling pain. It follows that better education about pain relief is still needed among doctors and nurses, especially those who do not have training in palliative care.

Strong pain is relieved by opioid medicines, the best known being morphine. Palliative care nurses report dying patients often resist morphine because of the social connotations of its use, even when this is the best drug to control their pain at the end of their lives.

Unfortunately, the belief still exists in some places that experiencing pain is ennobling, and a surprising number of nurses still carry this attitude, despite modern education on pain relief, which rejects the idea. This old belief is based on a few things – a distortion of the 'no pain, no gain' theory, a leftover of the belief in stoic self-denial that some cultures elevate to a virtue, and, often unspoken among some Christians, a belief that the pain we endure is only small compared to the pain Christ suffered for us, and therefore is something we should put up with.

In well-managed palliative care, today it is considered good practice to suppress pain aggressively. So the default position is to give pain relief continuously and extra as soon as the dying patient suggests they need it, rather than waiting for a professional to decide it's needed. The goal is no 'breakthrough' pain at all.

Since patients themselves have attitudes they've developed in life, rather than medical settings, many older people in particular are very stoic, and might say, 'Oh no, I don't need it yet, I'll just wait for another couple of hours.' While nurses working with the dying, possibly more than nurses in other settings, are expected to urge the dying patient to prevent pain from worsening, this doesn't always happen. Sometimes this is because nurses are so busy, they need to attend to higher priority issues than someone calling out because of pain.

It also tends to be a problem in aged care facilities. This can be because the nursing staff are dealing with old people with old-fashioned views. Or the staff themselves may have not been exposed to or don't have access to good palliative care training.

And often staffing levels are very low. Current Australian government regulations allow service providers to have only one registered nurse on duty at a time to cover large numbers of patients. This one registered nurse, often overworked, cannot attend to all their patients' pain management needs at once.

A specialist palliative care nurse would never say, 'It's good that you've gone six hours without having to have anything for pain.'

However, on rare occasions, there will be some people who will want to be excluded from pain relief, for example practising Christian Scientists, who for religious reasons do not believe in any medical intervention at all.

End-of-life care is full of individual considerations and choices. Sometimes people may want to experience a death unaffected by any medication, to be clear of mind, even though this may involve pain. If this is what you or your family member want then make it clear beforehand. Ideally, you will be working with a palliative care specialist who could align you with meditation or mindfulness techniques to achieve a completely drug-free, yet humanely managed, death. But set this up early in your disease management, since in many places, paradoxically it can be hard to achieve a completely drug-free death.

Sometimes families become apprehensive when they see the increasing pain relief levels of a dying relative, because of their own beliefs about managing pain with fewer interventions. If you are the person dying, make sure your family knows your wishes and aren't left in a position of guessing what you want.

If the dying relative is past the point where they can communicate and the family members want conservative pain management, the nursing staff will often try to find a balance between the needs of the patient and the family's wishes, unless the patient has discussed this with their substitute decision-maker or in detail in their advance care directive.

The advance care directive is discussed in detail in the second part of this book. But I will define two important terms at this point: an advance care directive is a legal document, written by the patient while they had capacity, which states their wishes about their future health care and treatment. Although in New South Wales just being written down makes it legally binding, some prefer the unambiguity of a legal document witnessed by a lawyer, a copy of which is lodged in their office. By implication, this person has had the advantage of going through a more thorough process of seeking advice. Advance care planning, in contrast, is the process of preparation that leads up to that definitive document. It might involve papers and notes you have written, with, say, the help of staff at a nursing home or relatives.

But despite these theoretical definitions, the lived experience is still muddy. Doctors and medical staff can override a patient's wishes on medical grounds, and individual experiences of negotiating advance care documents can vary, sometimes enormously.

Despite this – or maybe even because of it – it's worth spelling out in your advance care directive that you want proactive pain management, and researching a little information about this if you are up to it.

Basic details such as medication schedules to control physical pain will be different for every dying patient. Staff working with the dying person, in whatever environment, are expected to understand the need to explain medication schedules to those they are working with.

If you want to be in control of your medications, tell your family in advance, well before your symptoms are bad enough to need the care of others, what your attitude to pain relief is. You have the right to ask for your family to be informed about this on your behalf. So when the time comes when it's impossible for you to be thinking about this, ask them if they can step in at that time, articulating your position for you.

This is one of those discussions you may need to have with your family a few times, and the earlier the better.

As the supporting family member, if you don't feel you quite understand the medication schedules or what is being done for your relative, you're entitled to keep asking for information from the medical team until you are satisfied.

If you are dying when you are elderly, you're likely to have several medical conditions at once – for example arthritis as well as congestive heart failure, which is terminal. This means you are likely to be taking several medications. As the end gets closer, these will no longer be needed. The only drugs that will be needed are those to help you manage your pain and suffering.

But stopping certain drugs is something that will need to be managed by those who understand the impacts of both the medications themselves and of suddenly withdrawing them. For example, if you're on antidepressants, if they are suddenly halted will it have an adverse effect on you, complicating other psychological problems?

In the ideal scenario, all of this will have been discussed with you well in advance by your treating doctors – so try to encourage this conversation and be an active participant in it, as much as possible. Again, this may require setting up the circumstances for that conversation earlier than the doctors expect.

Relief of pain at death for everyone all over the world, no matter who they are, is now considered a basic human right, and it is a World Health Organization (WHO) goal.

Morphine and other opioids

A word of caution: this is not a medical guide, so for specific details relevant to yourself, you need to speak with your doctors about your own circumstances. My goal in this section is to show how complex the topic is, to encourage you to seek out as much information as you can and to talk with others. I will list more information sources in the resources section.

I'm focusing on morphine and other opioids here. This is because these are the drugs commonly used at the deathbed. The closer the person gets to dying, the more likely it is that other drugs will be dropped, leaving just one of these ones to be administered right until the very end. I'm leaving the subject of other painkillers and drugs to you to explore with your doctor.

The opioids have become controversial and the cause of anxiety for patients, society, policy-makers – and in turn for professionals.

'Opioids are a class of drugs naturally found in the opium poppy plant. Some prescription opioids are made from the plant directly, and others are made by scientists in labs using the same chemical structure', explains the US National Institute on Drug Abuse.

Often in Australia it is not actually morphine that is prescribed but a synthetic variant, one of the class of opioid drugs, such as oxycodone. But many people refer to morphine when they mean this range of opioids.

The opioids are one of the most important drug types in the treatment of pain at the end of life – and yet they are easily the most contentious. Basically, there are three reasons for this, all to do with fear: fear that when they're introduced it means death is imminent; fear of addiction; and fear that they could be used to hasten death.

You may or may not be surprised to find that attitudes to morphine and the opioid drugs vary from place to place, hospital to hospital, and hospital unit to hospital unit.

In broad, simplistic terms, it can be observed that the team of one hospital unit may not work with these drugs as much as another, because of the different physical systems of the body they focus on, for example digestive, skeletal, nervous, reproductive.

However, an intensive care team is likely to have more confidence with morphine and opioids than many other teams because they are very familiar with dealing with respiratory failure and respiratory depression. They are used to giving their patients oxygen and assisted ventilation, and their team is immediately able to start resuscitation, since that's something they do routinely, because the intensive care unit is where a patient is often transferred when their condition deteriorates.

The standard dose of morphine a dying patient will be started on is quite low, for example it might be 5 milligrams, every four hours. If the dose is to be increased, it usually goes up by small increments each time. Although, if the patient is only small and has never taken a prescription drug before, the starting dose could be much lower.

If morphine has become part of a patient's pain management schedule at a fairly early stage, for example to manage cancer pain or chronic pain, then the patient may have already exceeded the typical starting dose.

You could be a patient who is started on morphine for the first time close to death, say because of respiratory failure, or you could be a patient whose cancer pain has been managed with morphine for some time. The bodies of the patients who have been on morphine for a considerable period have, over time, adjusted to the higher doses of morphine they are receiving. If their morphine levels were suddenly withdrawn or dropped much lower, they would suffer from withdrawal symptoms and experience high levels of pain again, both unnecessarily.

Withdrawal symptoms include restlessness, watery eyes, runny nose, nausea, sweating and muscle aches.

Even though there are patient-controlled mechanisms for delivering morphine, these are not generally used in the palliative care setting, so you can be free to focus on more important things to you, such as spending precious time with your families and those you love, rather than becoming preoccupied with monitoring your pain levels.

The goal of healthcare professionals is to have a patient in the early stages of dying who is pain free and alert. If you are drowsy, then morphine levels might need to be reduced. This is not something you may be in a position to manage well yourself when in that state, so this needs to be discussed with your family and those companioning you at the end of life, so they can talk to the palliative care team about it.

Morphine's effect is transmitted via a complex group of receptors in the brain that are normally acted upon by the body's peptides, known as endorphins. Apart from analgesia, these drugs produce drowsiness and a sense of detachment. Other opioids, such as pethidine, can produce euphoria.

Associate Professor Richard Chye, director of the Sacred Heart Health Service, Sydney, explained that in the dying person sleepiness is increasing, separately to the introduction of morphine. But the effect of sleepiness needs to be discussed.

'To patients, I say, "Yes, morphine will make you sleepy but without morphine, pain will wake you up."

'Pain is a very strong stimulus and "wakes" people and deprives them of sleep. When pain is reduced, then patients may sleep whilst they catch up with their sleep deficit. Some misrepresent this as the drug causing drowsiness,' he said.

Many people fear the administration of morphine will lead to addiction in the dying person. But this is a long-term risk in a situation where there is no long term, and morphine addiction doesn't occur if there is pain to target and relieve.

Morphine addiction is a trick of the human brain.

'Morphine targets pain, so in someone experiencing pain, the pain counteracts the addictive effects of the morphine. But if there's no pain, it targets the brain. If we were to take morphine and we didn't have pain, then, yes, we would become addicted, because we are not using it for pain,' Dr Chye said.

Concerns about addiction to opioids are understandable and spread out from hospitals into the public domain, especially when there are worries about oversupply or that the opioids are too easy to access. For example, in November 2018, an article appeared prominently in the *Sydney Morning Herald* with the headline, 'They're not lollies: call for rethink on opioids'.

Its first paragraph stated: 'The over-prescription of opioids from hospital beds is putting patients at risk of lifelong addictions, pharmacists warn, with more than 70 per cent of hospitals supplying packets of tablets for people to take home "just in case".'

Too easy access to opioids is a real threat. But unfortunately, as a consequence of these discussions, the dying often find their access to these drugs more restricted, even though they will have no long life to be affected by addiction. So society's different needs in different situations clash.

Looked at from today's perspective, it's easy to imagine morphine and its synthetic equivalents were always regulated and hard to access. But nothing could be further from the truth.

Its use flourished freely in Georgian England, when the middle class was emerging and buying consumer goods for the first time. Paintings of that time show women in exotic finery in the foreground and what today we would effectively describe as 'junkies' in the background.

Centuries before, visitors to the Italian city-state of Venice used to observe that that place had a frantic, unnatural kind of energy to it. This was because many citizens took copious amounts of coffee in the morning, then copious amounts of morphine in the afternoon.

Opium has been used since 4000BC. It was commonly made into Theriac, an ancient Greek cure for the bite of anything wild that attacked a human – including a mad dog. Theriac's fluid viscosity came from honey. By the time Christ was born its formula had been refined. It included a wide and varying range of ingredients, but dead venomous snakes and opium were the essential ones. The ancients thought the snakes were the active ingredient, but the astute must have twigged the snakes could do nothing without the opium.

In Europe during the Middle Ages, Theriac had a surge of popularity because it was believed to protect against the plague. Futile as that notion was, the altered consciousness it evoked would have softened any disappointment. Venice, with its close proximity to Turkey's vast poppy fields from which opium was milked, effectively had a monopoly on Theriac's production, so the concoction became known as 'Venice Treacle'. Theriac's use wasn't abandoned as a medicine until well into the eighteenth century.

By then laudanum had emerged. It was made of 10 per cent opium powder dissolved in alcohol. It became a common remedy, administered to all and sundry, including children, for just about any reason.

By then the English, asserting their colonial claims, had gained control of most of the opium now growing in India and were trading it with the Chinese for everyday items such as tea and porcelain. This trade became so destructive of Chinese communities that the Chinese attempted to ban it, leading eventually to the two opium wars between Britain and China.

By the mid-eighteenth century in England, opium could be bought over the counter in corner stores and market places throughout the country. Georgian England was a place where high-functioning opium addicts moved everywhere unselfconsciously. They were respectable people such as lawyers, politicians and businessmen. Poets openly used the drug to help inspire them, and some described this in their work. The drug's usage was common in all classes: even many farm workers went about their daily work befuddled by opium.

In the late 1860s, the English standardised doses, driven by a growing awareness that opium could cause death in overdose, particularly in children and the elderly. But this drive to standardise had nothing to do with concerns about addiction.

Until the 1860s it would never have occurred to the English to fret about opium addiction. Eventually, in the late nineteenth century, as their politicians began to recognise its social cost, England and the rest of the United Kingdom began to wind back centuries of freedom for their citizens to dose themselves up to their eyeballs with opium.

The British dominance of the opium market gave them the lead in developing the modern licences on the drug, continuing to refine, develop and innovate with morphine, leading the way in the development of the morphine we use today. Many of the crucial commercial licences for it are still held by British pharmaceutical companies.

In northern America, opioids were freely supplied for pain relief by the British army during the American Revolution. Later, armies of the Civil War distributed it freely. Those soldiers who weren't addicted by the time the Civil War was over often became addicted afterwards. David Courtwright, a historian of addiction in the United States, describes how often the opioids were prescribed for 'pain management and sleeping problems'. There weren't many other painkillers available and little was known about mechanisms of disease. Regarded as a panacea, morphine was prescribed freely by doctors for all sorts of reasons.

In the picture painted by Courtwright, the doctor is significant, prescribing the remedy in the first place and then becoming the source to feed the continuing addiction. Addiction to the opioids was more of a problem among white populations than black ones, since black people had less access to medical professionals. At the risk of oversimplifying the story, he says the drug of choice for black people was cocaine, introduced to stevedoring workers as a way to help them labour for longer hours.

Following the Civil War, many young soldiers who had been wounded were now addicted. So, too, were many of their womenfolk, particularly in the South, whose families had suffered higher casualty rates than their northern opponents. Broken by grief, many women were freely prescribed opium at a time when the mechanisms of addiction were very poorly understood.

Social pressures played a role in the growing problem of opioid addiction too. With the slave trade abolished and, overnight, capital invested in slaves completely gone, labour markets collapsed, causing severe economic stress. Many of those in distress turned to opium as a distraction.

By now, the flow of opium in the United States was managed through medical practitioners, who made their living through prescription and supply. Pharmaceutical companies were already big businesses making healthy profits through the trade.

Plenty of quacks sold exotic potions and lotions too. In nineteenth-century America, it was up to the buyer to beware of any negative consequences of their purchases.

As the nineteenth century passed, the introduction of the hypodermic syringe needle to medical practice offered a smoother way of ingesting the narcotic, adding to more addiction.

The *Harrison Narcotics Tax Act* was introduced in 1914 to regulate the sale and distribution of these drugs. Application of this act by 1919 meant that addicts couldn't legally be maintained on these drugs by doctors, so as doctors who'd happily supplied narcotics dropped their patients, addicts turned to a growing black market.

By 1924, several municipalities had created narcotics clinics to alleviate this pressure, but by now the black market in opioids was well established.

Today, the main reason oxycodone is more commonly prescribed in Australia than morphine is because of our licensing situation, which gives us less access to morphine.

The idea of ruined lives caused by street drugs such as heroin understandably evokes fear and confusion about morphine. One British-trained palliative-care specialist explained she never uses the word morphine when prescribing in Australia, even though the oxycodone she prescribes is from the same family of drugs as morphine.

'Ironically, oxycodone is more popular with patients because its name doesn't have the same connotations as morphine – even though it's twice as potent as morphine, works in exactly the same way and has all the same side effects,' she said.

If a patient has been started on oxycodone by their GP, palliative care staff usually continue with this, simply because this is what the patient is used to. If opioids are being introduced late in the dying phase, alternative opioids are still usually preferred to morphine because of the fear the word causes in patients and their families who often become frightened that its introduction means they are just about to die.

Like many other palliative care specialists, Dr Chye hears this concern often. He explains to patients and their families who are worried by this: 'I have patients on lots and lots of morphine who are able to live for two or three years.'

Opioids can be delivered in various ways. For example, as an oral liquid. People who have difficulty swallowing can be given a patch to wear. People who suffer particularly badly from the constipation caused by their opioid can have it administered with a laxative. Morphine delivered as an injection, rather than by mouth, tends to work more quickly. It can also be delivered subcutaneously (under the skin), intravenously (into the vein) or intramuscularly (into the muscle) through injection. It can also be delivered via continuous infusion with a pumping system and perispinally (into the spine.)

Side effects usually include constipation, nausea, itching, dizziness, sleepiness and drowsiness. If any of these symptoms are noted, the dose of morphine will usually be cut back. Note that these last two are side effects of respiratory depression, which tends to loom large as a management concern.

But sleepiness, drowsiness and unresponsiveness are characteristic of people who are very close to death, so sometimes companions can become confused and believe it was the opioid that caused these conditions when in fact, they are features of the dying process.

There will come a point when death is imminent and a last dose of morphine or oxycodone is administered. Sometimes those companions who were with the patient look back on that last dose and assume this caused the death, even if the death was a coincidence. For some health professionals in this circumstance, that last dose causes anxiety, as they wonder if they will be accused of causing the death, maybe by other professionals or a distressed and emotional family. This fear comes from their teaching, lived experience and media reports about scandals involving abuse of morphine or other drugs at death.

British anaesthetist Dr Phil Jones believes that legislators, in Australia and many other countries including the United States, are overly worried about the effects, side effects and addiction potential of opiates, especially diamorphine, which is most commonly prescribed in the United Kingdom.

"Even if these drugs were to be severely restricted, in a general medical context, it is surely inhumane to extend this to those with terminal cancer pain," he argues.

It's a subject he's passionate about, not least because his Canadian-born first wife had the benefit of subcutaneous diamorphine infusion (managed at home) that allowed her a pain-free death.

In the United Kingdom, he feels, it is not theft of medical supplies that fuels the availability of addictive drugs on the street, it is the criminal industry.

'A change, one way or the other, in the medical supply of opiates, would be unlikely to affect the illegal trade', Dr Jones says. 'Drugs of all types are widely obtainable. If you want access to heroin, all you have to do is stand on an urban street corner and whistle.'

At a certain point towards the end of life, when more pain is likely, doctors and nurses will use their judgement to increase doses of morphine according to need. The doctor will write in the patient's treatment plan 'PRN', an abbreviation of the Latin expression *pro re nata*, which means the drug can be administered at the nurse's discretion. This frees the nurses to deliver the doses needed, without having to call doctors in to write scripts frequently, which would otherwise be necessary when the patient's pain levels are often slowly increasing because they are moving closer to death.

The ideal is that it will be delivered in such a way that the time lag between the delivery of the opioid and when the patient feels the benefit, usually half an hour, is avoided, so pain delivery is seamless, even in those who are already unresponsive, and particularly in those suffering from respiratory distress.

Did that last dose cause the death?

The dying often discuss their fear, not so much of death, but of what they will have to endure before they die. Good palliative care involves reassuring the patient and their companions that pain relief will be given as required, especially in those patients who have said pain relief is their top priority.

As mentioned before, some dying people, informed properly about pain relief and their access to it, choose to have very little, because they want to die in a state of conscious awareness, in line with a spiritual philosophy. These patients have usually been taught meditation skills or yoga practices to cope with pain.

In a patient who has requested as much pain relief as possible, the requirement for more morphine may increase as their death draws nearer, although not always. If more pain relief is needed, their healthcare professionals will ensure opioid dosage increases incrementally, rather than in a big jump, which could be fatal.

But is there a point where this drug becomes fatal?

Sue M's father died in a Sydney private hospital, and she believes his death was sped up with increasing doses of morphine.

'On his last day the hospital rang me and said, "He's had a really bad night, you better come."

'When I got there, he sounded like an express train. He sounded like there was some huge machine in his room and it was the one lung he had left trying to cope and it was full of liquid. He couldn't expel it, so he was basically drowning.

'The staff had been giving him morphine. The nurse said to me, "We're not doing the four-hourly, or once every four hours, we're now at the stage where we can administer as needed."

'Then, a little later, she came in with a younger nurse or orderly, and the nurse had the morphine in her hand and she said, looking at the other nurse then back down at my father, "I am now administering a threshold dose."'

Sue believes the use of the word 'threshold' was very deliberate: 'Through her words, her choice of words, through eye contact, I felt she was saying, "We will help him, I will help him along the way." And the other person was there as a witness.'

Less than four hours later, Sue's father died. To this day, Sue is convinced her father's death was helped by that nurse, and she's grateful for it.

Palliative care specialists who heard this story said that Sue misunderstood the experience she was having. One professor of palliative care offered an alternative explanation: 'It's quite possible Sue misinterpreted events, that the administration of his morphine and his death were in fact a coincidence.'

'People become very focused on the last moments of the lives of the dying. People lament, "If only I hadn't asked for that last dose of morphine for Dad, he might still be alive,"' she explained.

'And such are the emotions and sensitivities around death that people will reflect anxiously on other things done at the last minute too – for example, "If only I hadn't moved that pillow."'

Other professionals were equally emphatic morphine is not used the way Sue believed it had been, to speed up death.

'If morphine hastens a person's death it's either because the person administering it intended to do it or because they were incompetent and they got the dosage wrong. Morphine properly titrated to the patient's condition doesn't hasten death,' said one.

Another said: 'Most of our patients, particularly as they approach death, have been on opioids for a period of time and like lots of medications, your body adjusts to it in your system. So to facilitate a death we'd have to suddenly start giving a lot more for it to actually do that. The only way it will really hasten death is if we give a really big dose and we slow their respiratory system down completely. You don't see that happening.

'We also make a distinction between prolonging dying, which is what we would be doing, because we're not going to change the outcome. That's not hastening death. To me, whatever interventions we do for a patient have to have a very clear outcome that's going to benefit the patient.'

Doctors and nurses understand the risks of respiratory depression when opioids are used. But there were many more Sues who shared stories of the regular dose of morphine being given at the end of life and then death occurring within hours. So these conflicting stories seem confusing. Is it their perception, or is it what was happening?

The professionals' emphatic statement 'you don't see that happening' was contradicted by a small number of nurses and doctors who told me they knew it had been done or they had been involved in aiming to speed up death by delivering an extra dose.

The Victorian Parliamentary Inquiry into end-of-life choices final report stated that 'assisted dying occurs already in Victoria, despite being unlawful'. There's no reason to believe it isn't the same in the rest of the country.

This reflects the experience identified in several studies, including a 2014 interview of thirteen doctors who acknowledge and discuss the unofficial practice around hastening of death in Australia. Similarly, a 2003 survey of New Zealand general practitioners found 'Thirty-nine respondents had provided some form of physician-assisted death, and 226 had taken actions partly or explicitly with the intention of hastening death'.

This 'nods and winks' approach happens and it means our society can get away with not being honest with itself about how death sometimes happens, according to a prominent supporter of assisted death legislation in Victoria.

And this vague, ill-defined approach causes suffering.

In a typical example, one woman I spoke to felt she and her siblings had been robbed of the opportunity to say goodbye to her mother, because she had not known that a potentially fatal dose of morphine had been given. Was this a coincidence? Or was she right?

In another case, a woman who spent most of the previous three weeks at her mother's bedside, in an aged care facility, watched a dose of morphine being given, with the suggestion by the nurse administering it that it might be the last. But not realising the significance of what was being said, she went down to the canteen to have a cup of coffee. To this day she is devastated that she missed the moment of her mother's death.

It's true that there always has to be the 'last dose' and of course we don't know it's the last one until death occurs, in which case it might seem that that dose was the cause of death, when it isn't. But there's a gap between what the professionals understand about this and what the average person in the street sees.

The tensions around the issue abound.

When someone in the audience at a recent discussion on *palliative care vs euthanasia* said her relative's death had been nudged along by morphine overdosing in a hospital, the guest speaker became exasperated, almost shrill.

'Who said that?' she demanded to know. The woman in the audience wasn't prepared to say.

'I find that really frustrating,' the guest speaker said.

Sometimes it's a coincidence because the person was so close to dying anyway, but sometimes the incrementally higher dose did tip the patient into a slightly higher level of respiratory depression that made a difference. It can be confusing and seem contradictory. On the one hand professionals argue that it doesn't happen, yet on the other hand, families say they've experienced it. Did that last dose cause the death? Possibly, but not deliberately?

The key to avoiding distress and misunderstanding is good communication, according to a physician who does not work in palliative care but who is used to morphine being delivered in the hospitals he attends. He commented: 'I think we've just got to add one extra phrase: "I'd like to make your father more comfortable," – or whoever it is more comfortable – and "We'll do that by increasing the dose of morphine but there is a very real possibility he or she will die, even though it's not the intention. Don't go home. Get the family to come in."

'But doctors don't say that because they're fearful, fearful that it's actually illegal. In fact, it isn't illegal to do it or say it or to give the morphine in those circumstances.'

When faced with these questions, the healthcare professional and the family involved in the patient's care are supported in their decision to give a potentially fatal dose of morphine by the principle of double effect, as long as the dose given was proportional, incremental and not a sudden jump.

This ethical concept was first developed in the thirteenth century, when pain relief relied on opium, cannabis and alcohol, the most common mind-altering drugs, together with such things as gall of red ox, urine or live snails. The principle still holds today, even though some argue it's outdated.

The principle of double effect says pain relief should still be given, even if death is triggered by the administration of the drug, because the intention of relieving suffering was good, even though it resulted in the death, which was bad. The good effect outweighs the bad effect.

The American academic Timothy Quill sets it out this way:

- The act must be good or at least morally neutral.

- The agent must intend the good effect and not the evil effect (which may be 'foreseen' but not intended).

- The evil effect must not be the means to the good effect.

- There must be a 'proportionally grave reason' to risk the evil effect.

Over time, the original intention of the principle of double effect was gradually inverted, so that today, in every day hospital and nursing home environments, the doctrine is sometimes used to control and restrict the use of morphine. PRN, instead of speeding up the administration of morphine when it's needed by a patient in pain, ends up slowing it down. Fortunately, these views are being reassessed using a common-sense approach that, if applied properly, can act as a guide through the many considerations that make up this difficult ethical dilemma. The most recent case I was told about involved the mother of a doctor. She died slowly over a period of several weeks, in severe pain in a major hospital. It was something that he would never have allowed to happen to his own patients in his own hospital, in another part of the city. But he could do nothing for her.

If someone is not receiving the level of morphine needed to control pain at death, for fear of causing death, then the principle is being misapplied.

Doctors and nurses must not do anything that would deliberately take a life. They also have an obligation to relieve unnecessary pain and suffering. If the morphine is administered within the context of a regular, ongoing dose – for example, every four hours to relieve cancer pain when death is near – then the nurses and doctors have an obligation to continue that program.

They might also be in a situation where they've been given the discretion to increase the dose incrementally as the patient's pain levels increase, something that can happen the closer the patient moves towards death.

To withdraw pain relief, to lower it or to decide not to increase it to match sometimes surging pain because it might cause death would make no sense in these circumstances. For one thing, withdrawing the pain relief could itself cause death; for another, the patient would die in pain, an unnecessary – and cruel – additional burden for the patient and one that flies in the face of good healthcare principles.

In strongly supervised, confident palliative care units, usually within a major teaching hospital, morphine is administered appropriately. This tends to flow on to the community settings that are directly under the units' supervision, where families are taught how to administer morphine to control pain in the last days before death. Consequently, discussions with patients and their families are open about the use of morphine at this late stage.

But there are still too many situations in which there is confusion and a lack of openness about many aspects of the use of opioids.

When all these differences between theoretical knowledge and lived experience are resolved, the way the average person experiences death will improve and so will the experiences of their families.

The best palliative care teams encourage discussion about end-of-life care and the use of opioids. They talk to families about how opioids can contribute to a death that is free of pain and distress. This more forthright discussion is the big shift in palliative care education today.

Some medical specialists fear that talking about this subject will leave companions afraid. But not talking about it leads to fear and misunderstandings. Let's hope we can have the courage to talk about these issues with our treating doctors before entering the very end stage.

Palliative and terminal sedation

In some circumstances, when a patient's pain cannot be controlled, staff administer a level of sedation that renders the patient unconscious, so that they will not experience or be aware of experiencing any pain, right up until death. Depending on subtle differences, this is called either terminal or palliative sedation. Increasingly, the terms are being used differently. 'Terminal sedation' is being used to describe sedation and withholding food and water until death, starting when the patient can still absorb food and water, in conjunction with heavy sedation. By contrast, palliative sedation is done at a time when no further fluids and intravenous feeding can be given and the patient will not receive any benefit from them, along with heavy sedation. This is likely to involve a much shorter time, closer to the end.

Whatever the term, sedation of this type is not a strategy that is applied very often.

Those who argue for legalising euthanasia say that terminal sedation is just a lazy form of euthanasia. They say it is a distortion of compassion that simply prolongs death and suffering, that it technically allows those who practise it to, hypocritically, achieve the same outcome as euthanising the patient, but staying the right side of the law.

A recent review of several studies evaluating palliative sedation applied until death, showed that in those cases the sedation did not speed up the patients' deaths; rather, it left the patients unconscious while the dying process continued.

But this discussion depends on exactly what is being described and what drugs are involved. Some confusion in terminology occurs because of a lack of standardised definitions, even in studies and even among professionals. So a leading specialist in the area argues the term 'palliative sedation' should be abandoned altogether, for 'continuous deep sedation'.

Palliative care teams tend to do everything they can to avoid using this style of sedation, preferring to find a solution to the problem of a patient's pain or agitation. One palliative care specialist said she doesn't like it because to families involved it can appear that it is done to euthanise the patient, no matter how well it is explained beforehand that it is done to ease pain, and that death will not be hastened by it.

If the palliative care team of the person you are companioning is reputable and appropriately credentialled and they recommend continuous deep sedation, feel confident that they have given the matter considerable thought and that this is likely to result in less suffering for your patient. Feel free to ask: 'Will this hasten death?' and 'Is this legal?', if this course of action is recommended, since they will expect to be asked these questions.

Euthanasia, or assisted death

There is a very big discussion to be had about euthanasia (also called assisted death). In this section, I'll touch on a few of the main issues and make a few tentative conclusions.

In Australia, euthanasia – deliberately ending a life – is illegal, except in Victoria, which introduced the *Voluntary Assisted Dying Act* in 2017. Most of us have very strong moral, ethical and social beliefs against the taking of life, regardless of our stance on euthanasia. And there is also much confusion about what euthanasia is.

According to the *Oxford Dictionary* online, euthanasia is 'the painless killing of a patient suffering from an incurable and painful disease or in an irreversible coma'.

Some offer a further explanation, saying that in assisted death the patient completely controls the process, by performing the act. No one else is involved, although someone else might help by providing the means to carry out the act.

This is also illegal.

Social attitudes towards euthanasia and assisted death are changing, and it is argued surveys consistently find at least 70 per cent of the Australian community support it. However, what they actually support is not quite so clearly defined.

Apart from unrelievable pain, loss of control, desire for dignity and loss of independence are also reasons reported for requesting euthanasia.

Support falls in surveys if euthanasia for reasons other than terminal illness are offered, explained Emeritus Professor Colleen Cartwright, of Southern Cross University, in a detailed analysis of such polls in *The Conversation*, 'FactCheck Q&A: Do 80% of Australians and Up to 70% of Catholics and Anglicans Support Euthanasia Laws?' (1 May 2017).

And if the question is changed from one about physical suffering to mental and emotional suffering, support drops to as low as 36 per cent. As well, 'public support can drop significantly depending on the questions asked, how the survey was conducted and who conducted it', Professor Cartwright found.

In the lead-up to the change to the Victorian legislation in 2017, the *Age* newspaper editorialised that it supported legislation for physician-assisted suicide. Alluding to the ambiguities and lack of openness about purpose in prescribing drugs at the end of life, which I discussed earlier, it stated:

> *There is an overwhelming case to regulate something that*
> *happens widely but clandestinely and at the unnecessary*
> *peril of the compassionate medicos and family members who*
> *accede to the wish of such people to choose the means and*
> *timing of their death.*

Dr Bernadette Tobin is a Catholic ethicist at the John Plunkett Centre of St Vincent's Hospital, Sydney. She opposes euthanasia, arguing that better resourced palliative care would reduce the popularity for legalising it.

'The term euthanasia is a term that's invented for the purpose of persuading people. Literally it means "eu" which means "well" and "thanatos", which means "death". So I guess we can say literally it means dying well, a good death.

'We're all in favour of people dying well. Who's against that? And dying well will differ from person to person. What will constitute dying well for you, may well be different from what constitutes dying well for me. But there will probably be some things in common – such as, it is likely we will both want to be free of pain.

'There is no reason why people can't die well now, if they have the benefit of palliative medicine and care and if it is provided competently. There are a lot of problems with respect to competence and about access – in fact, there are terrible problems about access in this country at the moment.

'What needs doing is not any change in the law but training of people, a change of heart, different priorities.

'I think the desire to die well is entirely understandable. This is something a decent society should do something about. And it can. That said, the big challenge is to provide good end of life care for the poor and those who aren't powerful and don't have good connections and who live in remote places,' she said.

According to Tobin, the average Australian often does not understand that the law allows even aggressive intervention to control pain and ease the suffering of dying.

For example, it is legal to offer palliative sedation so that the person in effect sleeps out the last part of their life. It is legal to give effective doses of morphine, even if the side effect is to hasten death. It is legal to say 'no' to any treatment that would prolong life, for example, kidney dialysis or applying a defibrillator to kick the heart back into normal rhythm following a heart attack.

A number of people talked about harrowing experiences of watching someone they love die slowly in circumstances where poor palliation was offered, yet with a different management strategy, the person would have experienced less pain and less suffering.

One palliative care specialist said he can reassure almost all of the people he treats at his hospice, that they will have high levels of drug relief to avoid pain. Knowing this he can say to his dying patients: '"One day you will sleep and not wake up and then you will pass away very peacefully in your sleep and in 99 per cent of the time this is what happens." And this conversation is very comforting to patients – that they're not going to have a melodramatic death.'

Dr Chye is confident that the staff at the Sacred Heart Hospice can offer most people the possibility of high levels of effective drug relief to avoid pain: 'I can tell people you will go to sleep, you will experience no pain, but instead you will simply go to sleep. This is slightly different to what their family will see. But this is what we can offer the dying patient.'

This is in contrast to stories of patients – sometimes in regional hospitals, sometimes in aged care facilities, sometimes in other places – who suffered immensely.

One woman described the distress she suffered when her dying family member wasn't just able to 'slip gradually off into the ether with assistance from drugs, with us all there. For whatever reason, it wasn't an option'.

She explained that's why she now believes in euthanasia. But her family member was one of those people Dr Tobin mentioned, who live outside a major city and have poor access to good palliative care. Would better quality palliative care have changed her desire for euthanasia for him? The death she wished he'd had can be achieved in good palliative care environments.

Many people are surprised to find it is legal to refuse treatment, even if this means you will die, and there are also circumstances when infection is not treated. Sometimes pneumonia develops at the end of life. Withholding the antibiotics that would normally be given to treat pneumonia at this point is considered ethically acceptable because if the antibiotics were administered the infection may be halted but suffering will be prolonged and life will not be restored.

Arguments during the Victorian debate leading to the 2017 reforms in favour of euthanasia tended to focus on the issue of pain. I had a very intense discussion with a passionate advocate for the *Voluntary Assisted Dying Act*. He estimated that somewhere between 3000 and 4000 people in Australia each year die from horrible, painful deaths that don't need to be.

'That's a small but not insignificant number of people, who are dying terrible deaths, because there is nothing to help them,' he said.

Of those, the actual numbers who would avail themselves of euthanasia would only be very small, counter to the suggestion often made by critics of euthanasia that legislation would open the floodgates, he said.

The low proportion of those exercising a legal right to assisted death compared to those who've successfully petitioned for the right to do so, is important.

'We also find compelling the fact that while everyone given the choice immediately benefits because it reduces fear and anxiety, many of those people do not, in the end, exercise the option,' the *Age* said in its editorial supporting the 2017 Victorian act.

While some critics argue, without any evidence, that assisted death takes those societies where it is legal one step closer to the eugenics policies pursued in Nazi Germany, others argue it is not the state that's the problem in this debate, but people much closer to home – families.

In theory, the family is the first unit of society that protects and nurtures us. But top of its list of arguments against assisted death made by Hammondcare, an aged care provider specialising in palliative care services, is that legislation safeguards 'cannot detect coercion behind closed doors'.

'Safeguards cannot detect psychological pressure from family members and others with vested interests. This is particularly concerning for vulnerable groups such as older people, given more than one in ten older people experience psychological abuse in any given year.'

Our recent history shows that families are often the core centres of child sex abuse, domestic violence, elder abuse and other forms of exploitation and seriously dysfunctional behaviour. Maybe that means we are not ready to say that all our families will make objective judgements that protect the needs of the frail and infirm.

Palliative carers have observed 'bad deaths', in which families had an agenda of wanting a parent or relative to die so they could inherit assets. It might sound melodramatic but one nurse watched children plucking the jewellery off their dying mother, rather than offering her any succour. We don't know what the mother did to deserve such callous behaviour from her children. But the attending nurse was shocked by the attitude of the family, who she got to know. She suspected their attitude was driven by greed.

Kate White doesn't believe our medical system, with all its current potential for mistakes and mishandling, is ready for assisted death legislation: 'I just don't think you can build the safeguards in that we would all like. We supposedly have safeguards now and it doesn't happen.

'I mean we make decisions, particularly around the elderly where we say there's autonomy in decision-making but there isn't. And their decision-making is able to be influenced, even now.'

She argues that euthanasia advocates assume those wanting an assisted death can always independently come to a decision, when in fact, they may not have total control of the decision-making process.

In the meantime, the debate around whether we should introduce assisted death legislation continues. Whatever we decide as a society, the discussion is a good thing because it means we can all develop a better understanding of what really happens now, not what we think happens. I would also argue this extra reflection brings us one step closer to saying what we want when we die, and therefore one step closer to achieving a better death.

CHAPTER 04

What will companions see when someone dies?

*We learn what death looks like, so we are
able to face the death of those we love without being
afraid of what we do not know.*

To companion the dying person in all the stages right up until the very end, it helps to know what you will see. This means you won't be so afraid, which in turn means you can give more support to the dying person.

In reality, the part you're making better simply by being there is not the last moment of life. It's that time before, when the patient starts their intense solo journey. It's a journey that can take weeks, days or maybe only hours, a journey you can only be sure is over when the next breath definitively fails to come.

Even though it's a journey only they can go on, you can be a comforting presence.

For the terminally ill, there's a beginning point, when the active labour of dying begins. Some describe this as the 'pre-active phase.'

The dying person's focus will ultimately move inwards, as they become weaker and need to gather strength, simply to live through the day. This shift will not just be physical but psychological, since no one else will be going with them on the solitary journey they are about to undertake.

Kate White told a story that helped to illustrate this.

'We had a colleague we were looking after who was hilarious and the life of the hospital,' she said. 'When she was dying, she came to our hospital and we cared for her. Her little niece and nephew used to come in to visit and they would always put drawings on the wall for her and I remember coming in and looking at the drawings these children had done.

'And one day it just hit me that her niece had seen what I hadn't. My friend used to always be facing the door. You could never get past the corridor without her calling you in for a joke or chat or a story.

'But now she'd turned to the window and her back was to the door and her niece had drawn this and drawn it in this very childish way. But it really reflected that this person was pulling away. And I remember just standing there and looking at the picture and looking at her and thinking, "You are, you're pulling away from us, you are moving on, faster than we, her family and everyone around you had realised."'

Her journey to death was beginning, and she was detaching from those around her.

No two people will encounter death in exactly the same way. While there are some experiences in common, not everyone will have the same signs and symptoms in the same sequence, even if they are dying from the same disease. Some signs and symptoms will not be experienced at all.

A symptom is something the patient feels, while signs are physical changes that others can observe. Many of the physical signs indicating death is getting closer are, fortunately, not noticed by the dying patient themselves.

Some people will take several weeks to slowly pass through phases that others will take only hours to traverse. While staff attending a dying patient will do their best to help the family to understand when death is close, it is not always possible to know. When the dying patient stops eating, death will occur within the next few weeks. But it needs to be remembered the person is not dying from a lack of food but their underlying illness and their digestive processes have slowed down, so nutrients are no longer capable of being absorbed.

What your companions will see at the final stage

The following is a list of physical signs that the dying patient is likely to experience, although keep in mind that not all of them may be experienced. They don't happen in any particular order.

The risk with even documenting such a list is that it will raise more questions than it will answer. But I'd like to make a start. Inevitably, your experience will be different to what you see here, so please treat it is a general guide, not a strict rule. The reason for having a go at this is to try to help you understand what can happen and so be less afraid of those things that are either very rare or unlikely. If this list raises questions for you, please talk to your trusted medical professionals about it.

Sleepiness

As death approaches, the dying person will spend more and more time asleep. This is a normal part of dying. They may appear to have lost consciousness but be able to rally at times. There may be short breakthrough periods when the person is awake and lucid.

Deathbed visions

It is not unusual for a person at the end stage of life to have 'visions'. They may also talk of incidents that haven't happened. Are these hallucinations? Some palliative care specialists say not necessarily. As mentioned before, the dying sometimes speak in metaphors. It is common for people at this stage to have vivid recall of events and/or people from their distant past, and many palliative care specialists say it is common for the dying to see important people from their life who have died before them.

People sometimes worry that these deathbed visions are due to opioids. Most deathbed visions are not caused by medications. It might be hard, but one of the best things you can do when you hear the dying person talk as though they are hallucinating is just to sit and listen. It is highly likely that the dying person will find their vision comforting, although it may not seem so.

Changes in communication

Communication declines as the person spends increasing amounts of time asleep. If the patient becomes unconscious, it's now accepted that they continue to hear. For this reason, health professionals will continue to talk to the unconscious dying patient and encourage families to do the same. For conscious patients, the capacity to speak decreases and talking becomes difficult as the individual becomes weaker. However, occasionally someone who has said nothing for days can talk for brief periods not long before death.

Changes to the eyes

If the person is sightless due to unconsciousness, the eyes may have a flat, glazed look, even though their eyes are still open. The eyes can also stop tracking together before consciousness is lost completely. The blink reflex may also go before the person loses consciousness, but when the eyes are still open. The eyelids may appear half open and the eyes may appear sunken.

Confusion

Confusion has several causes. The cause of the confusion should be investigated carefully, because some triggers are unrelated to dying and therefore can be managed. Sometimes it is caused by lack of oxygen to the brain (hypoxia) as it shuts down, along with other organs. But is the confusion because of constipation or a urinary tract infection (UTI) that could be overcome, even at this late stage?

Or is the confusion one of language? Is the dying person trying to express something, the meaning of which is not apparent? Consider the possibility that the person is speaking in symbols or using metaphors. If this is the case, once again, if you can listen without expecting to understand, this can be supportive for the dying person.

Mild restlessness

This is a typical symptom of the dying and can have many causes. Again, a check needs to be done to ensure the person is not constipated or short of oxygen. Or the restlessness may be due to pain, a full bladder, discomfort from being in the one position for too long, medication or biochemical abnormalities. It may also result from a dream or have a psycho-spiritual origin. If a physical cause is found and it is treated appropriately this can mean a medication is avoided. If the restlessness is caused by fear, in the early stages the dying person can be helped with supportive strategies, such as listening and providing companionship. Drugs can ease symptoms. Care needs to be taken when medications the patient took every day during life are stopped, because stopping them suddenly can cause problems. For example, this can happen with some antidepressants, which are prescribed commonly today.

Again, if you are worried talk about this with the prescribing and treating doctors.

Severe agitation

As discussed in Chapter 3, some patients very near death experience severe agitation (called terminal agitation or 'the death throes'). They may pluck at sheets, pull at bedclothes and have long periods of distress. This can often be controlled by a variety of medications. If you are concerned, speak to your medical and nursing teams.

Changes to the pulse rate

The pulse rate might become more rapid or slow down and become erratic without feeling strong. This is because the heart is weakening. Sometimes the heart is one of the last organs to stop functioning. When it is the first to stop, death rapidly follows because blood flow to the brain ceases. The pulse rate becomes harder to feel the closer the person is to death.

Body temperature changes

Changes in body temperature can occur because the dying person has lost the capacity to regulate their body temperature. The person could become hotter than usual or cooler than usual, sometimes alternating between the two.

Hands and feet

As the person's condition declines, the body will prioritise blood flow to the centre of the body – to the heart, lungs and brain, and away from the extremities. This means reduced blood flow to the hands and feet, which can become cold to the touch. The skin can become very pale and the extremities can develop a distinct blue hue. This sometimes also happens to the nose. Gentle massage of hands and feet with hand or body lotions can be comforting for the dying person in the very early stages of dying. This can also be comforting to the family because it gives people a good reason to touch the dying, something we are often afraid to do. However, beyond a certain point, when the dying person has lost consciousness, these bodily changes – although noticeable – will not be uncomfortable to them because they are not aware of them, even though they may be disconcerting to those around them.

Rattling or noisy breathing

Although modern institutions don't like the term, this type of breathing is often referred to as the 'death rattle'. As soon as you hear it, you understand why. It occurs when the individual is unable to clear their throat because they have lost their cough reflex and small amounts of saliva or phlegm pool in the throat, which means that the air breathed in and out past it causes a rattling and crackling noise. Sometimes the rattle can be very loud. Although disconcerting to those around them, the dying person is not aware enough of their environment, or even their body, to be disturbed by this. Turning the dying person on their side can help quieten the noise. Medications can be given to dry up the secretions, although these are not always effective. The secretions can be suctioned off but this is not a popular strategy today because it's argued this actually stimulates their production.

Irregular breathing

This can come in a range of forms, the most common being Cheyne-Stokes breathing. Periods of rapid breathing alternate with periods of shallow breathing, and there may be little periods of not breathing at all. This is common close to death, but in the period before death is imminent it can occur and then correct itself.

Incontinence

A number of conditions, for example acute delirium, will cause the dying person to be incontinent of urine and/or faeces, well before they reach the end stage of life. Sometimes incontinence occurs as a person who previously had control of their bowels or bladder falls into unconsciousness. But as the dying person stops ingesting food or water, the likelihood of incontinence decreases. The dying may stop urinating or defecating altogether because they have stopped drinking and eating, so it is not to be feared as much as you might expect.

Decreased fluid intake

A point is reached when it becomes difficult for fluids to be administered by mouth because the throat muscles have weakened and the swallow reflex has gone. At the same time, any interest in drinking fluids usually decreases. This is normal when organs are shutting down. At this point, if not before, intravenous fluids are usually stopped because they cannot be absorbed by any of the organs. When the dying person has had no fluids for some time, long strings of saliva can form in their mouth. Palliative care specialists believe that even though the dying person may have no thirst, the build-up of saliva can still cause discomfort. Simple measures can be taken to alleviate this, such as cleaning out the mouth with gauze and spraying the mouth with misted water.

Loss of appetite

As death approaches, the dying person loses interest in food and no longer feels hungry because their metabolism starts shutting down. Occasionally, after several days the dying person can have a sudden interest in food for a short time before losing this again. This is a normal phenomenon in the period leading towards death. The dying person feels no hunger, pain or discomfort as a result of not eating, something that can be difficult for those around them to understand. However, people can live for several weeks after they have taken their last mouthful of food, and for as long as a week after their last sip of water.

Nausea and vomiting

Earlier in the process of dying, nausea can be experienced and vomiting can occur if there is a blockage in the gut, due to constipation, a tumour or medications. If vomiting and nausea are happening due to a treatable cause and death is not imminent, the medical/nursing team can investigate and institute appropriate treatment. Vomiting and nausea are not likely to occur close to death because the gastrointestinal system has shut down and all the by-products of that system are no longer being produced.

Bed or pressure sores

The time often eventually comes, close to death, when bed or pressure sores develop that will never have the opportunity to heal. Dying patients are regularly turned because of discomfort that invariably arises from being in the one position for lengthy periods. If the patient has a bed sore, the nurses reposition them to ensure there is little or no pressure on the 'sore'. While turning the patient was important before, the point may be reached where the person is so close to death that moving them or trying to treat the sore is more painful than the sore itself. Odour can be a problem, particularly for their non-medical companions at the bedside. In the dying patient, the wound will not get better. So the goal then is to try to avoid it getting worse, to keep the patient comfortable and to minimise the risk of odour to prevent companions from being discouraged to sit with them. If you are companioning someone dying whose bed sore has developed a strong odour, do not be ashamed of asking for something to mask or manage this.

Waxy skin

Once fluids are no longer being ingested, the skin quality changes, because the dying person is gradually dehydrating. The skin can feel waxy rather than dry. Subtle changes to the smell of the person's skin will occur with this. Breathing will also become shallow in response to dehydration.

Bodily breakdown

The weakest, most vulnerable tissues will break down first. The softest tissues of the body can start breaking down before death. Hence there can be fungal growths in mucosal areas, such as the vagina and mouth. If a person has suffered from neuropathy because of a disease such as diabetes, then blackness might occur in the feet. When the body breaks down in these ways there is no treatment. However, while it is confronting, try to take comfort from the fact that by now the person you love is unlikely to be registering pain, and death is close.

Open mouth

This common occurrence is caused when the lower jaw sags when the person loses control of the facial muscles. This, in turn, can exacerbate dry, cracked lips and a dry mouth. Once the mouth opens in this way closure is not possible. It creates one of death's most distinctive images, along with open eyes, a common occurrence.

The definition of death

With all the accumulating incidents that occur as a death gets closer, the mechanisms which finally trigger a death don't always follow a set pattern and are not completely fully understood, although the breathing and the heart stop.

At one time, the definition of death was very simple: death occurs when the heart stops beating and breathing ceases. But modern medical advances have changed this, and the definition is now the death of the brain, or more particularly, the brain stem. The brain is the source of all our functioning as a human being, and the brain stem controls the more basic activities, such as breathing and heart rate.

In the final stage, breathing can become erratic. Cheyne-Stokes breathing may occur until the slow pauses just get longer and longer. Breathing will either quietly stop, or, in other cases, after the last breath is taken, the dead person will let out a gasp-like noise as the last of the air from the lungs is completely expelled. In yet others, breathing just slowly comes to an imperceptible halt without either of these two experiences, giving a strong sense of someone just slipping away.

Once breathing has stopped for a considerable number of seconds, the heart stops beating. When the heart beat stops and does not pick up again at all, this is the traditional moment of death.

When the heart stops, blood stops circulating, and within minutes all the organs also stop or 'shut down'. Among those organs is the brain.

But in the modern era this definitive moment of death is now slightly more blurred than it has been for millennia. This is because the heart can be kept beating artificially, and with it other organs kept going, even though the brain is dead.

When the brain stem stops functioning, this is brain death. The person's awareness of self and power to be are gone. With brain stem death, as well as other organs continuing to function, hormones can still be produced and complete their interactions, fingernails and hair can still grow. Yet there is no life in a sense that has true meaning.

Every now and then there is a challenge to a hospital's definition of the death of a person. For example, when a child's heart is still beating due to a ventilator that is delivering oxygen to the lungs, from where the oxygenated blood is pumped around the body so that the organs keep working. But there is no brain stem activity. In such circumstances, distressed parents have taken hospitals to court to stop a child being declared dead. But, sadly, without the ventilator, even though blood circulates keeping organs alive, because the brain is dead, there is no viable life.

Sometimes something occurs that causes a reassessment of how we define death. A new development in heart transplant surgery in Australia in 2015, meant a heart could be removed from a dead person, then effectively 'restarted' in a new body after 20 minutes. So if the definition of death is the moment when the heart stops beating and it could be started again in a new person, was the person it was removed from really dead? The answer is yes. But the scenario left some wondering whether the legal definition of death needed to be rewritten in Australia. Debates and discussion still surface around brain death and cardiopulmonary death and their legal implications.

And even though when someone has died it should be obvious, this wasn't always necessarily so. In the past a great fear was that someone would be buried whose heart beat had slowed right down but who was actually still alive. In the eighteenth century in some communities a body would be buried with a bell on the toe, so that if the person 'came back' to life, they could ring the bell and get the attention of other people.

The wake, which in some cultures lasts for up to three days, apart from allowing mourners to gather and express their emotions about their loss, was also a convenient way in pre-scientific times, of giving the dead person an opportunity to move around and indicate if they were still alive, and so halt the proceedings before they were buried.

Fortunately, in the modern era, due to technology such as electroencephalography (EEG), we can read brain waves, respiration and heart beat. This means we can be extremely confident that someone is dead when this is claimed.

In the best of circumstances, the family's need to vigil at the end is respected. So important is this now considered, that some emergency departments are developing protocols for family to be present even when a person is being resuscitated with a defibrillator. Some medical professionals worry that such a family presence will obstruct emergency staff trying to do the job of saving the patient. The correct course of action is still evolving.

The vigil, the support of the dying at the deathbed, is a very ancient human ritual. It's history is longer than that of any hospital or medical system.

The dying will sometimes say they 'want to go home'. But is this the home they lived in until now? The home of their childhood? Or is it a metaphor for wanting to leave their physical body? If someone has expressed a wish to go home to a physical place before they enter the late stage of dying, can this be arranged? Sometimes it can't be because there is no one at home to look after them.

Otherwise, your support, your vigil at the deathbed can provide comfort. You can even encourage the person by giving them permission to go. The idea is to tell the person it is okay for them to go, not to tell them, 'It's time to go'. Death is about letting go and, therefore, their choice.

CHAPTER 05

What happens after someone dies?

We learn the 'housework' required after death – what's needed and what's not – so we can let go of the person honourably.

For centuries, and across cultures, it has been acknowledged that while death is a finite moment, the time afterwards is special; forces are at play. Some cultures and religious traditions argue it takes a while for the spirit to leave the body. Nurses, even with all their accumulated pragmatic experiences of death, see it as a time of great significance.

'In a nurse's mind, there is a sense for us that the person stays for a period. And whether we create that sense or not, I'm not sure. But it's a physical feeling, it's a feeling of someone being beside you, that they're there,' said a specialist palliative care oncology nurse.

'If you watch palliative care and oncology nurses wash someone after they've died, they talk to that person. They're very respectful. It's as if the patient was still alive, very much so, very much so,' she said.

Between death and burial

Care of the dead person and the family extends to the time after the loved one has died. You have the right to spend time with the person who has died, immediately after their death, in any institution where this occurs, although currently, in some places, this is something you might have to assert, rather than be encouraged to do.

If the person died at home, without any medical professionals around, before you make the necessary phone calls, it is okay to pause for a minute. Are there members of the deceased's family who would like to see them, to say one last goodbye before the body is removed from the house?

When Julie R's mother Joan died, most of Julie's five sisters were there. The family took the unusual step of keeping Julie's mother's body with them for nearly a day. She died at 5 p.m. and was not removed until the following afternoon, at 3 p.m., 22 hours later.

All agreed Julie's other sisters and grandchildren would want to say goodbye before anyone came to take Nan's body away. One of Julie's sisters was a registered nurse and the other two were enrolled nurses, so they were confident about laying out her body. They washed Nan's hair and changed her into the dress in which she would be buried.

'Everyone started gathering and so we all just had dinner, a huge big family dinner and a couple of the grandchildren went in and sat and had their dinner with Mum. And we were in another room and by the end of the evening all the sisters were sitting around the table in Mum's kitchen lounge area talking and we realised, "Well, where are all the kids?"

'And we went into the room where Nan lay and they were just chatting to each other, leaning on the bed and leaning into Nan, as if she was sitting there listening to them.'

Large numbers of the extended family stayed the night, sleeping in rooms aware that their mother and grandmother lay dead in a nearby bedroom. Julie said this was consoling, rather than unnerving. As the new day dawned, almost working at an instinctive level, the family members stayed on.

'For most of that day we were with her, until we felt ready to let her go.'

Julie believes this time with the beloved family matriarch helped everyone come to terms with her death. At a deeply fundamental level, they all, even the smallest children, knew that she had gone. But they felt peaceful and unperturbed by being with her.

Many argue it is cathartic to be with the dead body of someone you love and that it helps people manage their bereavement better.

'I know that being able to put my hands on the dead body of someone I love helps my body understand that they have gone – it's a cellular communication,' wrote Jenny Briscoe-Hough, Director and General Manager of Port Kembla's Tender Funerals, a co-operative funeral movement, in the book *A Matter of Life and Death: 60 Voices Share their Wisdom*, a powerful book of writing on death, edited by Rosalind Bradley.

She also made the observation: 'I was with [my mother] when she died and it was like having a hurricane blow through me. It rearranged me, which I think must be the job of this enormous life.'

This points to the spiritual value of being completely engaged with the death of someone you love when this is possible and appropriate for you.

More people today are reclaiming the old skills of attending to their dead. You can do this.

If the death occurs at home, straighten the person, putting a rolled towel under their neck and another one under their chin, to help keep the jaw closed since otherwise it will usually drop open, then contact the medical practitioner who has been involved with the patient in the time leading up to their death.

Since organising the death certificate falls to the doctors who were most involved, this could be the palliative care team who attended to your family member, or a general practitioner. Either way, a doctor will need to complete the first official task after the death, which is to write the death certificate. In some jurisdictions this has a more official-sounding name, such as 'Medical Certificate Cause of Death'. The death certificate is required for you to be able to register the death, something you are legally bound to do in most countries.

It is a serious offence for a doctor to give false information on a death certificate, so if there is any doubt in their mind about the cause of death, because they weren't involved and aren't convinced by the circumstances, they will not and should not sign the medical certificate. Sometimes, when a death has occurred shortly after someone is admitted to a hospital's emergency department, the medical staff can't say how the person died. In this circumstance, they will ring the police, who, as a first step, will ask family to identify the body.

The police will also ring the person's general practitioner. If the general practitioner knows the patient well, they can offer insights into the cause of death. But if they cannot be confident about the causes of death, they will pass the case on to the coroner. The coroner usually then requests an autopsy, which will be conducted by a forensic pathologist.

When someone dies from an expected death in a hospital or an aged care facility, responsibility for preparing the death certificate is taken by hospital staff and it's done as a matter of routine. If you want to take the body home, rather than to a funeral home, you will need to organise this in the period before the death.

Sometimes people think the police need to be contacted in the case of every death. But this is not necessary.

After the person has died, if you are in a hospital, nurses will come to lay the body out, observing any religious customs that are necessary. The opportunity to explain these customs is usually given to the family before death, and any reputable hospice or hospital will work to ensure cultural and religious requirements are respected.

For example, conservative Jews will want the body removed immediately, before it is handled by anyone else, to a *chevra kadisha* (spellings vary), a Jewish burial society, so that washing of the body can be done step by step according to ancient rituals, as biblical verses are recited. Muslims require the body to be washed by family members of the same gender.

For others, it can be a relief to think that hospital staff, usually the nurses who cared for the patient, will wash the body and prepare it for burial.

Nurses are taught how to wash and lay out a body, and it is reassuring to hear how respectfully and tenderly a body is treated by the nurses who had cared for the person when they were living. Many nurses value the opportunity to offer physical gestures of comfort in death, even if only symbolically.

'We wash the dead, that's what nurses do. It's where we say goodbye,' one nurse explained.

Viewing

US author and chaplain Kate Braestrup argues, citing her personal experience of those dealing with a death, that 'people are far, far more likely to regret not having seen the body [of a deceased loved one] than they are to wish they hadn't done it'. No doubt this will depend on each individual. In fact, she tells a very moving story of the reassurance it gave her to see her first husband's dead body when he died and then the story of a five-year-old girl, Nina, who wanted to see the body of her dead cousin and was eventually allowed to – with a good outcome.

There is something about the irrefutable evidence of the eye that helps the brain process the finality of death. For this reason, viewing the body is part of the death rituals of many cultures.

Many emergency physicians today believe that it is important, in most cases, for a child – and an adult – to see the body of someone who has died. This is because in their imaginations, people can conjure up an image of the person in death that is far worse than the reality. This, in turn, can have long-term effects on mental health.

Preparing a loved one's body for burial yourself

We asked the staff at my mother's nursing home if my sisters and I could wash and lay out my mother's body. Because we had no formal training in it – and because we were a little frightened of the unexpected – our sister-in-law Marie, a trained nurse, led us and showed us what to do. It was a peaceful time and, somehow, as we washed Mum's hair and cleaned her, I felt very soothed, as if we were providing some comfort and serenity, an antidote to the pain and suffering she experienced before she died, that we could not prevent.

But others have taken this a step further. The growing international movement to encourage and teach people how to clean, prepare their own dead and manage the funeral rites is built on the premise that it is only in the last 100 years or so that families have allowed this task to be taken from them.

American Elizabeth Knox, who as part of the Crossings group teaches people how to do this work, began her mission of revolutionising the Western attitude to this task after her seven-year-old daughter was killed by the release of a car airbag, that horror unique to the modern era. In very moving terms, she reports the overwhelming conviction that she should not hand her child over to strangers to care for in death, any more than she should have in life. Anyone who has read the very moving passage in Barbara Kingsolver's *The Poisonwood Bible*, when a mother washes the dead body of her child, would see this in new terms, understanding more the power of this small ritual in helping to come to terms with such a devastating loss.

Elizabeth Knox argues that as soon as a body is handed over to a funeral director, they have all the control and the bereaved very little. Her online booklet, *Crossings: A Manual for Home Funeral Care*, emphasises that the more people are involved and the more planning is done, the better those involved will feel.

Knox advises that more than one person should take part, to share both the heavy lifting and the emotional burden.

Rigor mortis, when all the muscles of the body contract and stiffen, begins anywhere between three and six hours after death. This happens because the cells of the muscles are no longer oxygenated. It eases off between twelve and 72 hours after this, as the cells of the muscles begin to break down.

It's ideal to wash the body in the time before rigor mortis sets in, and lay it out in a way that suggests rest and peace. It is natural for the jaw to drop open once someone has died. Sometimes a scarf is tied tightly from the neck up to the head, before rigor mortis sets in, in an attempt to keep the jaw closed. This is not always successful.

Preparing the body of someone you love may not be for everyone but these practices are a good example of us taking back the death experience from medical professionals and funeral directors. By being more active ourselves, we are more able to accept the loss, then let go.

The Natural Death Handbook, by Stephanie Wienrich, Josefine Speyer and Nicholas Albery, outlines in detail how to do this. The process is not so much complicated as confronting, since body fluids are expelled, and decay, particularly of the softer tissues of the body, has started. For this reason, many prefer to leave this task to others.

Even if you are not washing the body, you can be involved, and you can watch and take part in some of the preparation of the body. But be aware that you need to set this up with the funeral home, well in advance of the death, as attitudes to involvement of the family and the level of access the home will allow will vary.

Certainly, many people who have had this experience find it very healing, a spiritual experience.

Make sure that if you choose to do something unconventional like preparing the body for burial yourself, that you let the hospital or nursing home know in advance, so they do not automatically start a different process they expect you to follow. Also, ensure that what you have planned is legal. Having the right paperwork prepared in advance – for example, paperwork that allows you to transport a body – will help to make an already difficult time of grief a little easier, especially if you want to do something unconventional, like transporting a body yourself in your car.

When more time is needed

Wherever the death has occurred, the funeral director will usually be called so they can remove the body. In a hospital, after the body is washed, it is taken by lift to the morgue, which is usually located in the basement of the building. This is done discreetly, with the body covered in such a way that people don't realise what they are passing, when such a trolley is being transported.

Hospitals and other institutions such as nursing homes like to remove the body quickly, but make sure you have time for family members to gather and say goodbye if they want to. If the death has occurred at a nursing home or hospital, usually one of the staff will make arrangements with the funeral director. Make sure this is not so hasty as to be obscene. If someone dies in the middle of the night or in the early hours of the morning, you can insist on your right to have time for family to gather to acknowledge the death and say goodbye.

If the death has occurred at home, keep in mind that laws limit how long a body can be kept at home. For example, in many places in Australia, laws require that a body cannot be held for more than 48 hours if not refrigerated, unless it is embalmed. So this is a practical limitation on the amount of time you can have the body at home. Similar codes and regulations are in place in the United Kingdom and New Zealand.

New technologies are becoming available that enable the body to be kept refrigerated, yet still accessible. Traditional bags of ice can be used, but this method can quickly become troublesome as the ice melts, especially in hot climates. Dry ice is a better substitute since it is colder and doesn't drip while melting.

Australia's Natural Death Care Centre argues that by using cold plates, a body can be kept at home for up to five days. This five-day period is the amount of time in New South Wales that it is legal to keep a body with you at home before it has to be removed to a funeral home or buried or cremated.

The Centre's philosophy is that families should have the opportunity to be much more involved in every stage of death – which they argue is not new, but a return to a traditional approach.

When a baby dies, parents may feel they need to spend more time with their child than the hospital may allow. The CuddleCot was invented in the UK to allow families of a stillborn baby to keep their baby with them for longer, usually for several days rather than just several hours. It consists of a cot that includes a cooling unit to keep the baby's body cool.

It might be uncommon today, but the time might come when it will be considered socially acceptable to take a body home from a hospital to manage burial rituals from home. Today, those who want to attend to the body at home tend to be people who have nursed that person from home without involving a hospital.

Embalming

Embalming preserves the body of the deceased as well as removing liquid from the body to prevent leakage. The process means the body is presentable and does not disintegrate in the usual time, so burial can be delayed. It is also sometimes argued by embalmers that it is done for infection control, but this idea is open to challenge. For some diseases, embalming will not be enough to protect against infection, or embalming will not be recommended because of the risk to those doing the work. And likewise, Elizabeth Knox of the Crossings group argues infection can be prevented without embalming.

Embalming is not as common in the United Kingdom, Australia and New Zealand as it is in the United States, and it is traditionally even less likely to occur in Europe. The practice is thought to have first developed in ancient Egypt, where it became highly refined and was done so the body did not disintegrate before entering the afterlife.

It rapidly became part of US funeral practices during the mayhem of the civil war in the 1860s. Many young men died on battlefields, far from their homes. Parents who wanted to reclaim their sons' bodies refused to countenance them being buried without the intense rituals of the time, but the bodies' decay had to be prevented before they were put into coffins to be sent home. Embalming became the default service provided by most US funeral homes and, despite questions about its relevance, it is still popular today.

As a general rule, embalming is required if the coffin is to be placed in a crypt or a vault, or any other above-ground tomb, rather than buried in the ground, or if it is being transported overseas.

Funeral parlours are not able to hold a body for, typically, more than seven days unless it's embalmed to control infection, since some disease-carrying pathogens continue to breed after a person has died.

Embalming is also common if there is to be a viewing, especially beyond three days from the death, since this means the family can see the body and touch it, without being confronted by decay and odour. Embalming is also useful if the deceased had been disfigured by an accident, sometimes the cause of death. In these cases, subtle repair work by the embalmer means the family can view the body without gaping wounds adding an additional source of distress. But there is a growing attitude that embalming is pointless because it is not realistic or natural.

Notifications

In New South Wales, notification of the death has to be lodged with the Registrar of Births, Deaths and Marriages within seven days of the burial or cremation, and this is one of those tasks often done by a funeral director. Other states and countries will have similar requirements.

To a funeral director, completing such paperwork is a routine part of their job, and they have administrative systems in place to make this happen. For a grieving family, doing the same thing can be more difficult, at best a nuisance, at worst something that triggers great distress. But it's important to know that as a family, you are legally entitled to complete this paperwork yourself; doing so might make you feel better. According to the New South Wales Registry of Births, Deaths and Marriages, the following details have to be given:

   ❧ surname and first names

   ❧ sex

- date of death and date of birth

- place of death

- usual address of the deceased

- usual occupation during working life

- marriage particulars: the place, age, full name of spouse

- all children of the deceased, including their names and ages

- full name of both parents, including the mother's maiden name

- burial details.

A copy of the death certificate will also be needed by close family, such as a husband, wife, parent or adult child, so they can do things such as close down a bank account and cancel a driver's licence.

You will also have to advise, where appropriate, agencies such as Centrelink, Veterans Affairs, Home Care Services, Meals on Wheels, the Public Trustee, the executor of the will, the Taxation Office, Medicare, private health funds, the electoral office, insurers, the housing department, life insurers, the superannuation fund, the motor registry, banks and building societies.

With a bit of luck, the person you are companioning will have made this easier for you by organising their paperwork to ensure ease of access to these organisations.

Note also that the Australian Taxation Office has a deceased estate checklist, relating to the person's tax affairs.

Probate

When a person dies, they lose all legal power. A 'grant of probate' gives the executor the powers and duties necessary to administer the estate. The Western Australian public trustee has a good definition of probate:

Probate is the process of proving and registering in the Supreme Court the last Will of a deceased person. When a person dies, somebody has to deal with their estate.

It is usually the executor of their Will who administers the estate and handles the disposal of their assets and debts. In order to get authority to do this, they usually need to obtain a legal document called a 'Grant of Probate'.

New Zealand and Australia both have probate systems they inherited from the UK model. While US jurisdictions use different terms to describe the distribution of the proceeds of a will and there is slight variation from state to state, the principles are the same.

Although it is usually done by a lawyer, you can save money by doing this yourself, an experience those who've done it say is empowering. That said, estates with many and complex assets involved, such as property, shares and investments, are best handled by an experienced probate lawyer.

Mel has only one sibling, a brother. Dorothy had no debts and had stated in her will she wanted her assets, less a few expenses, to be split equally between the two siblings. Both were happy with the terms.

'So it was relatively straightforward and fortunately, my brother was happy for us to do the probate ourselves,' Mel said.

Mel and her husband Gav, who helped her with the paperwork, were lucky because her mother had talked openly about her will and what her wishes were, before she developed dementia about two years before she died. By then, for example, she had forgotten she had any shares.

'That saved us a lot of heartache. We had discussions beforehand that we would not have been able to have at the end, so I'm very glad we had them when we did.'

'Before she died, we were able to do a checklist with her. She had told us how she was planning to make the will – and it turned out there were no surprises in it. She had had a frank discussion with us about share portfolios and her superannuation arrangements.

She had her financial records all kept together, so when she said she had no debts, this was very easy for us to check.'

Mel and Gav live in New South Wales, so they followed the prompts on the NSW Supreme Court Probate website, www. supremecourt.justice.nsw.gov.au.

'The Supreme Court's website doesn't have a sign that says "Stop – appoint a solicitor now." By doing it ourselves we saved about $5800 in lawyers' fees – but be warned – you have to dedicate a good week of your life to filling in forms. The jargon is not of this world! But if you follow the links, and fill in the forms the way they say, all their links point you in the right direction. Remember, you need a certified copy of everything, so a JP (Justice of the Peace) is your best friend.

'Yes it was a bit daunting, but by working it through ourselves and discussing it with each other, we learnt so much. We understood why things needed to be done a certain way. It was very empowering for us that we managed to deal with this ourselves.'

CHAPTER 06

The unexpected death

We develop the skills, particularly the social ones,
to help when a death is unexpected.

'Julian's been in a motorbike accident and he's in Tamworth Hospital,' my father said in the official, clipped tone he uses to impart important news. He was talking about my brother.

'Oh? Any details?'

'Not really. Someone just rang. He said he'd broken his leg in two places. The girls have been crying and I can't console them.'

Julian's only daughter, fourteen-year-old Claire and her school friend were staying with Dad for the school holidays. I was alarmed. If Julian had broken his leg in two places, on a country road, that was serious – very serious in Australia with its distances so great that the femoral artery can bleed out and the victim die before help arrives. I rang Tamworth Hospital.

In a strange twist of fate, Marie, his wife and an intensive care nurse, worked at the very emergency bay where Julian was taken. She gave a nurse, a friend of hers, permission to talk to me.

'How serious is it?' I asked.

'Very serious. He was T-boned by a car on the Old Winton Road, riding into town on his motorbike,' said the nurse.

'What are his injuries?'

She rattled off a list of broken bones and ruptured organs. When she mentioned a pneumothorax, a punctured lung, I heard an obscure voice, almost behind me, say: 'Will he still be alive in the morning?' And then I realised the voice was mine.

I was expecting a rebuke for being so melodramatic but she said, 'We don't think so.'

We don't think so.

And so began my family's own very painful experience of sudden and unexpected death, something from which you wonder whether you will ever recover.

The role of authorities when death occurs

The coroner is involved when an unexpected death occurs. Sometimes these deaths are sudden and inexplicable, other times they could be the result of violence. So the police and ambulance have often attended the scene of the death before the coroner becomes involved.

The coroner's role is to investigate certain deaths to find out who the deceased was, the date of death, place of death, circumstances and the cause of death. In some cases the coronial investigation (that is, the coroner's inquiry) leads to an inquest but not always.

An inquest is a court hearing conducted by the coroner designed to investigate the circumstances and cause of a person's death. Now it's not just the coroner, working on the case on his or her own. Witnesses are called and can be compelled to give evidence. The coroner cannot find someone guilty of a crime. But if they start to believe a crime has been committed they stop their inquest and refer the case to the Director of Public Prosecutions, who decides whether criminal charges should be laid against someone, for a judge to hear, or a jury trial.

Coroners also investigate the cause of fires and explosions.

One of the coroner's roles is to ask: What can we do to avoid preventable deaths?

In Australia each year nearly 20,000 deaths – 12 per cent of all deaths – are reported to the coroner. There are about 5700 deaths reported to the coroner in New Zealand. While most of the cause of the deaths can be explained, some cannot.

If a doctor won't issue a death certificate, the death is referred to the coroner. When a death is suspicious and someone, maybe the doctor, has decided they need to involve the authorities, the death can be reported to the police or directly to the coroner. But in reality, most deaths in these circumstances are reported to the coroner by the police.

Coroners also have the power to direct police to conduct an investigation into a death. More typically, a police officer will report the death to the coroner, who will then have a forensic pathologist conduct an autopsy. A coroner will then look at the police report and the pathologist's report to decide whether the circumstances should be reviewed at an inquest.

A road accident death is always reported to the coroner because it's a sudden or unexpected death and there is always the possibility that someone may have committed a criminal offence in causing the road accident, and this needs to be looked into.

There is also the possibility that there was something else that might need to be scrutinised, so that systems can be improved – for example, a transport system or a hospital system.

Former New South Wales Deputy Coroner Hugh Dillon said an inquest can be of immense value for people, because it provides families with much more of an explanation about how and why the death occurred. Dillon is campaigning for reforms to improve the New South Wales coronial system and argues one way to improve it would be to have a standalone coronial court.

'New South Wales is an outlier in Australia and internationally in having no coroner's court. Our system is part of the Local Court,' Dillon points out.

One of the problems this causes is a wide gap between the skills of experienced full-time coroners servicing Sydney and the experience of country magistrates: 'Flowing from this, a significant variation in standards and quality of service across the state.'

An additional purpose of an inquest is to see if anything can be done to prevent a death in the future. Questions the authorities may ask include:

- Did the hospital system, or airline safety or road system treat this person as he or she ought to have been?

- Did the death arise because of something not being done properly or being done wrongly?

- Can something be done to prevent death occurring in similar circumstances?

The coroner may order a post-mortem to be carried out in certain circumstances.

In Dillon's experience, 'Coroners receive many reports of hospital deaths that trouble people, particularly in relation to children who die in hospital or mothers who die in hospital.' He gave an example:

An elderly woman who was in end-stage renal failure died in a major teaching hospital after she had required transfusions and dialysis. The family did not understand the cause of death. They made a request for the coroner to review the case, which the coroner agreed to do, although doing so is not mandatory.

Due to the nature of her illness the woman needed many transfusions and continuous kidney dialysis. For the dialysis, blood was pumped from a vein to the dialysing unit and treated blood was returned to the venous circulation, and there were already a number of places on the woman's body where an intravenous line had been inserted in the past. When the next place was found for the needle to be inserted, the tissue around the needle became very soft and started to bleed.

Even though she was being checked by intensive care unit nurses every twenty minutes, the woman very quickly lost large amounts of blood, went into severe shock and then died.

The exact details were explained by the treating doctors during the course of the inquest and it emerged that the family hadn't been told what was happening at the time and hadn't been given very much information about the incident.

The kidney specialist who had been treating the woman explained to the court the details of what had happened.

'Once the family heard the explanation, they understood much more, especially when he said, "I'm so sorry we lost your mother. I know it was shattering for you, but we really tried to do everything and it was a race against time." Later, they talked to the doctor outside the court room and went away accepting their mother's death.

'I see the coronial system as a way that our society has of treating human life with respect,' Dillon said. 'An inquest can be immensely cathartic and beneficial for people. But I think it's wrong to say that coroners and inquests ever give people closure, something you hear said quite often. It doesn't change anything.

'But it can give a degree of solace to some people in the sense that it provides some answers to some of the questions that they have. But I also think that the genuine benefit people get from this is that their concerns have been taken seriously.

'We can't do more except to show that the life of your loved one is valuable, was valuable; it's important and it's important not just to you, but the community has an interest in this life and we all have an interest in one another.'

How I wished for that show of the value of my brother's life when he was killed in his car accident.

In some cases, like Julian's, the coroner's inquest is dispensed with altogether. This was the prerogative of the court, since charges had been heard against the driver, which the magistrate had dismissed.

In terms of legal priority, the criminal case has precedence, a registrar of the court explained when I rang to ask about this afterwards.

'Duplication would be a waste of the court's time and resources. It's common for the decision to be made not to go to an inquest, if a related criminal case goes first,' he added.

This saves costs and stress on the participants, like my sister-in-law and her grieving family, he explained.

'I would have liked to have heard the driver answer the question, "Why do you think the accident happened?"' I complained.

The registrar remained calm. He was probably used to such harangues, and had developed customer-service strategies to cope: 'You could write a letter to the coroner. About 2 per cent of these cases are reviewed and an inquest does end up going ahead.'

But there was too much lead in my saddle. I didn't want to hound the seventeen-year-old driver of the car until she was broken. Life is too short, not just hers but mine, and I knew that if there was an inquest there'd just be some other point of order I'd want to call.

Acceptance eventually came, but that was some years later. At the time I fell into despair.

But it's encouraging to think that improvements can come out of the recommendations of a coroner: a set of traffic lights might be re-phased, bollards placed in danger spots, safety equipment on ships improved, a flaw in a drug delivery system fixed or better care provided in an aged care facility.

Since 2009, any NSW agency that has had a coronial recommendation made about it is legally obliged to respond with either acceptance of the recommendation or a reason why they shouldn't accept the recommendation.

Australia also has a National Coronial Information System, which collates coronial cases from across the country, so developments in one state can be shared with another.

If someone dies in the course of a police operation – which includes a car pursuit – then an inquest is mandatory. Inquests are also held into all deaths in custody.

Murder

Leigh Sales, the anchor of the popular ABC TV program 7.30, points out in her book *Any Ordinary Day:*

> *Notably, on the day of a terrorist attack, a mass-fatality accident or some other major news story, the number of viewers watching 7.30 will almost certainly be bigger than*

usual. A public disaster appears to make television ratings spike. People seem perversely but irresistibly attracted to catastrophe when it happens to others, while in our daily lives we do everything possible to shield ourselves from these poison darts of fate.

How true that is. Can't we all remember doing exactly this?

Thankfully, the closest many of us will get to the experience of a violent crime, such as a homicide, is to see it talked about on Sales' television program or acted out in a Hollywood movie. For those who've experienced it, it's very different. Not only has their life changed in a way that it will never return to, but they must experience grief and a deep level of trauma every time their thoughts return to the incident, which will be repeatedly, at least initially and possibly for a long time to come.

Many years ago I was preparing for a friend's child's birthday party when I took a phone call from my mother saying, 'Don't worry, I'm okay.'

Why shouldn't she be okay? It was a Saturday afternoon and she'd gone to the shopping mall. A few minutes before, I'd heard a radio report of a massacre in 'Sydney's western suburbs'. Seven people had been killed and six injured.

As we always do, I'd assumed that was in a place far away. But it was in the middle of the suburb where I grew up, where my mother was trapped while she tried to buy a cake. The owner of the shop had pulled down a security barrier and so she was protected but had to listen to the sounds of terrified shoppers banging on the screen, pleading to be allowed in.

A little while later, I took a call from the sixteen-year-old daughter of another friend. Her mother had gone to the mall to buy a present for the birthday boy: 'We can't find Mum,' Helen said.

Her mother had been taken hostage by the gunman. Fortunately, she was later released by him. When he fired the gun he'd been brandishing for hours, he shot himself, not her. The birthday party was abandoned.

I'd bought a beautiful wall mirror that morning but I could never look at it again. I donated it to the next school fete. Even now, when I think of that mirror, I nearly vomit. I used to take my three children to the mall. How would I have protected all three, faced with a gunman? I have been to that mall on a few occasions since. I've only stopped for coffee there a few times, if that's where a friend suggests we meet, but at the back of my mind is a feeling of repulsion.

Yet I was removed, had three degrees of separation from the story. The hostage suffered deeply and for a long time after everyone else had moved on. If I gag when I think of the mirror, how would I have reacted if my mother had been killed? It seems beyond imagining, yet people have to go through this and what they experience is nothing like a movie. And it's a world away again from the unexpected, accidental death, which is bad enough.

Analysing figures on violent deaths to put them into context is a good thing to do. Cover Australia is an insurance company, a business that needs to gather accurate data on the likelihood of a range of incidents, including homicides.

The 2014 Cover Australia report, available on the internet, shows that between 2010 and 2012 the three leading causes of external death – that is, death by a cause other than a medical one from within the person's own body – were:

- accidental deaths – 5867

- intentional self-harm – 2522

- assault deaths – 216

It also shows the three major causes of death by homicide in Australia were stab wounds (187 deaths), beatings (125 deaths) and gunshot wounds (69 deaths). The order of these events is the opposite to the order in the United States, where guns are more freely available.

30 per cent of these Australian victims were aged between 35 and 49, and 21 per cent were 25 to 34 years of age. 85 per cent of the offenders in all the homicide cases were male.

This shows that despite what we see on television, we're much more likely to die from an accident of our own making than by being murdered by someone such as an intruder. Our chances of dying through suicide are somewhere in the middle.

Cover Australia also says that in Australia between 2010 and 2012 there were 243 murder incidents. (The mismatch with the 216 figure is explained by the way the death was achieved and some assault deaths that weren't classified as murders.) In some cases, more than one person was murdered at the same time, so the total number killed in those incidents was 511.

The figures are therefore low, which is reassuring. That said, murder does happen and the people who love the victims have to live with the aftermath. In some cases the assailants are never found. Every now and then the police might still contact the family. This raises false hope of more insight into what happened, which never comes. The question remains unanswered, who did this? And when publicity occurs about the case, this raises anxiety for the family.

When the families of murder victims Anita Cobby and Ebony Simpson met for the first time, in 1993, they realised they wanted to unite to help other victims of homicide. With the support of the New South Wales Institute of Forensic Medicine and ongoing support (which still continues today) from the South Western Sydney Area Health Service, they formed the Homicide Victims' Support Group.

Two responses emerged – the urge to support others and the desire to bring political change, so that victims of homicide didn't go on to experience trauma at the hands of the legal system.

Trauma by travelling through the legal system is still a challenge for surviving families. A study done in the Netherlands by Anton van Wijk and published in 2016 looked at the experience of 28 'co-victims'.

He confirmed an earlier study which found the formal way police and legal authorities work can severely disturb the grieving process of the co-victims and the psychological and emotional problems they've experienced will worsen, continuing to grow during the criminal proceedings and sentencing.

None of this is surprising but it's an interesting, objective study that confirms what we suspect. In addition, he found the following about the co-victims:

- ❧ Their problems may be serious and long term.

- ❧ Psychological issues are worse than for other types of crimes.

- ❧ They are more susceptible to protracted and complicated grief.

- ❧ They have a higher risk of depression.

- ❧ They suffer a profound loss of self, which includes permanent loss of future, 'violating devastation', feeling like a different person now, loss of control and loss of innocence.

- ❧ They are likely to feel anger, not just against the perpetrator but against the world.

- ❧ They experience repeated intrusive images, nightmares, overwhelming feelings of anger and rage, fear, excessive alertness and guilt.

There has been a slight shift in the focus of community attention on homicide in more recent years. Yes, murder by strangers continues but domestic murders are now scrutinised in a different light. They are not happening more, they are just being noticed, talked about and reported more.

Again, we go back to the Cover Australia report for a clue as to why, although many long reports have been written in recent years on the subject. Of the 511 homicides in 2014, it found that:

- ❧ 39 per cent were classed as domestic

- ❧ 36 per cent were carried out by acquaintances

- ❧ 58 per cent were caused by the intimate partner in domestic cases

- ❧ 70 per cent took place at residential properties.

This tells us something chilling but well known: despite what television dramas and movies show, most murders are conducted by someone who knows us. But even worse, these figures point to domestic violence as the most likely setting for murder, something now drawing more media attention.

Rebecca Poulson's niece Malee and nephew Bas were murdered by her brother-in-law, the children's father. Rebecca's own father, Peter, was also murdered as he fought to his death trying to protect Malee and Bas. Her brother-in-law died later that day from self-inflicted wounds after being shot by police at the scene.

Rebecca points out that, as in her family's case, 85 per cent of child homicides in Australia are carried out by a parent.

She did not experience the revulsion of being a three-degrees victim, like me, but the emotions of being much closer.

'I suffered extreme pain and a need to know *exactly* how they died, so that I could carry some of their pain and work out how much pain they had before death came,' Rebecca explained.

She now lobbies, along with the Poulson Family Foundation, to help prevent child homicide. The Foundation focuses on police training to improve responses to apprehended violence orders and to increase the level of Department of Family and Community Services (FACS) caseworkers for children whose cases have already received a red flag.

In a recent piece Rebecca wrote for the *Sydney Morning Herald*, after a domestic violence murder in Western Australia similar to the one her family suffered, she noted that the father who committed the crime was often and repeatedly described by his bewildered community as a 'good bloke'.

Rebecca would like to see this thinking change – for the community to be more honest about what has happened, that the killer, although deeply troubled, has committed a crime of domestic violence.

'These are very rarely a "shocking" tragedy out of the blue but part of a long-term pattern of cohesive control and abuse, which the victim and her children would have suffered hundreds if not thousands of times before the final deadly "incident",' she said.

'Nearly always there are red flags. Various systems and bodies like police, FACS, schools or others were most likely flagged and aware that the women and children needed help.

'These are preventable murders, but the government, police, communities, FACS and many others need to work together to increase funding and change ingrained cultural attitudes and beliefs.'

When domestic violence campaigner Rosie Batty addressed the National Press Club recently, Rebecca was there, sitting next to Ann O'Neill, founder of Angelhands, a support group for people who have lost someone through homicide. Ann's two children were murdered by her estranged husband in 1994. Later she endured questions from strangers asking, 'What did you do to him to cause him to do that?'

Rebecca has advice for people who are co-victims of a homicide, especially one that has drawn media attention.

'Contact the Homicide Victims' Support Group and Police liaison officer. They will coordinate the media and police, whose involvement starts within hours of the death when you are still reeling in shock and disbelief,' she said.

'The Homicide Victims' Support Group also helps the people left behind to navigate and work with media. After murder, in particular if children are the victims or if there was more than one victim, the media scrutiny is intensive and unrelenting. Murder adds another different level to grief than most other deaths. There is the normal shock and grief the person is dead, then the police involvement. They were in my house within hours and continued to visit and take long and exhausting statements.

'Then there is the media camped on the doorstep, hiding in cars and approaching me when I was trying to select a grave site. I had immediate phone calls and people coming to the house to interview me – some programs pretending to deliver flowers, then when I opened the door asking for an interview. They came to the funeral as well and took photos of me and my sister.

'To keep this to a minimum and on advice from the police, we decided to do a press release and media comment two days after the murders. So I confronted a wall of flashing lights and recording media, when in reality I just wanted to curl up and hide.

'Another experience you don't think about until you are going through it, is the re-trauma and sheer sickness of going through the legal systems to try and get justice or find out why it happened.'

So Rebecca offers two pieces of advice for those who find themselves in her situation:

- ❧ **Get counselling:** 'In NSW this is free through the Victims of Crime Justice Board, if you can't afford it. Homicide will recommend the services organised through the Homicide Victims' Support Group or someone like this – as it really does require specialists. Some counsellors are out of their depth with these crimes. You can change or move counsellors if you don't feel comfortable and you don't need to justify or give reasons why.'

- ❧ **Take leave from work:** 'My work were great and gave me extended compassionate leave so I didn't have to use my annual leave. But use all the different categories of leave and use it for the following: to be with supportive family and friends, to go to your counselling sessions, to go on an easy mini-break after the funerals are done – like a beach with not too much of a commute. We went to an isolated farm the first Christmas, as cheery shopping centres and overwhelming advertising were just too much to bear – no TV, no shops. It was the best thing.'

Accidental death

When I asked if my brother was likely to survive his motorcycle accident, and the nurse I was speaking to said, 'We don't think so' my sister Cecilia and I did a frantic six-hour drive to his place to try to say goodbye. But we were too late.

The last thing he said to his wife, as he was loaded into the ambulance was: 'I can't breathe.'

Her last words to him were: 'Don't talk, just breathe.'

Hours later, he died, but not before an emergency team had worked hard to try to save him.

The doctors' report documents numerous blood transfusions. As fast as the emergency team could funnel blood in to him, it leaked out again, pouring out of every split organ and pooling in cavities such as his abdomen.

Julian fought his death hard. In and out of consciousness he went as he fought, consoled as much as he could be by his wife but still afraid.

And then, not surprisingly, given how hard his heart was pumping, his blood pressure fell, as blood pooled outside torn stomach, spleen, liver. He had a cardiac arrest at close to 11 p.m. Written in his doctor's hand at 11.03 p.m.: 'May He Rest In Peace'. It is finished, it is done. I didn't know until now that this ancient formula of words, passed along through the centuries, was still used.

I find it comforting, looking back, to think that doctors moved away from their functional tasks, even if only for a moment, to write this spiritual mantra.

For the next ten days our family huddled in a grief bubble. My two trips away from the farmhouse were like leaving a dark, cosy wolf's den and coming out into blindingly bright light.

In my memory, events there don't have a chronological order, like beads strung, the way they did with Mum's death. Instead, they hang in random clusters, like fruit on a tree.

This time I couldn't organise a thought, couldn't link words together, couldn't find a pen, and if I did, lost the paper I'd planned to write on. The effort of it all was too exhausting. There was only one word in my brain: Julian. When I shut my eyes it was there, like plumes of smoke from a motorbike's engine. If my eyes were open, the word was being sung over and over in my ears, as if by a cicada in the long, yellow grass surrounding his farmhouse.

So many lives, not just mine, were forever changed by it and his wife and young family took years to recover.

Sadly, his death, in 2012, was one of only many accidental deaths that had the same tragic impact.

In the 2011–12 year, in Australia there were 11,192 deaths caused by injury. In 2017 in Australia, 12,000 or 8 per cent of all deaths were caused by injury. In a typical year in Australia, a number of these injury deaths occur on roads. There were 1300 the year he died and in 2017 there were 1225.

Of course, roads are not the only place of accidental death.

According to Royal Life Saving Australia's *National Drowning Report 2018*, there were 249 drowning deaths between July 2017 and June 2018. Rivers and other inland waterways claimed the largest number of lives.

There are other causes of accidental death that may not seem obvious and in 2011, they spread out like this:

- 715 people died from slipping, tripping and tumbling

- 58 people died from falling out of bed

- 26 died after falling off a chair

- 34 died falling from a ladder

- 59 died from choking on food.

The impact of the unexpected death, particularly an accidental death, on those around them is more extreme than that of a natural death and likely not as intense as for a murder. But it is still difficult. It has its own label among psychologists: traumatic bereavement. Psychologists understand the experience of grief to be more intense and more prolonged among those left behind after an unexpected death than for those coping with a natural death. Additional anxieties that tend to surface among family and friends are:

- difficulty accepting what has happened

- feelings of responsibility and guilt

- questioning of religious beliefs

- worry the person suffered

- fear that they or someone they love will also die.

SIDS deaths and the death of a child

How often do we hear it said that it offends nature for a parent to have to bury a child? There could be no loss more difficult to bear

– yet so many are called upon to do this, despite all the advances in medicine and life-saving technology.

About 30 years ago, the category Sudden Infant Death Syndrome (SIDS) was recognised in countries across the Western world. This was characterised by death when a child was put to sleep in a bassinet or cot and simply never woke up. Today, the description has been refined to Sudden Unexpected Death in Infants (SUDI), which is a more inclusive term; SIDS is a subset of SUDI.

However, a study conducted in New Zealand showed there are quite a few variations from one country to the next in the way SUDI is defined.

The good news is that Australian Bureau of Statistics figures show a dramatic drop in SUDI since 1990. In Victoria, the incidence has fallen by as much as 84 per cent. New Zealand also reports a reduction over the same timeframe, as does the United Kingdom. This is partly because of the success of community education programs that promote safe practices, such as sleeping the baby on the back, using a safe baby sleeping bag with no hood or arms, and making sure soft toys are not kept in the cot.

But despite these precautions, SUDI deaths still occur. And the very success in reducing the risk factors amplifies the grief and sense of guilt of those parents who lose a child in this way.

Parents who've experienced a SUDI death can find support from doctors, including their own general practitioner, social workers and grief counsellors. But when the door is shut, the funeral is over and their shocked and saddened community return to their normal lives, this is the moment the parents will need more support and understanding from their family and friends.

When older children die

In Sydney, Lou Pollard – aka Dr Quack – offers palliative support to children dying at Bear Cottage, a purpose-built respite and palliative care hospice at Manly in Sydney.

Like other trained clown doctors who visit Bear Cottage, she has been with many in their final weeks, a consolation for parents who know their child shared precious laughter with their family before passing away.

Children can have powerful insights into death, and when they express their ideas it can be a good opportunity to provide them with reassurance and comfort. Sometimes they are more frank with others than they can be with their parents, whose emotions they sometimes try to protect.

'One seven-year-old asked me to do a role-play. The parents had left the room. The child asked me to lie on the other bed, I was to be death in its coffin, and I was not to smile because I was dead,' Lou said.

How can we be present for someone whose child has recently died? What is the right thing to say? Sometimes we are so afraid of saying the 'wrong' thing that we say nothing. No one wants to be the person who appeared uncaring and insensitive, yet so many bereaved parents have the experience of dealing with shocking and disappointing reactions mixed in with the kind and generous ones.

Sometimes a hug is a better way of communicating one's compassion. One eminent psychiatrist advises: 'When you don't know what to say it's because nothing needs to be said.'

Sometimes the biggest inhibitor is our fear that we will not be able to control our own emotions, our own tears, when seeing the bereaved parent for the first time. This causes people to avoid the person. Despite being lost in their own world to an extent, the grieving do notice those who've avoided them, who normally would not. This is partly because emotions are often heightened and there is almost a super-sensitivity in the person who is grieving.

My view is that if you are unable to completely stop your own tears, then that is not the worst thing. What is worse is your abnormal absence. While no one else knows what they are going through, they will feel supported by your empathy, as long as you can gain enough control to ensure the meeting does not become about you and your emotions. (One of the strains on the bereaved in this situation can be to find they have to console and reassure others, even though they are the person who has suffered the loss.)

One comment best avoided is, 'I know how you feel.' Even if you have had a similar experience, can you really be sure your experience is the same? It might be wiser to be a little less declarative, to say something more like, 'I think I know how you feel.'

We need to be careful about talking about the dead child 'being in a better place'. Is the person religious? If so, ask them whether they believe this, rather than stating it as a fact. Despite the best of intentions, this comment can be very alienating. Even someone who is very religious will prefer that their child was alive. If however, they state their child is in a better place, this may meet their need. Without contravening your own values, you can support them as they express this idea, encouraging them to share their thoughts about why this is so.

To say, 'I am so sorry' is okay.

Whatever you say, there is a small risk that the person will not appreciate it. But the risk of saying the wrong thing is not nearly as great as it can seem, and it is not as bad as being remembered for not saying anything at all, no matter how small. If you start gently, and be prepared to move on if that is the cue you are given, then the risk has been worth it.

One father who lost a child to SIDS many years ago said: 'The following is a personal view: it's better to make space for the grieving person to talk. In other words listening is more valuable than anything one might say. We fear silence and often fill this space with words which often stops the other from speaking.'

Zenith Virago, founder of Australia's Natural Death Care Centre, reminds us that it is a relatively new thing for death in early childhood to feel like an unknown. It has always been common. She suggests a radical approach to developing our empathy for those who experience the death of a child.

'Each day, just once a day, while you're having a cup of coffee or tea, contemplate and think about what it would be like to experience the death of your child,' she advises. 'You need do it only for a short time at first, and then as you become able to sit with that thought, it can be as long as it takes to drink the cup. If you are able to do this, and you're called upon to support someone in your family or community who is having this experience, you will be more prepared to walk that journey with them. It may help you not to have the expectation of yourself that you can make it better.'

If you are a close friend who will see the person often, then you face a slightly different set of issues.

One of the main ones here is that the supporting friends and family reach the point where they either want to move on, or believe the grieving parents should move on, before the bereaved parents are ready. Friends and family worry that the parents' grief is becoming unhealthy. This idea comes from Western society's cultural – and now challenged belief – that there is a set timeframe for grief.

A major issue is that people stop asking how the bereaved parents are, assuming that the grieving time is 'finished'.

Friendships change. Some people can't cope with the parents' sadness. If you don't want to be that person who walks away, maybe throttle back on the intensity in the early stages and then show up, consistently, much later.

By 'show up', I mean something as simple as the occasional phone call. Are the parents people you would have rung and chatted with in the past? If they were, do that. If they weren't, they are not expecting you to suddenly become close. Be consistent. When and if they start talking about their dead child, try not to redirect them. Try not to leave them feeling they have to defend themselves or their need to talk about their child. This is likely to add to their hurt. They may frequently want to say the name of their dead child or tell stories about them. This is okay.

Mary's baby daughter died more than 30 years ago, completely changing the course of her life. To this day, whenever she tries to talk about her daughter to her mother, her mother changes the subject. What is she left with after an adult life of this response? A thwarted relationship with her mother, as well as the loss of her child.

Sometimes we don't have the answers when a parent who's lost a child is standing among us, suffering. The least risky way of supporting them could just be to be completely honest about this, to say words to the effect: 'I really don't know what to say. I think

I can imagine what you are going through, but I know I don't completely understand. But I will stand here with you.'

Often, we don't need to say very much. Our support and compassion can be conveyed just by not walking away until they are ready.

We also need to be aware that grief can merge with anger and sometimes that anger can be misdirected.

It can sometimes be very difficult to stay loyal to someone whose grief makes you feel afraid – afraid that you now know 'too much' about the death of a child and this death will somehow 'infect' your own child, and then on top of that, that you have to deal with anger towards you that feels unjustified.

But the support you can give at this time will be treasured by those who need it.

The preterm death

Our instinct is that birth and death are opposite parts of the lifecycle. It's a terrible thing when this expectation is turned on its head. The loss of a baby before birth is always hard, yet invariably, the full extent of the loss to those immediately affected is poorly understood. It's not just that hopes and dreams are dashed – for the parents and also for their family – there has been a gradual identity shift. From the moment a first pregnancy is confirmed, the woman starts processing the idea of being a mother. And her mother is adjusting her self-definition to being a grandmother. Similar transitions occur for the men in the family too.

When the baby dies in the womb, all those who made these fundamental shifts in their identity, have to grieve their loss of a new way of being, in addition to the loss of the baby. To the casual observer their lives haven't changed, yet nothing could be further from the truth. They had started to become someone else, and the new life was leading them there.

It can be very hard for outsiders to realise that two huge shifts occurred – the first into parenthood, the second into grief, mourning and despair. Someone who sees the young woman on the train nearly every day sees no difference. Some outsiders will make the judgement that no birth had occurred, therefore no life was lost.

The emotional issues are slightly different if this is a second or subsequent baby. The role of being a mother is already established. But many mothers in this situation report being hurt by the nonchalant statement: 'Oh never mind. At least you've already got one baby.'

To the mother who has a baby and has lost this one, one child's life does not compensate for the loss of that of another.

Due to major changes over the last 30 to 50 years, minimising the mother's experience is now recognised as a very poor response to the family's grief. First to acknowledge this are maternity hospitals.

If your maternity services appear to be nonchalant about your loss, then this is not acceptable. While it's difficult to change services at such a time, remember that accountability standards of modern hospitals demand that there are processes for making complaints. This means if you've had an experience that you don't think was acceptable, for whatever reason, you're entitled to make a complaint about it, to be respected when you make the complaint and to be informed about what the institution has done in response to this.

Fortunately, many maternity units and their staff handle preterm loss with understanding and compassion.

Eloise was excited that her daughter Tracy was having a baby and was looking forward to the birth. However, complications developed over several weeks and Tracy was admitted to hospital for observation. Sadly, at eighteen weeks' gestation, Tracy's waters broke.

This meant Tracy would go into labour, if not straightaway, then some time over the next three or four weeks. At eighteen weeks, the baby was too early to be viable but too late to be defined as a miscarriage. Tracy asked the staff: if it could take up to four weeks, wouldn't that be just long enough to be defined as a premature birth? Wouldn't they be able to get further enough along to just get over the line? But the doctors explained that even though the baby was still alive at this point, it had lost all the fluid that cushions it and gives it space to move and grow. It was being squashed and was not going to be able to grow properly. Although it wasn't spelled out, the inference was that the baby was suffering and would continue to suffer unless there was an intervention. The doctor gave Tracy a choice between waiting for the miscarriage to occur naturally at some point in the next month, or to choose a termination. If she chose the latter, the birth would be induced. As the baby's tissues and body structure were not strong enough for the baby to survive the powerful force of the birth contractions, it would die during the process. Nor were its lungs and body developed enough for it to be able to live if Tracy had a caesarean.

Unfortunately, at this point of a pregnancy, a curette to terminate it is not possible. The young mother must go through labour, knowing that she will not take home a live baby at the end. In very rare circumstances, some babies born at this stage survive for a short time, which can add to the parents' distress.

If Tracy waited for a natural birth, she would risk complications, because the baby would now not survive and as the baby's body broke down, it could trigger infection in Tracy. She opted to follow the hospital's recommendation and have the baby's birth induced.

The hospital recognised Tracy's emotional needs and the long-term impact this situation could have on her, and she was brought into a birthing centre for the birth. She was treated as a woman having a baby, an important acknowledgement so that she could go through her grieving process.

The nursing staff had been trained to deal with a young mother who was simultaneously experiencing delivery of a baby for the first time, with all its excitements and physical challenges, and preparing to bury that baby.

Ordinarily a woman's partner accompanies her through the birthing experience, but as Tracy had lost her partner, the supporting role fell to her mother. Her mother was allowed to stay with her for several days and nights, before and after the birth. Her sisters also attended during the day. They did a lot of crying together as Tracy processed the information and made her decision, but they also did a lot of laughing. This acknowledgement of the social needs of the grieving young mother is relatively new and intensely valuable.

The staff explained what the baby would look like: small, with very translucent and very dark skin, so Tracy wasn't shocked. When her baby was born, Tracy talked to her using the name she had chosen. Tracy and her mother were given a family suite, and Tracy was allowed to keep the baby with her for as long as she felt she needed. The baby was placed in swaddling clothes and the family took photos together – an acknowledgement that Tracy had given birth.

When she was ready to give up her baby for an autopsy, two days after the birth, Tracy and her family were invited to lay the baby to rest. The hospital had prepared a special room for the event. It was decorated as beautifully as any home nursery and contained a lovely bassinet. Tracy laid her child in the bassinet, along with a teddy bear and a letter she had written, and she and her family all said their final goodbyes.

Tracy's experience of being a birthing mother as well as a mother burying her baby was dignified and made real by everyone involved.

The burial followed. By going through the rituals of a funeral service, the family was able to honour and show its respect for the baby, in a way that solemnified and gave focus to their grief, but also gave them a pivotal point, from which they could move on.

There was a funeral service, and cremation, then a week later a scattering of ashes, and the place was marked by the planting of a flowering shrub.

Preterm and infant deaths are memorialised on 15 October every year with remembrance ceremonies and candle-lighting vigils in Canada, the United Kingdom, Western Australia, New South Wales and Italy. Tracy's family now takes part in these. For more information on this go to the Sands website: www.sands.org.au.

Termination

While pregnancy termination is available and the reasons for needing one vary, terminating a pregnancy can be a major source of grief for the mother, father or others, regardless of the factors that drove the decision. A parent's grief in this situation needs to be respected.

Suicide

A family I know well are now asking themselves, 'Why?' A beloved daughter-in-law took her own life and everyone close to her is devastated. No one in her family has any insight into her reasons for doing so. Each person is reviewing the last conversation they had with her, searching for clues, but nothing matches the enormity of what she has done.

Those closest to her are angry. It's something hard to admit to easily, but it is a very strong emotion mixed up with their grief. They are angry because none of them would knowingly have hurt her and yet now all are left with a range of emotional burdens to carry for the rest of their lives.

For those wanting to help someone who is coping with a suicide loss, don't be afraid to acknowledge the death and ask how you can help. The most important things is to show the survivor that they are supported and not alone.

It helps for you to know that the survivor is likely to be feeling shock, anger, confusion, guilt and despair. Their anger and guilt are likely to be greater than those experienced with a non-suicide death.

When supporting someone suffering from the aftermath of a suicide, remember that they will also be dealing with social stigma or the fear of social stigma. This will contribute to their anxiety and grief.

More women than men will harm themselves, but in Australia, the United Kingdom and New Zealand more men than women will suicide.

Within that broad generalisation, there are some groups whose members are particularly vulnerable. And remember statistics on who's likely to suicide are almost irrelevant when we realise that anyone can be vulnerable to thinking of suicide, given the lining up of circumstances – the old woman, the young man, the glamorous person who looks as though they have everything.

That said, it's more likely to happen if someone:

- suffers from a mental health disorder, such as schizophrenia

- has tried to suicide before

- suffers from mood disorders (that is, very low and high moods at times)

- has a substance abuse problem

- has access to lethal means such as a gun.

Protections against suicide include having:

- access to mental health care

- a sense of connection – to individuals, family, community and social institutions

- life skills

- good self-esteem and a sense of purpose or meaning in life

- cultural, religious or personal beliefs that discourage suicide.

So protection can be boiled down to making sure you have someone (or something) to love, something to do and something to look forward to – no matter what age you are.

It's true we can all be vulnerable, but there are certain groups who we need to look after and nurture in this regard.

Due to social stigma, lesbian, gay, bisexual, transgender and intersex people experience poorer mental health and have a higher risk of suicidal behaviours compared to the community at large. This is despite greater openness about and awareness of gender orientation, and tolerance in the form of gay marriage in several countries.

'These health outcomes are directly related to experiences of stigma, prejudice, discrimination and abuse on the basis of being LGBTI,' argues Australia's National LGBTI Alliance.

The LGBTI community in New Zealand has recently criticised Statistics New Zealand for not asking the appropriate questions about gender and sexual orientation in the 2018 census to elicit accurate information on their community. Doing so would include important insights into LGBTI people's mental health pressures, depression and suicide rates.

Ex-soldiers are also vulnerable. The suicide rate in the period 2002–16 in Australia was a quite significant 18 per cent higher among ex-serving men than all Australian men after adjusting for age. For ex-soldiers, high suicide risk was associated with younger age, involuntary discharge, short length of service and non-officer rank.

When someone suicides the experience of those left behind is sometimes described as 'disenfranchised grief'. Those close to the person who has suicided often feel they can't be open about the experience, can't talk about it, and are often anxious about the responses of those around them, because suicide is taboo. Their grief is not acknowledged.

'They incur a loss that cannot be openly acknowledged, publicly mourned or socially supported,' explains Christopher Hall, director of the Australian Centre for Grief and Bereavement.

In three recent cases I know of personally, no suicide note was left, so there was no explanation. In two of those cases the suicide came after a minor tiff with other members of the family, not enough to suggest the response of suicide was proportionate. One person appeared to have everything, the envy of those in her social circle. In two of the cases there was some suggestion, when the family analysed events looking back, that there might have been deeper issues. But in all three cases, there were no clues to indicate the person was planning or even thinking about suicide. In each case the person's demeanour beforehand gave no hint of what was coming.

Children, husbands, wives and partners were left behind with a crippling sense of confusion and guilt. That question 'why' will haunt and torment them, long after the period of mourning has gone.

In each case could the opportunity for one more conversation have made a difference? The answer is 'yes', according to Australia's

Beyond Blue, a not-for-profit organisation that addresses a range of mental health issues.

And Don Ritchie, who for many years lived near Sydney's notorious suicide hotspot, The Gap, put that approach into practice. Before his death in 2012, he saved around 160 people from jumping to their death by talking and listening to them.

The Australian media in recent years has had to face the challenge of how (or if) to portray suicide in news reports. If we talk about suicide in the media, do we actually contribute to the suicide rate? It's argued that, unlike almost every other area of health, the problem is worsened rather than improved by public discussion. This concern is based on a 1995 study of coverage in Australian newspapers, and others since, which have shown male suicide increased following reports of suicide, with suicides peaking on the third day after the story first appeared. Other studies have shown that if the suicide is presented as a waste of life, with emphasis on the negative aspects rather than romanticising it, the rates go down. As a consequence, today media reports follow strict guidelines – for example, they don't include details about the means of death and always include the telephone number of a support hotline.

But we are left with the social problem that this strategy contributes to making suicide seem mysterious. Are we stopping the development of a more pragmatic approach to solving this mental health problem by ignoring it because we don't see it? And if we don't talk about it openly, does this mean we don't get to explore the reasons it occurs?

'Suicide contagion' is a relatively new concept. This theory argues that people who have experienced a suicide are more likely to suicide. This is not those who read about it in the media, but those who are personally exposed to it.

The Australian organisation Wings of Hope says that suicide results in more deaths each year than road deaths and that each suicide will have an impact on eight or more people.

'Direct and indirect exposure to suicidal behaviour has been shown to precede an increase in suicidal behaviour in persons at risk for suicide, especially in adolescents and young adults,' the US Department of Health and Human Services explains.

This is a problem compounded by access to social media, which is fluid, direct, has no 'conscience' and can deliver its message in a rapidly expanding way, particularly among adolescents, who, just like everyone else, can be vulnerable to suicide but are also particularly vulnerable to online bullying that erodes self-esteem.

The US Department of Health and Human Services recommends that, because of the risk of suicide contagion, if someone within a close circle of family or friends has suicided, then those within that circle should be assessed for their suicide risk.

Male suicide rates are high. Australian radio personality Gus Worland made a television series in 2017 called *Man Up* in response to a good friend's suicide. Worland expressed shock at the figures for male suicide, asking: 'The number one way for an Aussie male between the ages of 15 and 44 to die is to kill themselves. Why don't people know about this?'

One of Worland's interview subjects is John Harper, who poignantly explained how with labour-saving technology, fewer farmers work with other people on their farms today. Where once six people worked in the paddocks and had smoko together – an opportunity to talk about their problems, even if accidentally – now the farmer works by himself, in isolation, an opportunity to stew on his problems. He carries a gun to kill sheep and farm dogs that can no longer work.

'It's not a short straw between putting yourself down, when you think you ain't worth a cracker,' Harper explained.

It is highly likely that the true level of suicide is higher than the figure reported to the coroner, since other causes of death that may have been suicide were classified as accidents, such as drug overdoses, single vehicle accidents, falls or drowning incidents.

The pattern that consistently emerges in suicide is a set of problems that leave those suffering from them feeling isolated from others. Be in no doubt, that sense of loneliness can be a killer both when it manifest as suicide and because of the poor health and disability it contributes to.

More research is highlighting that suicide is now considered a major killer of men in old age and questions are being asked about whether deaths previously labelled as accidental in older men may in fact have been deliberate.

Creeping into the discussion about suicide is the description 'rational suicide', used to describe those cases where, whether there is an apparent mental health problem or not, the determination to suicide is seen as a rational response to the circumstances, such as intractable mental or physical illness.

Personally, I cannot agree with this argument, since to do so would mean accepting that the problems our society confronts cannot be solved with all our combined resources – intellectual, scientific, emotional and financial. Until the last dollar, idea and solution has been thrown at the challenge of making life better, this will not be good enough for me.

So, for me, reading one particular article – easily accessed on the internet – that argues for the right of old men to choose suicide as a response to their circumstances, was a chilling experience indeed.

CHAPTER 07

Saying goodbye

*We learn how to say goodbye. We strip away dross
to say our own authentic goodbye – so we discard and recycle,
sometimes going back to the ancient, sometimes
moving away from it.*

New ideas about saying goodbye

Funeral planning – by you, before you become the dearly departed, is an area where there has been a major shift in thinking in recent years, and there are more changes to come. As people step outside the traditional formulas, they invent something new. Of course, if you're going to say 'No' to the old, it will help your family if you tell them exactly what you want for your 'New'.

Innovation is everywhere – even in, or especially in – funerals and burials. There are many aspects of the funeral and burial that you might want to make a choice about, and this is more possible than ever before.

The traditional ways – old and cosy

Before we explore the new, let's look at the old. Ancient cultures might have something to offer us – or even just to tell us. There is so much more for us to learn about death – or is it that we need to go on a journey of rediscovery?

In Victorian times, attitudes to death were very different. The Victorians were as obsessed with death as we are with sex. Their front room, the parlour, was where the dead were laid out and prepared for burial, something they did from home. The link is still there today in the term 'funeral parlour'.

They were so obsessed that when the camera was first invented it was used to capture images of the dead, ideal subjects given the clunky technology of the time because they didn't move. They made mourning rings encasing fingernails and lockets woven of the dearly departed's hair. Women proudly wore their black, signalling to the world in one of the period's loud yet unspoken codes that if their behaviour was a little odd, grief was the explanation.

But along with the funeral photos, our society gradually began to hide from view pretty much everything related to death. We shed the mourning clothes, we reassigned the parlour to a better use and over time we gradually abandoned many of the rituals around death.

Some aspects of the Victorian burial and funeral practices lingered. For example, until only recently children were often excluded from funerals. This is something many today argue is harmful.

Christine was only seven when her father Fred died, an event she will never forget. One emotion that loomed large for a long time after was anger – not because Fred had died but because his death was kept a secret from her.

'It wasn't until my mother died, more than 50 years later, that I was able to somehow work through all that that entailed. As Mum was lowered down into the same grave to be with Dad, I was able to finally say, "Well I am now saying goodbye to you too Dad."'

Today Christine teaches meditation. She has a beautiful mandala on the wall of her home, painted by a dear friend. An exotic script encircles it. To my eye it looks decorative, but Christine knows the language, and the words are about love. It expresses a personal philosophy that Christine has used to overcome the hurt she experienced all those years ago.

'My brother, who was ten, was an altar boy and he served at the funeral Mass for Dad. But I was in the school playground. I remember that day looking out and saying to the girls I was playing with, "Hey, those people over there look like my relatives." They said, "Come on Christine, let's go over to the back fence to play over there."

'Well-intentioned people had decided I was too young to cope. So they'd ordered the girls to distract me. I'd been told that Dad went on a holiday, so I thought he'd gone back to New Guinea, where I was born.'

Christine kept waiting for her father to come back from that holiday, feeling bewildered that he'd simply left without saying anything.

'They didn't trust the resilience of a child. But they did much more harm than good.'

Others tell similar stories of exclusion on the grounds that children should be protected from grief – and if truth be known, based also on a belief that young children shouldn't be allowed to distract in any way from the mourning rituals of the adults.

Adults in their fifties, sixties and seventies cried as they shared stories with me about the denial of their grief as children.

But in broader terms many now say we've swung too far away from the rituals and obsessions of the Victorians, that the social pendulum has swung too far in the opposite direction. One of the first to make this argument was Elisabeth Kübler-Ross, in the 1960s.

By 1979, commentators were observing that modern culture had moved from the sacred to the profane – and as a consequence our culture began to 'worship' the new and the young and as a consequence old age was devalued. They argued that 'secularisation' – the move away from religion – and death denial go hand in hand.

Novels that explored the idea of our 'collective narcissism' include, for example, Tom Wolfe's satire *The Bonfire of the Vanities*.

Today our Western culture's death denial is a widely discussed subject.

'It's almost total,' said Margaret McHarg, a student counsellor with a special interest in anthropology. She sees the effect of this on her students, when they are grieving. She believes they are particularly susceptible to the negative impacts of this because death comes so much as a shock to the young today. And as a separate but related issue they can't take much comfort from the old. Partly she says this is because our culture doesn't value and take comfort from the wisdom of the old.

She argues that cultures that value their elders aren't as frightened of the next stage – what she calls the 'ancestor stage', that is, the time beyond – death and being gone forever.

Margaret pointed out that for centuries in most cultures a person's spiritual life or an afterlife was more important than their earthly existence, and it is only in relatively recent times that this has shifted.

'As a culture today, we don't want to acknowledge death because we're so materialistic, in the sense that the material life is everything to us. And we spend so much time frantically achieving, being busy, because of our radical individualism.

'The individual is the locus of meaning, rather than the group or the family and so I think there is also not that sense that you get in, for example Indigenous Australian and Pacific Islander communities that "I will go on after I die in the hearts of the people around me". That in turn feeds the death denial.'

But green shoots of a reinvented spiritualism are emerging. Interesting things are happening that may suggest our culture is swinging away from its earlier death denial.

Many cultures or people living in modern contemporary societies have found ways of holding onto old rituals that they find soothing and deeply healing. Instead of abandoning them, they are holding on to them with more determination. Irish-Australian Martin and Scottish-Māori New Zealander Thomas are two examples. They live very modern lives, but despite that, maybe because of it, they value the traditions of their ancient cultures.

Traditionally in Ireland when someone died the family sat with the dead for three days until their burial. The family would sit with the dead in the front parlour, neighbours taking it in turns to keep the body company on the first one or two nights so the family who'd been nursing the person or sitting up in a vigil at the deathbed could get some sleep, which still translates today into someone always sitting with the body. Martin told me this is done in deference to Jesus Christ, who rose on the third day.

Irish friends accompanying the body would sit in clusters of at least two or three to keep each other company through the long nights. No one was impolite enough to sit with a neighbour – dead or alive – without the courtesy of sharing a bottle of good Irish whiskey – hence, the Irish wake, which was not finished until the body was buried.

Martin went back to Ireland for his father's funeral. 'After Dad died, when he was in the house before the burial it was a lot more restrained than those occasions used to be.

'After being embalmed, he was lying out at home in the front room, where he used to watch TV, in the coffin, but with it open, so anyone could come along and pay respects. Friends, family and neighbours popped in and my cousin, Father Martin, came around and said some prayers.

'Although Dad lived in Dublin he'd bought a plot down in the country, at the Roscommon border with Galway, near where he was born and grew up.'

The Roscommon funeral director, who ran several local businesses, including the local petrol station, drove up to collect the body, and many of the family drove in procession behind him as they went back to Roscommon.

'We stopped at a town called Moate in County Westmeath for lunch at a pub restaurant.

'The funeral director parked the hearse in the square and joined us for lunch. My sister said, "What about Dad?" and we all said, "He'll be fine where he is."

'My cousin and sons had dug the grave beforehand. They weren't official gravediggers but that is the Irish tradition – for family to dig the grave. After the prayers around the grave we did a very Irish thing; everybody shovelled the dirt in after the coffin was lowered. Everybody takes a shovel and shovels all the dirt back in and presses it down, and that's the end of it. It doesn't take long, ten minutes at the most. When you put him in the ground and fill it all in and pat it down, it helps you feel closure.'

Again, another hint of old ideas migrating. This is reminiscent of the Jewish practice of mourners taking it in turns to shovel earth over the casket.

Martin says the traditional Catholic Church rituals of the Irish have changed, mostly in recent years, eroded by disillusionment over the way the Church has managed the problem of paedophile priests: 'Attitudes to religion and even to burials are rapidly changing, especially in the large cities.'

The traditional Māori funeral, the *tangihanga*, brings people together for a long period of ritual and celebration, usually for a week, although in modern times this can be compressed into three days. The *tangihanga* soothes the living, helping with their grief, as much as it honours the dead.

The body is not left alone between death and burial. The family will gather at the *marae*, the traditional meeting place, with the immediate family surrounding the body. Mourners are welcomed with a *karanga*, a special, lilting, calling of the spirit, done by women trained in the art, with the call sometimes thrown from the family to their guests, other mourners, and then back again.

'The major protocol among most of Māori tribes, is that the body is carried feet first through the door, as if he or she still lives,' said Thomas.

'Every visiting party or individual always goes and greets all the living, relatives first. Then they stand at the foot of the casket and generally tell a humorous moment they shared together.

'The funeral is always finished with a *waiata*, a song or hymn to see them through to the next lifetime. When we leave the grave-site we always wash our hand to cleanse ourselves of the dead.'

In the past, Māori mourners spent the whole week together, singing, telling stories and farewelling the dead, although in some traditions, the immediate family did not speak.

The night before the burial, the mourners also meet for a special feast. Having had such an intense emotional experience together, people were able to shed their grief and adjust quickly.

'We do a lot of grieving in that time, but we also do a lot of healing. It's very intense but spiritually renewing. You come away from it feeling as though you've been part of a really life-affirming celebration,' said Thomas.

Honouring your traditions is important, said Matt Poll, Sydney University's Museum and Heritage Studies curator.

He pointed out that it is considered a basic human right for communities to be able to express their own mortuary practices. That's a major reason why Australian museums have now committed themselves to returning human remains to Aboriginal communities.

'To watch a community develop the confidence to honour their dead, no matter how long ago they died, is an exercise in watching that community grow,' he said.

Non-Indigenous Australians still have much to learn about the cultural heritage of our first peoples. Maybe one day we will be a nation that embraces the best of our 'newer' influences and combines these gracefully with inspiration from spiritual traditions that are at least 60,000 years old. It's a powerful and attractive idea.

Dr Anne Poelina, a Nyikina Warrwa (traditional custodian) from the Kimberley region of Western Australia, confronts death on a regular basis as part of her work with young Indigenous Australians.

'Much of my work is about creating the opportunity to live and promote life especially for our young Indigenous people in the Kimberley who have the highest rate of suicide, also described as "self-murder". The continuing impacts of colonisations are so destructive and there is very little recourse for hope for these young people,' she explained.

'My views on death and life are grounded in my Indigenous lived experiences and they are not a generic Aboriginal world view. But one view I do share with many senior elders – Aboriginal mentors – is that we must "call people to us". Calling people to us is an important part of our resilience, resourcefulness and spirituality. It is part of us becoming human through building empathy, with both human and non-human beings – all vital ingredients for building greater humanity, firstly in ourselves and then through the wisdom of others.

'You learn to call people to you from the moment you are born, if you are brave. This braveness is carried through your life journey right up to the moment you are ready to die. We all have loved and special ones we can call on to help us to have the strength to say: "See you again when we next meet."

'Death is indeed a big part of life, and at some point we will all need to come to that destiny.

'I believe when someone dies, they do not leave us. They continue to communicate with us. I still speak to the life energy of significant people who have died and feel and believe they communicate with me and show me 'signs' and come to me in dreams – as their life force continues.'

Hers is a belief in remembrance many of us share. In some cultures intense rituals of remembrance continue. Each year on All Souls' Day, from which modern Halloween evolved, Mexicans honour the dead with bones and skulls at mini altars, as reminders of the dead that also keep anxiety about death at bay. Although just because people derive ongoing comfort from these rituals, we shouldn't presume that they still don't experience as devastating the death of someone they love, Mexican mother Marisa pointed out. She lost her four-month-old son to SIDS, an experience that many years later she still grieves over.

Australian Maria says the same thing. Maria talked about the Sicilian approach to death. A month after the burial everyone gathers for a Mass and then everyone gathers for another Mass a year later. Sicilian women, like other Italians, traditionally wear black from the time of death.

'From the day a person dies to the day they are buried, whether it's five, six, seven days, family and friends stay with the bereaved. They cook, they shop, they are there every night. Some stay the night,' Maria said.

'The night before the burial there is a viewing. This can be done at the funeral director's place or the body can be taken to the church. The coffin's opened. People can come and see the dead person.'

She is aware of how migrant communities sometimes develop customs they believe are from the old places but in fact are different.

'When the Italians came to Australia, because they came from a very poor country they wanted the best when they came here. So they wanted to keep their bodies whole. In Italy they don't always do that, they just bury them without embalming them. But here everyone was embalmed. So in Australia today when you go to the cemetery you see all those big vaults, and the tradition now is that Italians living here are usually embalmed.'

'When my family were back in the old country, when someone died there you wore black and you wore it for the rest of your life. And that's how you were supposed to respect them. Australians didn't know what it meant when my mother's family first arrived here. A friend of my mother was wearing black all the time and her Aussie neighbours all put money in to buy her new clothes because they thought she couldn't afford any.

'I don't wear black though because my mother always used to say to me, "You respect someone when they're alive. Black doesn't prove anything," and I think she was right.'

The new ways – bright and exciting

But sometimes we take the old and we mix it with the new, and so forge the next way forward. In the modern era we have much more access to different ideas and freedom from strict religious conventions. We have more freedom to express ourselves in our own way.

Amy Sagar, from Tender Funerals of Port Kembla in New South Wales, is an enthusiastic embracer of the community movement that involves people reclaiming the rites of death and dying for themselves, to create something unique and special for them. For those who want to participate in this last significant rite of passage, she said, it can be an enriching and life-affirming experience.

'I've developed a sense, after ten years in my work, that people who create a funeral ceremony that expresses something of how the dead person lived their life, and where family members take more control, seem to go away with positive attitudes towards the funeral and farewelling the person,' she said.

Ultimately, how you choose to do this will depend on your personality and your life experiences.

Some people argue they don't need to do any funeral planning. After all, it won't make much difference to me, I'll be dead, they say. Yes, that part is true: it will not make any difference to you at all, you won't be there – in a conscious sense – to experience it. But a little bit of planning by you, even if it's just indicative, will make it a lot easier for your family.

I've decided I don't want mine to have to think about it all too much.

Of course it may not happen the way I visualise. I don't think I'll care as much as American filmmaker Nora Ephron did. She organised a 'A Gathering for Nora', and meticulously laid out all the details about how this was to be done in a folder she called 'Exit'. Some mourners afterwards said they weren't sure whether they were at a funeral or a cocktail party.

Mine is only coming together now. I'm not going to pretend I'm entirely on top of it, but the notes are starting to take shape. At the moment I'm distracted by the births in rapid succession of grandchildren. Recently, at my nephew's wedding, I heard my favourite pink silk coat dress tear under the arm. I had bought it to last forever, but it wasn't to be. I don't want to throw it out, I love it too much. But I'm going to add a note to my funeral planning. I want to be buried in that dress. It's a coat dress, so hopefully it'll be easy to wrap around my body.

I like the idea of returning to the earth in a dress that I love. And I'm starting to make other notes.

While generations have listened to 'The Lord Is My True Shepherd', sung as a mournful, colourless dirge, the words are the most joyous and optimistic you will ever hear. So I've made a note: I want it played as a light, Celtic jig, the sort where you'd swear everyone will fight the urge to get up and dance. The note is in a folder marked 'My funeral' on my computer, along with the names of the other songs I want played – Led Zeppelin's 'Stairway to Heaven' is another one, and there are a few more.

It might not turn out the way I visualised it, but if there's an opportunity for everyone to spill out of my funeral with a smile on their face, I absolutely want them to take it. If I've chosen my songs, my children don't have to make any guesses about what they think those might be. If they don't pull it off and somehow the day doesn't work, then there will be no opportunities for recriminations between them, they'll be able to laugh it off and blame any failures of the day on me, which is exactly what I want.

Let's get down to tin tacks – or nuts and bolts, or wood and wicker

Even though it's the usual practice in our culture to rely on a funeral director to arrange a funeral service, in Australia there is no legal reason why you have to. It's just that coordinating all the things that have to be done, and bringing all the elements together, is usually easier with a funeral director involved because they effectively act as event planners.

Some people don't want a formal funeral service. Steve and his partner of 30 years, Grace, decided that when she died they would have a small gathering at home, attended just by close family. Grace died at home, after a short illness. There was no church and no community hall involved. Steve and Grace's sister said a few words and then everyone drank a glass of champagne to celebrate Grace's life.

'Grace didn't want a formal funeral, she just wanted close family and friends around. That's how she wanted it; she didn't want any fuss; she didn't want any service – we weren't religious, that was all sort of irrelevant. She wrote a list of people she wanted to come and that's what happened. We had a gathering here at our house. I stood up and gave a eulogy about Grace and her life and how perfect she was. It was hard for me to do. But I talked about what a really fantastic person she was.'

By that stage Grace's body had already been cremated, with only Steve and their three children present.

In another example, Judy chose to be celebrated by her family and friends with an afternoon tea at an elegant function centre. Her two children had been present at a private cremation in the days before. There was no body, just a small speech made to honour Judy by her son Tim.

To some people, though, a funeral without a ritual leaves them feeling deprived of a ritual that helps them move on.

Ritual is an important psychological tool. Recent research suggests it is employed across cultures even though each community and culture differs in having unique observances.

Some worry that now that we have parted way with the Victorians, we've thrown the baby out with the bath water.

We have few mourning rituals or codes and fewer that are universal, to give us a moment longer to cling on, to create a buffer and to help us discreetly signal that we are grieving, once the funeral is over.

Our approach has changed. We've lost many rituals associated with death, but some argue we need to bring a little ritual back, even if it is not at the same intensity as the Victorians.

Ritual helps many people shift gears because of the external authority projected onto each step. There might be a particular step or series of activities that help achieve this. To a traditional Catholic it might be the moment when the body is blessed by the priest at the Rite of Committal just before burial, or it might be the cumulative effect of the Requiem Mass, the burial and the wake.

But it doesn't have to be associated with religion and it doesn't have to be so conventional that all sparks of imagination have gone. The Dutch architectural firm HofmanDujardin has designed a completely new style of funeral home, with the idea of making the space beautiful (with beauty defined by a refreshing mix of the contemporary and 'green'). It has a zone for wall-to-wall collages of images of the deceased person, a centre for the coffin where people can gather and then a reception room. It is not the spaces, so much as the way they have been designed, that is impressive, shaking free of all the drabbery that is so often associated with funerals. It is stunning and beautiful. What a way to go.

While Australia, the United Kingdom and New Zealand are still dominated by culturally Christian values, this is changing, as are attitudes towards religion. We live in a pluralist society and many people are reconsidering their religious values.

Almost every aspect of the traditional funeral is open to challenge.

Muslims (and Jews) still observe the cultural tradition of burying the dead as soon as possible, something appropriate to the extremely hot climates where these traditions started, and many people will still want to do this. But for others delays not only allow people to gather from distant countries but also give time for those close to the deceased to come to terms with the loss before the formality of burial. In cold climates, a mid-winter death could result in a spring burial because the soil is frozen, something one Englishman told me is common practice in the village he comes from. Others report that such delays can be confronting. The difficulty arises if the family wants to bury and move on emotionally but feels suspended in grief by processes out of their control.

These days, it is more likely that funerals will be delayed not because of the climate but to accommodate the family's needs, both psychological and practical. Due to better, more efficient long-distance travel and cheaper airfares, families live further away. But many still want to gather for the funeral. Like Martin's Irish family, they sometimes need to gather from three different continents. Some people want more time so that they can be more composed when they face the friends and well-wishers at a funeral. They need to wait sometimes for up to ten days after the death.

One Australian family recently delayed their father's burial until one of the sons returned home from a long-planned overseas trip. The holiday was not shortened, his family badly needed it and business the son had to do while away could still be attended to.

His siblings were happy, no one else minded the delay. It not only meant they could all be together to bury their father, but everyone's frame of mind was better.

Funeral celebrants offer a range of burial services, ranging from the spiritual to the non-spiritual. They can be done in environments outside churches.

A casket is not needed, and chemicals can be avoided. As attitudes towards the rituals of death change, so too do other details. For example, members of the Kiwi Coffin Club of Canterbury, New Zealand, design, make, paint and decorate their coffins.

Working on the coffins in the club's workshops is very much a social activity. Far from being morbid, it allows people to open up and discuss their funeral and burial with other people who are at the same stage of life and thinking in the same way. Members take their highly decorated coffins away with them to keep until they are needed.

Apart from giving people an alternative and cheaper funeral service than was available to them before, the club's activities mean members retain a greater sense of control over the elements of their funeral.

The idea has now spread, with Coffin Clubs inspired by the New Zealand model emerging throughout the world, including in Australia and the United Kingdom.

Do you want a traditional burial? Do you want to be buried in a conventional cedar wood casket? Once it might have been inappropriate or just felt inappropriate to ask these questions, but today it is not.

Burial methods, unless for occupational health and safety reasons, are being re-thought, largely because of environmental concerns. Recyclable coffins, made mostly of recycled newsprint, are now available, for example. They have been available in the United Kingdom and United States for nearly ten years.

Many people are opting for a 'green' burial, also called a 'natural' burial. There are no caskets and no chemicals. The aim is to reduce the environmental impact of burial, particularly to reduce carbon emissions.

The body is buried and, often, a tree is planted, so that the nutrients from the natural breakdown of the body fertilise the tree. I'd be worried that my family will have a crisis if the tree died, so I won't be suggesting this, but some businesses are now producing containers to grow the tree indoors, with the body packed tightly inside and sensors to help maintain the plant's growth.

Green burials take place in special cemeteries called natural burial parks, which offer simple burial sites with minimal disturbance to the natural environment. The Natural Death Advocacy Network, an Australian advocacy group working to expand opportunities for natural choices during death and burial, can provide information for those who want a natural burial.

The network also advocates for those who want a 'family-led' funeral, in other words, one without a registered funeral celebrant officiating. They will negotiate with cemeteries for this on behalf of families, helping cemeteries make suitable arrangements.

In fact, in most places, we are legally allowed to handle all aspects of the body's preparation for burial and cremation, as well as the funeral, although many people don't realise this.

Living on

The lives of those we've loved seep into us, becoming part of us forever more. No matter how fast the pace of change in the world around us, we continue to have the urge to honour and love those who've gone. As the role of religion is questioned by some, the spiritual connection to those we grieve endures.

Milo died of a brain tumour when he was 68. Some time before he died he wrote a story about a leaf.

'I'm only now actually coming to terms with his death,' his widow Cherie said. 'It's been so busy, so much has happened and I pushed it all away.'

'The thing was he never acknowledged death. If he did, it was a throw-away line. He never made any preparations, he never wanted to talk about what would happen after, you know what sort of funeral and that type of thing. He never asked me, "How will you manage, what do you think you'll do?" He never went beyond it.

'One day I was looking for something and I found in some pigeon holes in his study, a folder. In it, in his handwriting, was the story of a leaf. He claimed he wrote it before, in the office of a stockbroker that he used to do some analysis for, but I don't believe it. I think he actually wrote it sitting there on that lounge and looking at those leaves out in the courtyard.'

Cherie didn't read the story until about a month before Milo died. It was about how the leaf felt its skin go dry, with the changes of the seasons and it was barely hanging on to the vine.

'Until then, it never occurred to me that this was about him, that he was looking at himself. Later, it was his first anniversary and I saw a leaf fluttering against a window. There was a bit of a breeze outside but it kept coming up against the window and I couldn't believe the persistence of this leaf.

'It was just swirling, like you know a whirlwind, so it was sort of dancing in amongst all of these other leaves and none of the other leaves were moving. It was just dancing in a little zephyr of its own and the others around it were perfectly still. It was just this one moving and I made a connection with Milo straight away.'

'I have no spiritual beliefs at all, none at all, I'm a total atheist. But I just thought, well there's more than just a leaf here. It was very evocative.'

When Mum was in her nursing home, we continued to play Scrabble with her at this time, the word game that had shaped Mum's most enduring relationships. Despite all her other cognitive losses – her short-term memory, her knowledge of who we all were – she had still retained this skill, could still play competitively, and win.

Now that she was in a nursing home, if there were just the two of us playing, I faced temptations. One day, I looked down at my tiles and the letters 'E' and 'D' jumped out at me. They would create the perfect scaffold to reach a triple word score, in my next move. I checked the cheat sheet and the word 'ed' wasn't there. I checked the dictionary, but the full stop beside it told me it was an abbreviation – it was not an esoteric, old English word.

Mum's knowledge of obscure words had once been so good she could challenge most dictionaries, so I asked, just as I would have done in the old days, if she would allow it.

She looked at me with wide open, trusting eyes and said: 'Yes, of course you can have it.'

But I couldn't do it. I couldn't exploit this reversal. For all the bluffing and poker-faced strategies playing Scrabble allowed, without honesty the game was meaningless.

But then the moment came when Mum slowly started losing her word power. During Scrabble she put out 'quean' and, when I challenged, changed it to 'quena'. I decided not to patronise her.

'I don't think that's a word,' I said.

She withdrew the tiles.

But a little while later, she scored 24 for 'zoo', each one of us fighting hard throughout the game. Finally I scored 309 to her 239. She was not upset about losing, just refreshed by having had a challenging game. Afterwards, she sat reading a book – a rare sight by then.

I never really expected to have an experience like Cherie's, to feel the spirit of a loved one coming to me, as a bird, leaf or feather. But then something like that did happen to me. I picked up a copy of a New York newspaper. An article about the meshing of pop and South American music caught my eye.

The photo caption described a quena as a South American flute. So not surprisingly, Mum had been right after all, when we had played that game of Scrabble together all that time before. It was a word. And now of course it occurred to me, she had come back to me through words, a Scrabble word no less.

'Hello Netti,' I smiled.

CHAPTER 08

Coping with grief

We find new ways to reach out when grief strikes – for the sake of others and also for ourselves.

At first it seems impossible to put one foot in front of the other. One step forward and two steps back is more like it. Sometimes, the safest place seems to be in our bed. But then we get to the stage where we can make the bed and lie on top of it. We have made progress.

Life after loss

Following the expected death of my mother after a long life, I coped, although I was very sad. Mixed with grief was a sense that she was now no longer suffering and a powerful conviction that she had found a deep sense of satisfaction and contentment as her long life inched towards its close. This was the bigger context of her life, before illness and chronic pain cast their shadow. Eight weeks later, when Julian was killed in his motorcycle accident, the emotions were very different, and among them were ones that were completely unexpected.

Before long I developed something I called my 'grief anger'. Looking back, I realise I took out on my husband all the anger I felt towards others about Julian's death. I realise I was angry with Julian too for dying, but it felt taboo to admit this, so I unwittingly redirected it. Valuable insights into this came from a gentle and little book about grief that has become a classic, *Coping with Grief*, which, seeing my need, my friend Bec gave me.

I realise, looking back, how important support for the bereaved can be, both informal and formal.

Support groups for the bereaved can be found through a range of avenues, although Jane, who's distraught at the moment and attended one recently, found that it did not work for her. Somehow, nothing anybody said felt right.

Sometimes the challenge is to find the right time to intervene. Grief writer Doris Zagdanski explores this in her book, *Now That the Funeral Is Over*, republished in 2018.

'After the funeral we shut the door and everyone's life is supposed to go back to normal. But it often doesn't. That's when grieving people often need the most support, when the busyness of the funeral is over and they're left on their own,' she wrote.

'How can we make that better? It's a challenge for all of us.'

Melbourne's Springvale Cemetery is addressing this. The cemetery's Centre for Care and Wellbeing provides yoga, meditation, grief counselling, and sessions on wills and estate planning.

'In today's lifestyle we don't have the ritual, the ceremonies, the traditions we used to have, so people are a little bit lost, the isolation is prevalent,' Dianne Lee, who runs the Centre, told ABC radio's *Life Matters* program.

Once upon a time we would have said a cemetery was the worst place to find such support, but maybe it makes perfect sense that the people we will meet and interact with there, will know the depth of darkness we are traversing.

Without sounding glib about it, and painful as it may be to acknowledge this, new theories (or are they very old ones?) about grief tell us that loss is an opportunity for personal growth. My own grief journey, after the unexpected death of my brother Julian, led to very dark places – grief, depression, the incapacity to work, questioning my marriage because I was angry with my husband about the way he dealt with my grief, and a fundamental shift in family relationships. None of these would I want or ask for again. But through the personal pain I was forced to learn, shed old ideas and adapt my thinking, so I could find new ways to live again. I saw counsellors, learnt about mindfulness. I read books and met people I would not have met before. In a strange way I grew up.

I realise my life divides into two: pre-Julian's death and post-Julian's death. In the first half, when I looked at an old person walking down the street I saw someone withered, decrepit and decaying. These days, every time I look at an old person I ask myself how much loss they have bravely endured. I wonder how many friends they have had to bury, how many siblings. And I see remarkable strength and powers of endurance. I see warriors. They have learnt to let go and survive the letting go. They have understood what it is to be alone.

The wise tell us this is the positive that comes from loss. Mapped out, philosophies about the changes grief brings go something like this:

- The change of life's course results in opportunities. These opportunities are not the ones you thought you were going to have. The 'new' life you are experiencing may not have occurred to you before the traumatic event but, paradoxically, it can feel more true.

- Closer relationships, with greater empathy, develop. Before this life experience, we felt a little smug when we thought of certain people or certain styles of people. That smugness has now gone, to be replaced with humility. We don't need the glamorous, the wealthy, the fashionable quite as much as we thought we did. In fact, they can seem hollow. We treasure the authentic more.

- We gain greater awareness of our own inner strength; I will survive, I can survive.

    ▢ We appreciate life more. Once we have experienced the lows forced upon us by personal tragedy, such as the sudden, unexpected death of someone we love, we appreciate the good times more.

    ▢ A spiritual awakening may occur. This doesn't always mean 'finding God'. For some people, it actually means losing God, which can be a form of spiritual growth. Some would argue that losing a romanticised view of God and gaining a more realistic one is part of religious growth.

When in the middle of the worst phase of grief – especially if several losses have been experienced at once, or in close succession – it can be hard to believe that life will ever get better. But it may be enormously comforting to know that most people will eventually lift out of despair. Life will be different, but you will get better.

Psychologists now talk of 'Post Traumatic Growth', an idea that developed in the 1990s. This is when you not only survive your personal loss but also experience personal growth because of it.

It can have artistic elements. Australian author Gail Jones says it's often assumed people write from a place of plenitude: 'But we write from a place of loss,' she explained once at the Sydney Writers' Festival, arguing that loss and grief are greater triggers of our creativity.

The Reverend Graham Long, whose son James died from a stroke at the age of 31 in 2009, argues in his lyrical and unconventional way that no matter how low your grief has taken you, 'the awesome will come for you'. This is his way of expressing the Christian spiritual concept that growth that can come from despair and grief.

It's important to fight the impulse to let past losses define us, even though it may be difficult to imagine the grief lessening in the immediate aftermath of loss. As German thinker and spiritual writer Eckhart Tolle said, 'The past has no power over the present moment.'

According to Richard Tedeschi, author and Professor of Psychology at the University of North Carolina, who has written extensively on overcoming grief, at least 75 per cent of the population will experience trauma at some point in their lives and of these around a third will grow from the experience. The three personal characteristics that will ensure growth are openness, optimism and extroversion. Researchers are now asking to what degree these characteristics are genetic.

But whatever conclusion they come to, we can survive. If it's too much to say life will be better, it's reasonable to say we can grow from our experiences – even the very sad ones.

This message echoes with the theme of 'resurrection' in both this life and the next, which forms the basis of hope in the Christian religions. But the idea of challenge, exploration and rebirth is fundamental to the 'lessons' of storytelling across cultures and was evident before the birth of Jesus Christ. The story of Jason and the Argonauts and other ancient Greek myths are examples. Jason explores, he tests himself, he is cut to the quick. He survives, he triumphs, he is victorious over self. The reward for shocking experiences is a deeper understanding of life.

Men and grief

People who are unable to express grief are more vulnerable to depression. This is especially true of men, who in our culture are expected to be stoic, to be strong and supportive, and it can be particularly painful when dealing with grief over a child. It's the model of masculinity that Gus Worland, mentioned before, put under the microscope – and found to be flawed – in his television program *Man Up*.

He argued that the tough guy image – projected by men in many cultures – leaves our men vulnerable to holding on to grief without finding enough support. He concluded it's okay for a man to cry, that it doesn't mean his masculinity is threatened, that seeking support from others when a man is down – sometimes about the loss of a mate to suicide – is not a sign of weakness but of strength. However, ingrained ways of thinking and behaving can be slow to change.

Fathers can be overlooked when tragedy strikes their home. Men often experience and express their grief differently to women.

This is despite the changes in our society that mean fathers are more involved in parenting and expected to show more emotion than before.

'We spend our whole lives being told we need to be strong, look after our families, be successful breadwinners and providers,' Tony explained at a men's grief forum.

'We learn this from our fathers and in our schools. Then in addition, our wives want us to be emotional, just at the right pitch, just at the level that they need at that particular time. Suddenly making that switch can be incredibly hard. It goes against what we've been taught and what we know. Women have years of experience at opening up for each other but for us it's much more difficult,' he said.

But sometimes the problem for a grieving father is not so much the way he sees himself but the way others see him.

In certain types of work (firefighting, policing, even medicine), men see their identity as protectors and people who will take charge in a dangerous situation. In their families they often take charge – sometimes even if it is only wielding the barbecue tongs – because this is what they feel they are expected to do. This mindset can lead to a brusqueness when confronting the death of someone they love, which can be misread as anger: frustration and grief can look like anger. And for a man to be angry in our culture today, with its rightful heightened sensitivities about domestic violence, is problematic.

In a poignant letter to *The Lancet* medical journal, a young mother, Rebecca Goss, whose sixteen-month-old daughter had died, wrote: 'My husband and I have been treated kindly, by friends and strangers alike. But in the weeks and months after our daughter's funeral, my husband was often asked "How is your wife coping?"'

But what about him?

And the wife is often treated as though she has lost someone she loved, whereas the man is treated as though he has lost some-one he was responsible for, she wrote, quoting Ann Chalmers, Chief Executive of Child Bereavement UK.

When encountering a grieving father, asking an open-ended question such as the late Gavin Larkin's 'Are you okay?' is a good way of showing support, without putting pressure on the person to open up to us.

Guilt about moving on

Are you feeling guilty about not being able to move on? Then don't.

Back in Sigmund Freud's day, 'getting over' grief and getting back to normal was considered the goal of therapy and indeed of life, after the emotional trauma of the death of a loved one. Any unusually long attachment or focus on the dead person was considered abnormal, and if this continued, psychotherapy was recommended (at least for the elites, who had access to it).

This led to the concept of normal and abnormal grief.

Elisabeth Kübler-Ross came along in the 1960s and suggested a 'stages of grief' schema. These stages are: denial, anger, bargaining, depression and acceptance. This schema was designed to help busy professionals understand the typical reactions of someone who has just been given a diagnosis of terminal cancer, and to support them. The concept was later applied to grief, all grief.

Kübler-Ross's teachings did us all a great service because death had become completely divorced from life. Rapid technological developments after World War II fed into medicine and hospitals, which began to take on a more disciplined, can-do aura that was positively death-defying. Now, if people died, somehow that was a failure, a mistake. America was particularly vulnerable to this way of thinking, and Kübler-Ross showed first Americans and then us all, that death is not the enemy.

But she herself later expressed great regret that what started as an observation about how people behave – the stages of grief – turned into a rule.

Kate White told me a story that illustrated the limitations of this rule-based way of thinking about grief. She was sitting in hand-over at the end of a busy nursing shift and the nurses came to a patient who was struggling with the enormity of her impending death. One nurse said, 'She's still in the stage of anger and she needs to move on.'

As Kate White says, 'Well, it ain't that neat.'

To suggest there are stages someone has to pass through is to suggest there is some kind of reward for getting to the last stage. But how can there be? As I travelled, listening to stories of grief, I talked with Maria whose stories about her Sicilian traditions were discussed earlier. Maria lost her father, her niece, her mother and her husband, all in quick succession.

'My husband Pat developed brain cancer just after his 54th birthday. Then my father died. I didn't have time to grieve for him because Pat was having so many seizures each day and I had to be strong to care for him. My niece died suddenly shortly after my father, then my mother, then Pat,' she explained.

Maria loves her children and granddaughters, but she believes she will never get over these losses: 'I look at my granddaughters. I look at the way they look at life and I see their innocence, which is so beautiful. But I'm shut off.'

She says she will never feel rewarded for moving on – and she feels angry when people suggest she should.

The reality is that people skip stages, do their own thing, and behave as the individuals they are. The five-stages concept has therefore been pushed to one side to allow room for new thinking. And grief over loss is now accepted as complex and messy, although theories about it still have a place, to help those immersed in it.

Grief experts now no longer talk in terms of a predictable movement through grief, from beginning to end.

While psychologists, and our society generally, want to urge us back to a happy and full life, we're entitled to be cautious about this, and then re-engage when we're ready.

When to seek help with grief

In the immediate aftermath of a death, rather than seeing stages, psychologists now see people switching between emotional responses (breaking down, crying, not being able to get out of bed, 'the bad days') and practical responses – moving forward, getting out and about, going back to work, achieving small goals during a day, then larger ones.

It is acknowledged that people can ping from one to the other of these two responses, randomly and in no set order. Generally, if people are making some progress towards re-establishing a meaningful life – not necessarily the old one – then psychologists are now confident that they will eventually get through their grief and move on to a safer emotional place.

Referrals to counsellors have been shown to have no success in helping healthy but grieving people manage terrible experiences that lead them to distress, if they don't want it or believe they need it. Some experts even argue that sending people, who believe they are coping, to counselling can be damaging, as well as a waste of time and money.

About 10 per cent of us will have intense grief reactions that persist for more than six months. If this 'prolonged bereavement' lasts for more than twelve months, it's considered unusual.

It is the same thing as 'complicated grief', the term psychologists prefer to use today, since this expression is non-judgemental and more accurately reflects that there are many factors involved in how someone grieves. The woman who buried a sister, then a mother, then a child, in a short space of time, has a more complicated set of circumstances than another woman who experienced a single loss.

Psychologists also talk of prolonged grief disorder (PGD), when people develop mental and/or physical afflictions due to prolonged grief. These afflictions include sleep disruption, high blood pressure, and increased risk of cancer and substance abuse. Over the years following a death, these afflictions evolve to become their own, separate physical or psychological problem, but in each case they can be traced back and directly linked to the death.

Many people also have concerns about the 'medicalisation' of grief. If grief is seen as a problem to be managed, then does this mean we'll be offered the latest drug from a pharmaceutical company to help 'solve' this problem?

Sometimes, offering a pharmaceutical drug to solve an emotional problem is entirely appropriate. But there is still much debate about whether talking therapies can work better. While studies warn that seeing the wrong therapist is worse than simply being prescribed drugs without much thought, a recent review of a number of studies concluded that, on balance, there wasn't much difference between the effectiveness of pharmaceuticals and psychotherapy. However, the author of a more recent commentary argued that we have to be careful, because the level of care in community settings for patients taking antidepressants is drastically less intense than it is in drug trials.

Should antidepressants be used to treat grief? Certainly a therapist will deal with grief in a different way to depression, watching to make sure it doesn't become abnormally and destructively prolonged.

This is a vexed issue, which only the individual working with their doctor can judge. However, Australian specialists tend to recommend talking therapies much more than drug therapies, say, compared to their American counterparts. This is particularly so in dealing with grief.

What of the religious issues? 'There is an undercurrent that sadness is a sin, a punishable sign of weakness,' said Rebecca Goss in her article in *The Lancet*, in which she discussed attitudes to her husband's grief.

One idea talked about by psychologists today, for the first time in a very long time, is that successful grieving doesn't necessarily involve 'letting go' of the dead person. Is it okay for people to want to maintain their bonds with the dead? Academics and researchers are divided on the answer. But despite this – probably because of it – as many as 50 per cent of people in studies report when asked that they believe the deceased can be 'present' after their death.

Few people admit to having a sense of the presence of someone who has died because this is not considered acceptable in our culture. But what if it is a healing mechanism, even if poorly understood?

Psychologists today are more aware of the bond with the dead – whether that bond is expressed as a memory, or as a firm belief that the person grieved over has never really left, Christopher Hall points out.

My sister-in-law Marie talked of my brother Julian's presence long after he died, in fact she still does. It threatened me at first and

I didn't like it. But now I accept that this helps her cope with his loss. She is deeply religious and has found purpose in his death by believing he guides her, her family and others through their problems, particularly in marriages.

This firm conviction that he is still with her helped her manage her grief in the early days. It cannot be shaken and continues to shape her life.

On a lesser scale, Brian and his wife Jan buried their daughter Kim in 2017. Brian believes he copes better than Jan with her death because he believes Kim is still present. 'She hasn't really gone. I talk to her all the time – and she talks back. Last week I looked at myself in the mirror and Kim said, "That tie looks terrible Dad. Take it off and put another one on." So I did.'

Many people report wanting to express ideas about the deceased for the rest of their lives. When we become uncomfortable around those who want to talk about the deceased, whatever the timeframe since they died, they often feel judged. In some cases this distresses them or makes them angry. We need to be aware that wanting to keep the dead person present is not considered mad or stupid by psychologists who specialise in grief. That said, psychologists say depression is separate to grief. These two states can look very similar, and grief can turn into depression.

A crucial question is whether the person seems to be finding a way, in their own time, to make sense of their experience. It's a hard idea to express, but sometimes grief leads to a new understanding about life. The period between the incident and the equilibrium that comes with insight into what we are looking back on can be frightening and lonely, no matter how many other people are around. But if people can give meaning to their experience of grief, this will help them to recover.

There is a lot to consider here. But here are some simple considerations to support someone grieving:

- Don't be too worried if someone doesn't seem to be 'getting better'; don't feel you have to hurry them.

- If you are concerned that they just can't move on despite an abnormally long time in despair, question whether their grief has turned into depression. Be aware that they might reject attempts to move them into a different space.

     ♚ Be with them.

How to talk to those who are grieving

Here are some good suggestions from the helpguide.org mental and emotional health website.

     ♚ Don't let fears about saying or doing the wrong thing stop you from reaching out.

     ♚ Let your grieving loved one know that you're there to listen.

     ♚ Understand that everyone grieves differently and for different lengths of time.

     ♚ Offer to help in practical ways.

     ♚ Maintain your support after the funeral.

Blogger Sarah Parmenter makes some invaluable points in her article, 'The Things Nobody Tells You About Grief', at the website LifeHacker.com.au:

> *Don't say 'Anything I can do, please shout/call' or similar. Offer to do something, anything. Real tangible things. 'Can I come over for a coffee?' or 'Can I bring you anything from the supermarket?' – anything that's an actual do. You learn to hear 'anything I can do, please call' as 'I have no idea what to say and have no intention of doing anything.' Don't put yourself in that bracket.*

This is a slightly edited version of a few more of her tips:

     ♚ Understand you're now dealing with a muddled mind.

     ♚ Everything and anything can set the griever off on an emotional downward spiral. But often, talking about the lost loved one is the thing that brings the most peace – yet it's the one thing people skirt around.

   Ꝭ Speak about any triggers. Often the griever has triggers associated with death. Mine is ambulances or sirens, among other things. This is not so you can tread on eggshells around the griever nor baby them, it's so that you can understand a change of behaviour if in the presence of the trigger.

   Ꝭ If the griever tries to tell you of a change in behaviour, or something they've noticed as being different about the way they cope, listen. Intently. Read between the lines.

   Ꝭ Understand they can function perfectly normally too.

   Ꝭ Tears. They make almost everyone uncomfortable don't they? I've had one person shake me, physically, and tell me I had to get a grip and move on (it had been three weeks since my mum had died), while others have sat and quietly listened and passed tissues. It will help to know how you deal with people who are crying before you put yourself in a situation where it's likely to happen.

   Ꝭ Remember that friendships can be changed by the grieving person's experience. The person grieving feels different to the way they did before. Having faced the enormity of loss, they may feel impatient with those who do not know what this feels like. To the grieving person, others' lives can seem trivial.

Is the person angry? Sometimes they are angry with God for taking away the person they loved, angry with the world for not being as sad as they are, for not coming to a dead halt, angry with other people whose lives seem to go on regardless of their own void – and hardest of all – angry with the person who died. This is the most difficult to deal with because it can shock others who hear them express this anger.

Sometimes the grieving person is experiencing all of these angers at once.

This anger tests everyone, the griever and those trying to deal with them. Some relationships will change as a result, some will be lost and some will get better. Relationships between spouses can change if they respond to the grief differently.

There is one other person to consider in this: the person who is grieving in advance, because they know they are to die soon. Maybe this is the hardest person to talk to.

Their journey is painful. It can make our own concerns look foolish. Yet when my friend Helena was dying she always asked for a chat about the subjects we would have raked over before. She said, 'These are the conversations I want, these are the conversations that I miss.'

As we begin to recover, we find that traditional cultural supports have changed: the neighbour over the back fence hanging out washing at the same time as we do, the good priest ready to offer a prayer and blessing we believed in. How do we replace these?

Let's find a cultural solution, in our own communities. The definition of community has changed, but the need for it has not. Where once we would have met for a craft group in the local church hall after being invited by a fellow parishioner from the same church, today the knitting group might be found through an app on your phone.

Sometimes social media can be seen as threatening – especially when we see it mining our data without our authorisation, or we look at its potential for use by politicians for social control. But we can make it a force for good. Paradoxically, we can use it to create meaningful communities. For example, stitch.net is a social networking community designed for those aged over 50. Despite being global, it's goal is to create local connections between people.

There is also Meetup, a platform used by members to invite others to attend activities. For example, you might go to meetup. com to look for a group to cycle with on the weekend or find a group to train for a marathon with, or learn to cook.

If you want to work at a slightly more local level, see what your local library has to offer. Once upon a time a library was strictly about books and 'Silence please!' Today they are recognised as important social hubs. Often book clubs are organised through libraries, as are other social groups.

The people you meet will come from different places and the ideas you'll be exposed to might be unexpected. But the opportunity to grow with others, through joint activity, is there. The app has not replaced the opportunity for connection, it is simply the means that allows it. Remember, don't confuse connectivity with connection.

The grief of a child

The belief that children should – or can – be protected from the consequences of grief is now challenged. In fact, there is a powerful argument that the more they are given the opportunity to discuss the death of someone who they loved, the better they will cope.

Author Doris Zagdanski points out in her book *What's Dead Mean?* that adults often don't know what to say to children because they don't know what to think themselves.

She makes the following points:

- Parents generally underestimate the need to inform children.

- Children need to be able to share in family grief.

- The opportunity to participate in farewells is important.

- The grief of a child will involve lots of questions – when they feel safe enough to express themselves.

- Schools can help – but their staff may need advice about how to do this.

- Children remember details of a death many years afterwards.

- Children can be confused when it looks as though adults have stopped grieving because they have, for example, gone back to work.

Children are most likely to ask two questions: What is death? And why do people die? The best answers are simple ones. For example, 'When people die, everything in their body stops.'

We need to use simple, concrete words and be prepared to keep repeating our answers.

The grief of an adolescent

Adolescence remains a time of immense growth – physically, emotionally, psychologically – a time when we juggle emerging adult responsibilities with the needs of the child within. It is a time of intensity.

'Adolescents enter into a time of testing, of exploring unknowns – sex and drugs, and sometimes death of a peer – all of which can take them into the profound and expanded consciousness,' Zenith Virago explained.

In funeral rites and burials, Virago has supported adolescents when a peer's exploration has, unwittingly, gone too far. We need to allow adolescents their opportunity to learn the lessons when others' attempts at experimenting and pushing limits go wrong.

There are other stories of adolescence and grief, too, of the child on the verge of adulthood who experiences a great loss, such as when a parent dies.

My nephew, Evan, was nearly fourteen when he lost his father, in the motorcycle accident that changed our lives. His brother Christian was seventeen, his sister Claire was fourteen, all very young to have to deal with such a loss. Now, at nineteen, Evan still vividly remembers the day his father died.

'When I was told he'd been in an accident, my first reaction wasn't to panic,' Evan said. 'My impression was that he'd been bumped in a roundabout somewhere in town, and that he'd broken a leg. When my mother and brother Christian came back from seeing him, just up the road, they were grabbing blankets. I thought it was because he was cold, but he was bleeding out.'

This is something he has only recently been able to talk to Christian about.

'I didn't realise how bad it was until we got to the hospital. When a nurse told me there was a small chance he would die, then I panicked,' he said.

Time stood still, yet there are patches that he doesn't remember.

'Then later, in the hospital waiting room, a family friend and one of the doctors each took me by one arm and then Mum started screaming, and that was what happened for the next fifteen minutes. That time is just like a dream, it's so surreal,' he said.

After struggling through the disorientation of the immediate impact of the news, as well as thinking about his father and feeling the intensity of that experience, he became aware of the implications, struggling with his concerns about how others would see him and his family – realising that he was about to receive a lot of attention that he didn't know how to deal with. This added a dimension to the experience that he didn't expect. Maybe it's something adults can be aware of when dealing with an adolescent's grief.

'I worried about everyone finding out – all my friends and family, all the teachers, almost everyone in town,' he recalled. 'I could see what was just about to happen. Telling people was like waiting for another punch and that was played out over and over again, every time. I felt like my stomach was dropping, every time. It just felt like being strangled, and just waiting for that moment to be over.'

'Even going to the hairdressers to get my hair cut for the funeral, the hairdresser asked me where I went to school and when I told her she said, "Did you know the teacher from there who was just killed in an accident," and I said he was my father. She misheard me at first.

'"He was your art teacher?"

'"No he was my father."

'And she crumpled up and apologised and it was so hard dealing with that moment. She was upset and it got really awkward but I had to hold it together.'

In a moment when Evan just wanted to sneak out and have a haircut, to zone out and not be conspicuous in his misery, he felt himself under scrutiny. He quickly realised this would keep happening: 'I just had to go through that over and over again, to see the same reaction again and again.'

Each time it happened, as he watched other people struggle to deal with it, reminded him of his loss.

But he feels positive now about the way the adults around him handled it.

'I wanted to hide but I also knew it would be worse if I hid. I wouldn't have been able to see how people felt, they wouldn't have been able to let me know they cared.'

Even now, six years after his father's death, it still hurts: 'It's the little things that really hurt the most, like setting the table – there's one less placemat, one less knife and fork.'

'The grief doesn't go away. It gets better – although I don't think that's the right word,' Evan said.

Some things change. I remember Evan at the time saying he felt left out of the adult conversations, and felt angry about the assumption that he was too young to cope. His perspective has shifted and he doesn't agree with that now.

'The whole nature of the situation is bad in itself, so the interaction with all the adults around was all helpful, really. I can't think of anything that was done that could have been done differently.

'At the time, I didn't want to be pampered and the last thing I wanted was to be at the centre of attention as the kid who'd lost his dad. But at the same time, I knew I needed it. People were keeping an eye on me.

'One of the first things that was done was that I saw a child's grief counsellor at the hospital where my mother works as a nurse. I had a really hard time opening up to her because of a weird mix of a teenage boy going through that experience, and then all the other issues of the early teenage years.

'I feel as though when Dad died my older brother and sister grew up really quickly, but I did the opposite. I became really insecure and afraid of everything – it amplified all the fears I had before Dad died. I became really afraid of doing things and really dependent on Mum. If I didn't do something, it wouldn't hurt me, that was my mentality. I didn't want to try new things, try go to new places. I was terrified because of what had happened to Dad.

'Because Dad was a teacher at my school that was an added element. I went through a real identity crisis and felt as though I couldn't develop my own identity because everyone in the school knew I was Mr Rice's son, and now I had to grow up being the son of Mr Rice who's died. In that environment, there was no way I could escape it.

'So I felt a mixture of things. I felt I was on display, that I was being tip-toed around, that the adults and children around me were being told not to upset this child, not to talk to me unless they could say something nice, and that didn't feel genuine. Right from the get-go, I could feel it.

'Looking back I don't think anyone was doing anything wrong, no one messed up. It was just inevitable because of the situation.

'Coming into puberty and changing as a person, that was when the grief was running its course, too. So for me they went hand in hand – growing up as a person, and growing up struggling with Dad's death. They went hand in hand, one came with the other. So I'm left all the time to wonder how I would have been different.

'For others who find themselves in the same situation, I'd say everything about who you are going to be, who you're going to become, is completely changed by that one incident. That's inevitable, but all you can do is go with it. You're going to grow up being affected by this but try not to feel too intimidated, let it run its course but don't feel hopeless.'

PART **02**

WHEN YOUR
OWN TIME COMES

CHAPTER 09

Planning for your own death

We plan ahead, taking what we've learnt and applying practical steps, to help ourselves and to help others.

Having companioned a death, something happens. We are now more able to think about our own death – we're more ready to do some practical planning of our own.

Planning for our own death might be confronting, so some of the things I say next might make you feel uncomfortable. Soothe yourself. Pour yourself a cup of tea, pause between sections and do something gentle for yourself, and maybe even talk with friends about what I'll say in the next few chapters.

Planning for death opens up many big and challenging questions about what you believe and how you want to live your life. Yet it begins with a housekeeping style of checklist, so let's start with the more practical issues first.

Creating a non-medical checklist

Paradoxically, in order to have a simple straightforward death, one over which we have the most control that's reasonable, we need to do some forward planning. As the seventeenth-century French poet Jean de La Fontaine once wrote: 'Death never takes the wise man by surprise, he is always ready to go'.

Some people don't like the idea of planning for or even thinking about their death. That's fair enough. But this attitude can create problems. I know an old couple who do not like talking about their deaths. They're pretty typical of many people of their generation in our culture. But because they don't talk about it, they can't plan anything. Some people don't like planning for or thinking about their financial future either. That's a way of living, but it's a way that can lead to vulnerability and much worse, continuous stress, all of which can be avoided. Planning for a good death can serve a similar purpose to good financial planning – avoiding unnecessary bother and achieving personal goals.

When planning for your death, how early is too early? A Buddhist monk or anyone else who has devoted their life to spiritual contemplation would say it is never too early.

But we're not all so focused on the ethereal, so what's best for the rest of us? The best time to make plans is much earlier than any of us would like to think.

Planning ahead is the first step, because a little bit of forward thinking – and sometimes a lot of it – is needed to make every step that follows work. Planning ahead underpins most other things in this discussion.

We could die suddenly, in an accident or from an unexpected illness. It's not too morbid to suggest that because of this, we should have at least a few notes, however informal, set aside. The good thing is that because of the resources available to us today, through our computers and other electronic devices, much of our reading, studying and planning can be done on the internet – so we don't need to leave our homes, our familiar desks. We can cut and paste the ideas we like into our own documents and then explore a few weblinks. If you are not computer savvy, that's not a problem. There are other ways to collect the information that's needed.

What's documented in our planning notes will depend on personality and personal choices. But the more descriptive you can be, the better for the friends and family left behind, who will want to follow your wishes.

Forward planning will make it easier for those who have to manage our affairs after we're gone. Leaving a mess behind will be seen as part of our legacy. Some people don't mind this but many others would rather make life easier, not harder, for those left behind when they die.

When Vanessa's mother was diagnosed with a terminal illness, she told the family that all her relevant paperwork was on the top shelf of her library desk. When she died and it came time to look for these papers, her family were still shocked and distressed.

'I can't tell you what a gift her act of organising these things was for us. When I opened the library desk, there was nothing else except these essential documents in it. She'd put everything that was important in that one place. She'd taken out everything that wasn't essential to our tasks and duties at that point.

'I was the one in the family who had to work with them, and she made it so straightforward,' Vanessa said. 'I've got friends who've been in a similar situation, but because nothing was in order they spent weeks and many sleepless nights just trying to sort things out, before they could take the first step. I was so grateful to my mother for that final and important gesture. It sounds boring and officious to talk about gathering a set of papers together, but when I sat at that desk working, I felt her love.'

Inheritance lawyer Michelle Johnson says that messages can be left behind and these can be important. This is not just the pragmatic messages about, for example, financial matters but other, softer ones.

'The importance of a message left behind is twofold. From a legal perspective, detailing information which will assist with estate administration cannot be underestimated. Indeed this avoids family members and others searching records to enable the completion of death certificates and probate applications at a time when dealing with emotional sensitivities. They know where things are.

'It can feel wrong to be searching for and preoccupied with documents at a time when you are preparing for a funeral, so this is really an invaluable and supportive thing to do for your family.

'But there's another perspective – the emotional one,' Michelle said.

'Words of reassurance and comfort are something richly cherished – and those thoughts and reassurances can never be underestimated.'

Michelle says through her work she often noticed the way war veterans left their affairs. Usually, this was in a very orderly way, which she found really touching. They had often been forced to reflect on their mortality at a very young age, as young men going into battle.

'I was frequently able to identify members of the RAAF or RAF by the manner in which their affairs were left and usually with a note headed "When the time comes", "If you read this note then" or "The things you should know if".

'Not only were details of financial interest but things lovingly documented were left in the top drawer or in the family bible, including requested requiems, tributes and wakes.

'One only has to read the beautiful letters in the war museum to family from young airmen to know how much comfort they provided.

'One such young man said: "If I die in flight I would do it again – flight is freedom in its purest form."'

Michelle's stepfather left such a note: 'And I will treasure it forever, for it let me know just how much our relationship meant to him.'

Organising your paperwork

Let's make a list of the documents your family will need. It's a good idea to list them under two headings, or layers, one for general documents and records (the outer layer), the other for things that relate directly to your death (the inner layer):

The outer layer:

- ❧ Birth and marriage certificates

- ❧ Property deeds or lease agreements

- ❧ Insurance policies

- ❧ Loans

- ❧ Bank accounts

- ❧ Investments (including superannuation).

The inner layer:

- ❧ Your will

- ❧ Power of attorney

- ❧ Substitute decision-maker – name and contact details

- ❧ Your advance care directive.

Important documents such as birth and marriage certificates, property deeds or lease agreements, insurance policies and details of bank accounts and other investments or debts should all be kept together.

Having all the important documents in the one folder in the one place is not just a go-to resource for others in the event of your death, it's also a good thing to do for yourself. If you suddenly had to pick up a handful of documents and run, what would they be and where would they be stored?

Make your own folder, tailoring it to your needs. Or buy a ready-made one from stationery stores and hip designers, such as kikki.K, which have files in them for categories such as:

- ❧ Certificates – birth, marriage, passport

- ❧ Health – vaccinations, medical records

- ❧ Home – title, lease, insurances

- ❧ Finance – banking, shares, superannuation

- ẽ Career – contracts, CVs, references

- ẽ Education – credentials, certificates

- ẽ Will – legal records, forms

- ẽ Tax – returns, group certificates, tax file number.

As part of your *ars moriendi* planning, you need to make sure your significant other knows where this folder is stored.

Keep a list of all your financial records and insurance policies with the documents. Give a copy of this list to your partner or other person you would like to manage your personal affairs if you die. Once again, this is handy to have for your own needs.

Never put any passwords, particularly internet banking passwords, on this list. But do record all account numbers that currently appear on your records – for example, your account number and your BSB (but not your secret PIN!)

It is also worth adding your:

- ẽ tax file number

- ẽ ABN number.

If these two are listed, then it will be much easier for authorities to help family track assets and obligations.

The list will include all your insurances, for example: professional, life, home, contents, car, third-party, public liability. Include all the dates they are due to expire. If you don't have automatic debiting organised for regular bill payments, listing due dates will also help make it easier for you to keep your payments up to date – another reason it's handy to have them listed together.

On this list also put superannuation details and any loans. While some loans, such as personal loans, are extinguished when you die, most other debts, including credit card debt, will be transferred, in one shape or another, to those who inherit assets from you. It's therefore really helpful for those who will be dealing with your financial affairs not to have any nasty surprises. Where there's a co-signatory – someone else whose signature is on the loan documents – the responsibility for the debt falls to them.

Beside the name of each policy, it would be even better to have the name and direct telephone number of your contact person in the business that issued the policy, so that your relatives can speak to them as soon as they need to.

Be mindful of your personal security, though. If your important documents are collected together and you are concerned about identity theft, you might like to store them in a more obscure place than the main drawer of your study desk. What about the middle drawer of the laundry cupboard? But if you do this you need to let someone close to you know where they'll be able to find them when they need to. Some people store such items in safety deposit boxes in their bank, although these are less common today.

You can also upload copies of these documents to the cloud as a back-up. But you need to ensure the security of your computer when you do this. Make sure your computer has a proper security program.

If you are in any doubt about the security of your personal documents, written or electronic, you can talk to your local crime prevention officer. In New South Wales, these officers, located at various sites, are happy to talk to individuals and groups.

To reassure you, the Crime Prevention Officer at a busy NSW command centre said that documents are not usually the target of house break-ins. (The gold and bullion are.) And most identity thieves ply their trade over the internet, not by stealing real documents.

Who needs to be told when you die?

Keep a checklist of those who need to be told. It can be hard to work this out, especially if it's the first time your family members have had to organise events after a death, and it can be doubly hard when they are grieving. It may not feel necessary and it may be the last thing on their minds, as they cope with their sadness and loss and the process of planning a funeral.

But letting the appropriate people and organisations know will stop these institutions from sending unnecessary mail and making wasted, irritating telephone enquiries later. Some organisations, such as banks, may need to know so they can release funds or reveal vital information. Banks usually have a deceased estate and bereavement officer who can talk this through with the surviving spouse. If there is enough time beforehand, the dying person might even want to pre-empt that moment and see what they will be told.

These organisations will usually require formal, written evidence of your death, such as the death certificate.

Some of the other organisations that will need to know of your death are:

- credit card companies

- employers

- health professionals

- insurance companies

- the local council

- utilities such as electricity, gas and phone companies.

All of this may seem officious and unnecessary, especially when we don't want to have to deal with it. But it does matter.

My friend Kristin tells a story about something that happened to friends of friends. We can't tell whether it's an urban myth or not. It doesn't matter – it illustrates a great fear. She was told a story about a Scottish couple who decided to go on a trip to Europe. At the last minute, 80-year-old Mabel asked if she could join them. They drove to Dover to catch the ferry across the English Channel and at that point realised Mabel didn't have her passport with her. They all decided Mabel could be transported in the boot of the car. But when they got to Calais, Mabel had died. They immediately went back to England to report the death to police. While they were in the police station the car was stolen. Mabel had disappeared and the car was never found.

The feature I picked up from the story is that a death had occurred and there was no way of noting it. It seems unlikely, but the fact that it's been told repeatedly points to a deep fear – that our death will go undocumented, not noted, that we could simply disappear. It's reassuring to think that would be hard to achieve.

Your will and power of attorney

How you plan to provide for those left behind can have a big impact. Your will needs to be part of your planning very early in life. The ideal is to make your initial will when you first have a family to support, and then to update it at regular intervals throughout your life. Managed this way, it is not an added pressure when you're old, but an idea that you're used to and comfortable with.

Your will is a legally binding, written statement in which you name who you would like your assets to be given to after you die. Your property and other assets can be distributed without a will, but if you make a will you're actually deciding how you wish your estate to be distributed, rather than leaving it to set formulas imposed by the legal system.

Your will must be written voluntarily – that is, it needs to be free of duress and undue influence – and it must be signed by you, in front of witnesses, usually two, who then must also sign the document to validate that they witnessed you signing it. The witnesses can't be beneficiaries, otherwise this makes the will invalid.

A will may be changed by way of a codicil (an amendment to the original will) or by making a new will.

The most practical way to ensure that your will is legally valid is to consult a solicitor and be guided by their advice. There are many issues to be considered in making a will, such as the suitability of a prospective executor, the nature and ownership of assets, the care of minor children, and funeral directions.

Keep your will with the solicitor who draws it up, because it is easy to lose the original. Wills used to be kept in a safety deposit box at a bank, but today, this is less likely because banking relationships tend to be conducted online. Make sure you keep a copy yourself.

Your executor or executors is a person or persons you've nominated to be legally responsible for executing, that is following through on all the wishes outlined in your will. They can be family members and can also be beneficiaries of the will. It might seem obvious, but before you make your will you need to ask prospective executors whether they'll take on this role, since they could be involved in quite a bit of work on your behalf when you die.

These people should also have a copy of the will because they're the ones that are going to be called upon to activate the will when you die. Their first job will be to locate the original copy of your will.

Remember, once you have written a will, it is quite possible you will want to change it, as the years pass. Do not expect to be able to do this over the phone. When you tell your solicitor that you want to change it and they suggest you go in to their office to discuss it, this is essential, so do not treat it as an inconvenience – or an excuse for them to make money, as someone suggested to me recently about her solicitor.

Your solicitor has to be confident that you are of sound mind, whether this will is the first you have written or the last of many. It will be during the course of a face-to-face meeting with you that they will be able to fully consider your state of mind, whether you have 'capacity' to sign one. Making the assessment that you are mentally competent is their major responsibility in this process and no matter how many times you have seen them before, each repeated rewrite has to be done scrupulously and thoroughly, in order to protect your interests and ensure you have a valid will.

Capacity is more subtle and complex than it might first appear. Is it the person's legal, mental or physical capacity that is being examined? They might be capable of buying food at their local shopping centre but not of making a financial transaction like buying or selling shares.

Arguments about capacity and whether someone had it are fought out in the law courts all the time, and sometimes cases are taken all the way to the High Court, which means lots of lawyers have argued about it – so the right answer couldn't be too obvious, or there wouldn't be two opposing teams spending money fighting over it. But in most cases it can be straightforward and it needs to be resolved when a will is written, when power of attorney is signed and when guardianship or substitute decision-making documents are signed, to protect us when we have become vulnerable.

And the basic question is: Can this person understand the general nature of what they are doing? A valid will can only be made by a person of sound mind, memory and understanding. The person making the will must understand the nature of the act of making a will and have an understanding of his or her assets and a comprehension of who they ought to provide for in their will.

If the solicitor has difficulty deciding that, then they can ask for the advice of a range of medical professionals such as a psychiatrist, a geriatrician or the Aged Care Assessment Team (ACAT) of the major hospital in the area.

Probate is the area of law that determines the validity of wills and administers the distribution of assets of a deceased person.

Whenever property, for example a house, is left by the dead person to a relative the probate process, supervised and administered through the courts, ensures the title deeds are transferred correctly from the name of the person who died to the name of the person who is inheriting.

Contesting a will

A surprisingly large number of wills are contested, making probate a busy area of law. This is because, for example, siblings expect a parent's division of assets to be fair, but they don't agree on what is 'fair'.

Lawyers in Australia, the United Kingdom and New Zealand all say the major factor causing an increase in contested wills is the greater frequency of remarriage, which leads to greater diversity in the way families are structured, bringing in step-children, full brothers and sisters and half-brothers and sisters. Changes in legislation also put more emphasis on protecting the rights of a dependent second wife, for example the changes to the NSW *Succession Act 2006* (amended in 2008).

Lawyers warn that contesting a will causes lots of distress in families, and that your children are more likely to contest your will if the will has been poorly written.

As a general rule, children, including quite elderly adult children, have the right to be provided 'for the proper maintenance, education or advancement in life', in the words of the *Succession Act*. This is known as 'family provision'. This right doesn't extend to the brothers and sisters of the dead person.

Wills legislation across Australia provides a framework for people who meet certain criteria to make a claim to the court for a share or greater share of an estate. The terms of the legislation are not uniform, so check your local legislation.

New South Wales is governed by the *Succession Act 2006*. Under the Act, people eligible for provision in a will include a spouse of the deceased, children of the deceased, a former spouse of the deceased, and a person who was dependent on the deceased and who was a member of the deceased's household.

New Zealand led the way in family provision, enacting laws to ensure it in 1900. This undid the previous notion of 'testamentary freedom' – that a man could leave his assets to whoever he wanted to. In an era when wives didn't work and spouses and children were very vulnerable to destitution if their father didn't provide for them when he died, these laws were designed to ensure fathers took responsibility for their children. Similar laws were later adopted in Australia and the United Kingdom.

Are the assets of your will something your children are entitled to or should they just be seen as a gift? This question goes to the heart of many costly legal battles over the proceeds of wills. If you decide to leave a child out of your will because they made no contribution to your family life, or caused heartache and suffering because they removed themselves from your family, you can protect this decision by inserting a clause in your will explaining why you are estranged, since 'estrangement' is a legal term and will be taken into account by the courts when they are deciding whether they should intervene to change the way you divided your estate.

But there are a few non-legal issues that are worth thinking about. Such a decision, made by you, is going to cause a new round of division and heartache among your children, unrelated to any family tensions that existed before you died, since any changes will need to come from their assets.

Legal battles of this nature are expensive. Do the financial benefits outweigh the costs? But more importantly to most families, will the financial benefits outweigh the emotional costs?

The flip side of the decision to leave a child out is the perception of unfairness when some children are left better off financially under a will than others. NSW barrister Therese Catanzariti sees potential clients who believe their parents were too generous to another child. But time and again, when she reviews the situation she sees parents who have provided well for a child who is far less financially secure than the others. From the point of view of the law, this is reasonable, she explained.

'It's what I call the "Mamma Bear" complex. I've got a child who is doing really well and I've got a child who's doing really badly. When I pass away, I won't be around to look after the one who is doing badly, and no one else will look after them. So I look after the one who is doing badly. This is the last thing I can do for that child.

'And this is often at odds with the expectations of that person's siblings who worked hard all their lives, built up their finances and would like their labour acknowledged by their parent.'

She says it would be better if people saw anything left to them in a will as a windfall.

'Sometimes people feel betrayed by their parent and they blame their siblings. I have to remind them that it was the parent's decision,' she said.

Power of attorney

There are two types of power of attorney: a general power of attorney and an enduring power of attorney. The difference is that an enduring power of attorney continues to operate if the person loses capacity.

A power of attorney is a legal document in which you appoint someone to look after your legal and financial affairs. This person will have a very important and powerful role to play in your life because they will control your money, usually when you are incapacitated by old age and/or dementia, and they won't be able to consult with you or ask you for your input. The person you appoint for this role has to be someone your trust completely. If there is no one you trust completely – a surprisingly common situation – you can organise for the state (the public trustee or guardian) to do this.

The alternative, which is to do nothing, usually leaves people in a situation where informal arrangements are made. For example, an adult child is given access to PIN numbers or credit cards or becomes a signatory on the account. This can work – but it can also fail. Control, or the perception of it, can subtly or quickly be taken by the person with access, leaving the elderly person uncertain about making financial decisions. It can also leave others, usually siblings to the elderly person, uneasy about the arrangements.

If you want to minimise distrust between your dependents, a formal arrangement with its more transparent protocols, and the opportunity to change the power of attorney, will achieve your purpose more effectively.

Next of kin

The next of kin is the person you nominate on papers when you enter hospital. While in some US states it is a legal term used in relation to inheritance, it isn't a term with a legal meaning in Australia, the United Kingdom or New Zealand. Rather, it is a convention, referring to the person you want contacted in the event of a medical emergency. This person doesn't have to be a relative; they could be a close friend. He or she will be contacted by the hospital if they need someone to come in to be at your bedside. If they have to restrict visitors, the next of kin will have priority. So assign this role carefully.

Ideally, don't nominate the person that you feel you *should* name; nominate the person who you really *want* at your bedside. But be practical. If this person is different to your substitute decision-maker, a role to be discussed in more detail later, it works best if they can work with each other. For example, your next of kin might be your husband, but your substitute decision-maker your eldest child.

There have been some very sad situations in recent history when people who lived alone died and no one even knew they were sick or noticed they'd gone missing. In response, NSW police are encouraging people who live alone to register the name of their next of kin, someone who the police can contact if there's an emergency or the police have become concerned about your welfare.

Social media

How should those who have electronic lives organise their exit from social media when they die? For these people, a high priority is to have some mechanism for others to access our passwords to social media sites so that these can be shut down.

But the dilemma is, you don't want to make your passwords widely accessible, sharing them with other people. Maybe the solution is to give select passwords, such as to your Facebook account, to your partner or a close friend or relative, who can be trusted to go in and either shut your site down or put a notice up on it when the time comes.

Facebook's policy is that, upon request, an account can either be memorialised or deleted after the person's death. Memorialising the account removes sensitive information, like status updates, and restricts profile access to confirmed friends only. However, this can be harder to achieve than we'd like, partly because users, the friends and associates who are shutting your account down, have to work through Facebook's electronic help centre and do it themselves. No one from Facebook will take responsibility for completing these tasks or ensuring they're done for you.

Memorialised Facebook accounts are sites where people can post memories after a person has died. Facebook says memorialising an account also helps keep it secure by preventing anyone from logging into it. According to Facebook:

'If Facebook is made aware that a person has passed away, it's our policy to memorialise the account... Please keep in mind that we can't provide login information for someone else's account even under these circumstances. It's always against Facebook's policies to log into another person's account.'

Reduce, reuse, recycle – even in death planning

Early reflection on death, so early that it feels like an ever-present part of life, is a key aspect of many forms of religious and spiritual belief – an awareness of the cycle of life. But it can also be profoundly practical.

Author Margareta Magnusson in her book *The Gentle Art of Swedish Death Cleaning* argues that continuously decluttering with the goal of shedding possessions, instead of accumulating them as we get older, is profoundly liberating and life-affirming.

For many of us this will require a major U-turn in our thinking. Deliberately letting go takes practice, which is why Magnusson sees it as a philosophy to embrace and develop from early middle age, rather than an activity to suddenly adopt late in life.

In an age when we are becoming more aware of our impact on the environment, and people are striving to lower the size of their ecological footprint, the idea of putting a check on accumulation is appealing.

For many of us holding on to items we've accumulated connects us with happy memories from the past. But this can gradually shift from being a good thing to a cause of trouble, as we become mired in mess.

George is an elderly gentleman who held on to a lamp for many years and wouldn't be parted from it, even though its electrical cord became so frayed it was dangerous. It turned out it was only really the shade that he was attached to, because his wife had made it. But he wouldn't let the lamp go. He had not challenged his own assumptions about what the lamp meant. After he died, his wife was left with the daunting task of removing this and many other similar items from their garage, which he'd turned into his storeroom.

All that anxious energy consumed over what to do with many possessions, how to store them, when it could be spent living in the moment.

Yes, a dining room setting that a family grew up with is an important symbol of all the meals the family shared as the diners were shaped into the adults they became. But does that mean the table and all six chairs have to be squeezed into a little retirement village unit? Will holding on to only one item serve the same purpose?

I'm training myself to challenge the argument that items hold my memories, making exceptions for only a small number of items, such as my wedding ring. (I don't think I'll ever be as good at it as Marie Kondo, the Japanese expert on decluttering and author of *The Life-Changing Magic of Tidying Up*.)

Today we can easily hold our memories in different ways, for example in our photos. We can do this more now, in an age when images and memory triggers are collectible on a phone and can be stored in the cloud. But I know I need to be careful that I don't simply transfer the problem and end up with too many photos that I will never see or remember to look at ever again.

Why there has never been a better time to be alive – or to die

You sometimes hear people talk about the pressures of modern living and how stressful life can be today. But for someone who lives in a Western democracy, in health terms there has never been a better time to be alive. We have clean, drinkable water, and ample, good quality food. Medical care is excellent. We are treated with antibiotics when we get an infection, and expect all our children to survive beyond their first five years. The average age of death has stretched so that we now expect to live much longer than the biblical three score year and ten.

Of course, the challenge is to make these benefits universal, so that all people across the globe can benefit.

Sometimes people fret about the evils of the internet – how social media makes us lonely, with people sitting at cafes working their phones rather than chatting to each other. Or how there are new opportunities for political manipulation and control, which present political challenges we have to address and in some cases fight against.

But in fact the internet has created more opportunities for connection, not fewer.

Royal Trinity Hospice in London is taking technology a step further, trialling virtual reality equipment to give patients who are too sick to travel a virtual reality travel experience on their bucket list, a program that has already reported bringing an increased level of joy to the dying.

It's said that technology is even changing the way we grieve – for the better.

New and exciting ways of communicating our needs are being developed every day. How they are harnessed is up to us. We are getting closer to a world where you can be sick and dying in one place but still be within reach of those who can respond very specifically and immediately to your needs in another.

While it's impossible to imagine the needs of a dying person ever disappearing – the human touch, the comforting voice, the reassuring smile – services leading up to death can be housed at a distance and then delivered as needed because of better technology.

Another really good thing about being alive – and dying – today is that we're encouraged to ask questions, to seek answers. Not that long ago, we would never have felt we could question the authority of those working in a hospital. Now, when we sense there's major – or even slight – confusion between 'law' and 'policy' at the institutions we're involved with, we can ask questions. The same applies when we observe something go wrong – or appear to go wrong – at someone's bedside.

Change has come. In hospitals now, quality end-of-life care, including as someone is dying, is a standard – not a gold standard, just an average every day standard – and patients' experiences are monitored and reviewed in relation to this standard. A hospital will have, for example, a clinical governance unit that looks after community participation, patient liaison, patient safety, complaints procedures, and quality and risk. If your hospital doesn't have a clinical governance unit, or has a poor track record in this area, today you can tell your family, carers, doctors and ancillary healthcare workers what your issue is. You can use written resources, guides and internet sites to give you more power and autonomy than people in your situation have ever had before.

In terms of treatment and outcome, more older people are undergoing treatment and surgery for, for example, heart disease – and we know more now than ever before about how to avoid it. Heart disease used to be major killer but now is no longer. There are still some communities where public education programs about, for example, diet but most importantly anti-smoking still haven't penetrated, but numbers dying of heart disease have gradually but significantly dropped.

We have new opportunities to hold on to our independence, even though we have to be brave enough to make decisions, such as focusing on our death planning, to get there.

Your substitute decision-maker

What happens if you can't say what you want? In that case, you'll need to rely on someone else, a substitute decision maker, to talk on your behalf about your concerns. Depending on where you live, this person is also called 'interim power of attorney', 'statutory health attorney' or 'enduring guardian'. This is a person who negotiates on your behalf at your bedside when decisions about your treatment are being made, if you have lost capacity or are unable to communicate.

The reality is, whatever less important decisions they find themselves making, a substitute decision-maker is the one who ultimately decides, on your behalf, whether to withhold or withdraw life-sustaining treatment.

Each year, about 40,000 adult deaths occur across Australia following a medical decision to withhold or withdraw treatment, according to End of Life Law in Australia's website discussion, 'Stopping Treatment'.

So among the first people to think about when you are planning for a good death are your substitute decision-maker or makers (the role can be shared).

Substitute decision-maker roles are activated more today than ever before because the number of elderly people developing dementia is growing, due to the significant mismatch between medicine's power to keep us alive for longer, and its ability to help us keep our brainpower as we progress through that longer life.

People often think the substitute decision-maker is the same as the power of attorney role, or at least part of it. But it's very different. As mentioned before, a power of attorney is a legal document in which you appoint a person to look after your financial and legal affairs when you are past the point of being able to do this. But the substitute decision-maker is appointed to think about your medical wishes – particularly when you are dying. Like 'power of attorney', though, these documents are signed in front of a lawyer. This person will liaise between you and the strangers you are meeting in a hospital and make decisions on your behalf to ensure your care. The person is expected to make the same decisions they believe you would have made.

So this needs to be someone you really trust to interpret what you'd want in this situation, someone who really knows what a good death means to you. You need to be communicating with them enough so that it's easy for you to let them know you've updated your thinking, without that having to be a formal or awkward conversation. You've also got to be practical. If you've appointed your favourite niece to be your substitute decision-maker because you get on so well with her but she lives in London and you live in Auckland, then you've got to think about whether she's going to be able to get to your bedside quickly enough to help you effectively in a sudden medical emergency that requires the presence of a substitute decision-maker – or whether she can be present enough if you slowly and gently decline.

In Australia, each state and territory defines the role of the substitute decision-maker slightly differently. In New South Wales, for example, an enduring guardian is a substitute decision-maker who is appointed under the *Guardianship Act 1987*. Be aware that not every state recognises the legal standing of a substitute decision-maker from outside that state.

In New South Wales, a lawyer must witness the appointment of an enduring guardian. He or she will certify that when you signed the document you were of sound mind. Once again, just as for your will and power of attorney, if the solicitor doesn't feel they've got enough information to make that decision, they will talk with your medical professionals, especially doctors, to establish your capacity.

If you've got a lawyer managing your will and power of attorney, they're quite likely to raise the subject of a substitute decision-maker document, since all three are often filed together.

The person who you appoint as your substitute decision-maker needs to know they've been given the role, to accept the appointment of enduring guardian and sign legal the paperwork documenting this.

Substitute decision-making can be done – and will be – on your behalf if it is needed, even if you haven't signed a legal document. The person assigned the task will be nominated by the hospital. If all your family and companions agree who that is, this is helpful. But that person will be left to guess what you want.

Your advance care directive

Just a reminder about definitions: in broad terms, an advance care directive is a specific document, whereas advance care planning is the more general process around that.

Advance care directives are being developed and increasingly implemented wherever complex hospital systems exist.

An advance care directive is a specific direction advising your health professionals and your family as to the health care and treatment you wish to receive when you are not able to communicate these wishes due to incapacity.

It would be good if we could simply say that advance care directives are legally binding documents that indicate in advance all the treatments you will consent to if you wind up in hospital having medical treatment. However, it is not quite this straightforward.

This is the goal of current thinking but the outcome varies slightly from state to state, as does the terminology.

Advance care directives go by several different names in different jurisdictions, such as 'living wills', 'written advance directives' or 'statement of wishes'. In the United Kingdom, an advance care directive is called an 'advance decision' or, more formally, an advance decision to refuse treatment (ADRT). In New Zealand, it is often referred to as an advance directive.

Most particularly, your advance care directive should be as straightforward and unambiguous as you can make it, covering all the treatments you definitely don't want to have – the treatments you want to refuse – even if this refusal will result in your death. Development of these directives has been driven by very real but relatively new fears – in terms of human history – about being kept alive by technology.

Only 5 per cent of the Australian community have a written advance care directive. But this proportion is beginning to increase as the directive's advantages become more widely known.

Advance directive writing has come a long way. Ten years ago, there was a fragmented approach. Doctors tended to be suspicious of those who came to the subject from a legal background, and lawyers didn't talk to doctors. And hospitals were divided about whether a patient–doctor conversation was better than a piece of paper.

Nowadays, doctors and hospitals are more accepting of written documents that give directions. The consensus is that a conversation between your family and you, the dying person, is still the most important thing – to ensure your family understands your desires. This talk should be backed up by you appointing one or a number of people as substitute decision-makers, and reinforced with a written advance care directive – a copy of which you should pop into your handbag or wallet, so that if you're suddenly transported to hospital, it's easily accessible.

It's important to know that writing down how you want to be treated, in advance, holds legal weight in Australia, the United Kingdom and New Zealand. But what 'written down' means varies slightly from state to state and country to country. For example, in the Australian Capital Territory, you can make a verbal 'Health Direction' if this is witnessed by two people, one of whom is a doctor. But if you make a written one, it has to be on a particular 'Health Direction' form, otherwise it is not valid.

These variations may seem trivial now. But you don't want to get trapped in red-tape by choosing one that's not valid in your state or territory or follows a protocol that's not valid in the place where you live.

In New South Wales, as the result of a common law case in 2009, anything that's written down and clearly intended as an advance directive is legally binding. The case that set this precedent was between the Hunter and New England Area Health Service and Mr A. It clarified, in New South Wales, that if someone has written advance care instructions, clearly intended as a directive, even if it's only written on the back of an envelope, this informs the direction of that person's treatment if they are no longer conscious.

Mr A was a Jehovah's Witness who did not want renal dialysis. He entered hospital, lost consciousness and went into renal failure and was put on dialysis. Shortly afterwards, a friend who was also a Jehovah's Witness asked the hospital to stop dialysis because it was against Mr A's religion. The friend had with him a hand-written document in which Mr A had said he did not want a blood transfusion or renal dialysis.

When the hospital went to the NSW Supreme Court for clarification, the judge decided that having written down his wishes and with no proof that Mr A had changed his mind, his advance care directive still held, even though it was a fairly informal document.

It is now mandatory for staff in NSW hospitals to follow an end-of-life care directive, if one has been written. For this to be valid, the person who wrote it must have capacity to write it, understand what it means and be aged over 18 when it was written.

A written directive gives staff confidence that the dying person is being cared for in the way that he or she would have wanted. Even better, is when that directive is supported by an actively engaged substitute decision-maker who has talked through the patient's wishes thoroughly when they were well. This is in contrast to dealing with a family who have no preparation for the situation (because it was an accident or because they didn't discuss these things) and who, in very emotionally fraught circumstances, say something like, 'Do everything you can, throw everything at it because this is what my father/mother/sister would have wanted'.

The NSW decision had a ripple effect, redefining and updating thinking about the role of advance care directives in most states and territories of Australia.

But even with all this investment in finding legal protections around their advance wishes, people can still enter an intensive care unit and be in there for a whole course of treatment without anyone ever being asked if they had an advance care directive.

However, the more lay people, like you and me, discuss advance care directives with our medical teams, the more this will change. And that's getting easier.

In the early days of advance care directives, there was a tendency for the patient to look at or try to imagine a whole series of likely scenarios. This sometimes resulted in a long or a short advance care directive that didn't quite work. After all, based on what you remember, for example of your parents' deaths – the ones we've usually have had most experience of – you might put detail in about what you want and what you want to avoid, only to find yourself in an utterly different scenario.

You run the risk of outlining 2000 different scenarios and then hitting Sod's law – the 2001st is the condition or circumstance that puts you in hospital.

Intensive care specialist Professor Ken Hillman explained that a new approach informs today's advance care directives: 'We ask people to look at their values and to look at long-term scenarios that they would not want to be in. For example, you might say that if you were elderly, incapacitated, suffering from dementia, and these had been established for some time, that in those circumstances you would not want to be put on a respirator in intensive care.'

A broader benefit of advance care directives is that studies show they not only help the person who is dying but also the bereaved family, who suffer less stress, anxiety and depression over the death than they otherwise would.

There are many advance care planning resources that can be found on the internet. One of the best is the End of Life Directions for Aged Care, found at www.eldac.com.au. This set of advance planning documents became available in 2018, after hospital and academic teams from around Australia put their heads together to come up with a uniform, standardised, easy-to-manage advance care directive tool, which can be accessed by everyone, particularly the elderly. It guides the user in discussions about advance care and locating the best advance care document for your area. (For these advance care directives, see the ELDAC website: www.eldac.com. au/tabid/4971/Default.aspx.)

As the ELDAC resources and toolkits are introduced and used more commonly across Australia, and easily downloaded from the internet, older people, including those in nursing homes/aged care facilities and in remote areas, will be empowered.

One of the exciting things about this new work is that IT systems will be used to collect information to make sure people are not lost to care systems and so we can better understand – and respond to – people's needs, particularly as they age and especially if they are on their own.

Making your own directive

There are many factors to take into account when filling in an advance care directive form. For example, what if you're being treated for heart disease but you also have kidney problems? If you don't want a bone marrow transplant or chemotherapy does this mean you wouldn't want a blood transfusion?

Here are a few questions you might want to think about:

   ♼ If I receive life-saving treatment for one disease,
      what about my other medical conditions?

   ♼ What will best create the right environment for me
      to die in? Do I want to die in an acute care hospital?
      At home with family around me? In a palliative care
      hospital? In a nursing home?

- What can I afford and will there be any financial limitations on my decision?

- If I am likely to die, what will make me comfortable as I die?

- Do I understand the difference between having a treatment to prolong my life, such as a heart operation, or having treatment to make me comfortable and to lower my pain levels, but which won't cure me?

Some people make their advance care directives extremely detailed, for example to the point where they state, 'I don't want to have special blood pressure stockings'. Other people simply write, 'I don't want to have my life prolonged if I develop a terminal illness. I just want to be given palliative care treatment'.

Palliative care is going to be an important part of this discussion. Here is a definition of this area of medicine that I really like, from the World Health Organization. Palliative care:

- provides relief from pain and other distressing symptoms

- affirms life and regards dying as a normal process

- intends to neither hasten nor postpone death

- integrates the psychological and spiritual aspects of patient care

- offers a support system to help patients live as actively as possible until death

- offers a support system to help the family cope during the patient's illness and in their own bereavement

- uses a team approach to address the needs of patients and their families, including bereavement counselling if indicated

- will enhance quality of life, and may also positively influence the course of illness.

However, whether you want to write a very broad directive or a very detailed one, it's worth discussing this with a few people, particularly doctors and nurses who have seen these situations before, and also with your own doctor, who knows your set of diseases.

It is important to discuss the contents of your advance care directive with your family, because what you've written could be quite different to what they thought you wanted – or believe you *should* want. And they could be looking at your wishes and considering the implications of them in a very stressful situation, for example if you've described a scenario where you want life support turned off.

And remember, you're entitled to nominate life-saving and life-prolonging procedures, if this is what you want. If all the people around you are nominating to stop all treatment but that's not what you really want, then advance care directives can give you a sense of security about your opposite choice.

It's important to understand that an advance care directive is not a guarantee that something will be done in accordance with your wishes. Medical teams want to be proactive in saving a very ill person, but if that person is clearly dying, a point may come when the patient is still breathing (through a ventilator), but monitoring shows there is no brain function. The patient will never get better and cannot be revived. Even if the patient had an advance care directive stipulating that the ventilator be kept on indefinitely, the doctors are not legally obliged to initiate or continue treatments that won't offer any benefit. While they don't easily reach that point, eventually they will make the decision, despite the advance care directive.

And be aware: there's something slightly paradoxical about advance care planning. What is documented will carry weight. This is necessary for those times when you don't have the capacity to speak or to communicate what you want, or because you are no longer conscious. But aside from this, you have the right to refuse medical treatment and this may or may not be recorded in an advance care directive.

So as long as you are alert, you can contradict your advance care directive by, for example, refusing a treatment that you'd said you'd wanted. Remember that doctors have no legal obligation to initiate or continue a treatment if they think it's futile.

But for the sake of everyone, particularly you, it's best not to be confusing – that's when mistakes and misinterpretations are more likely to occur. So it's good to remember that you can update and change your advance care directive at any stage.

Your family, carers and the people looking after you in hospital, a palliative care unit, at home or in a nursing home should have systems in place so that you can review and update your directive. You can ask them about this to check that you're satisfied you have the options for change that you might need.

So keep in mind that advance care planning is a process, rather than just a piece of paper with a signature on it. The planning is broad, the directive is a specific piece of paper.

Your substitute decision-maker will be expected to know whether you have an advance care directive, so when filling out your directive, make a copy for them. If there is not a written one, the substitute decision-maker will work with what they believe are your wishes.

A word of caution needs to be expressed at this point. Some families have had bad experiences with the person appointed substitute decision-maker dominating and controlling the process. In one case, the siblings of a substitute decision-maker believe the person appointed used his position to put undue pressure on their mother to move out of the family home and into a nursing home. She had lost capacity in a legal sense but was still able to interact quite well with others. He underplayed and diminished her powers of reasoning, then insisted on using his position to monitor and control her interactions with the other siblings.

A Sydney lawyer who deals in probate cases said this is happening more often. He believes that as the use of substitute decision-makers increases, allegations that the role has been abused will increase. He argues the way to protect sibling relationships at this point in a parent's life – which can last for several years – is for at least three siblings (if there are that number!) to be given the role, forcing discussion between siblings about what will happen next to their parent.

If you are a parent setting up these arrangements while you're fit and enjoying good health and the family is functioning well, keep this potential problem in mind. Taking action to safeguard against it is an important step.

While it could be argued that the very tools developed to protect vulnerable people against abuse can themselves be misused and lead to mistreatment, this shouldn't be an argument against the increased use of roles such as the substitute decision-maker, which are designed to protect your rights. Instead, it's a cue to make sure that as a society we develop ways to protect against the misuse of these powers, and that we develop methods for exposing errors in systems and abuses by individuals, so that our rights and opportunities as we reach extreme old age and are dying are maintained and protected.

Your health

The more accurate our knowledge about our health, the better our advance care planning will be. Understanding what is most likely to cause a decline in our health which could be fatal means we need to find out about old age, infirmity and vulnerability, and their impacts, and at the same time work out how to acquire the information without losing our optimism.

Seeing ourselves as having a full and active life, despite our health problems, is a good and positive mental approach that helps to keep us physically well and actively engaged with living, well into old age. But being engaged with life needn't be the same thing as denying we will one day die and therefore not planning realistically for it, the position many people leave themselves in today, sometimes without even realising it.

Maybe it's best if I say nothing and take my chances at the end, when I'm dying, rather than try to control the way medical events play out, some people argue. After all, I won't be around afterwards to regret what happens, so the logic goes.

However, even if it makes no difference to you, information you have collected and decisions you have made in advance will definitely make dealing with your death much easier for your family and/or loved ones, and free up their time to focus on grieving for you and working their way through this period.

Another important factor to consider is that lack of awareness of what is likely to happen means what could have been straightforward becomes complicated.

While your actual death is a finite moment in time, the period beforehand, the dying, is a process. It is likely to occur over time, unless you are involved in a sudden accident or sudden fatal illness. And it's possible to take the opportunity for that particular stretch of time beforehand to be a better, smoother, less stressful experience, rather than one in which pain and illness are compounded by confusion, stress and mismanagement because of other fears.

The first step in this is to objectively think about your disease state. Does this seem morbid? That's understandable, but consider looking at it another way. What if researching and thinking about these won't make you as morbid and frightened as *not* thinking about them will.

Your frailty index – a reliable guide to mortality

Here's where you do something simple yet extraordinary: *forget about your age.*

Age is irrelevant to the idea of planning for a good death, for two powerful reasons.

First, you could die younger than expected, not when you're old. It makes sense not to overplan when young: we are entitled to believe that an early death is anathema, something for our society to fight against. In *A Matter of Life and Death: 60 Voices Share their Wisdom*, by Rosalind Bradley, the Reverend Desmond Tutu quotes Swedish statesman Dag Hammarskjöld: 'Do not seek death. Death will find you'. I tend to agree. You don't want to overthink it, but a few notes and ideas, reserved in the right spot, would be helpful should it come.

The second, more significant reason is that chronological age doesn't count. Today, some people do their first skydives at 80. You can still be skiing and playing tennis at 90, like my father was. We live in an age in which we are encouraged to stay fit, challenge ourselves and break our own boundaries every day, including the physical ones. We want to grow old disgracefully. And why not?

It's not your age that will make you vulnerable to death in old age. What's relevant is how *frail* you are.

Geriatricians employ a frailty index to predict when a person may die. Their work has percolated through to other medical specialties, including intensive care. Professor Ken Hillman, an intensive care specialist who has studied and written about end-of-life expectations, now talks about the light-bulb moment when he realised how significant the tools of his geriatrician colleagues were: that nine indicators on a frailty index before they came into hospital could reveal whether his intensive care patients would survive surgery or a major event in his hospital. He also explains how he realised the frailty index has a more than 90 per cent accuracy rate for predicting death.

He and his peers routinely use the Clinical Frailty Scale, which is very easy to read and understand and can be accessed from the internet. Another good one is the Edmonton Frail Scale, which can also be found on the internet.

In fact, there are several different frailty indexes, but anyone can understand these two, think about what they mean for them and then work with them. You don't have to have any medical knowledge. Using these indexes, instead of waiting for someone else to tell you you're frail, you can work out a few important details for yourself.

The Edmonton determines the level of frailty (from 0 to 17) by asking questions about a range of activities that relate to categories such as cognition, general health status, mood and nutrition. If someone has a high score, close to 17, they will have the following problems either as standalones, or in several combinations:

- they will have poor cognition, that is their mental processes will be very slow

- they might have been admitted to hospital several times already in the last year, for any number of reasons

- they are unable to look after themselves, in other words,

> they need help with showers, feeding and going to the toilet

- they need other people to buy food for them
- they're taking several medications for a number of diseases
- they are either unable to eat or not interested in eating
- they are incontinent and bed-bound
- all of these conditions have left them very unhappy.

Many people with this combination of permanent impairments would say their quality of life is very low.

In addition, the closer our score is to 17, the more frail we are and the less likely we are to survive the next medical crisis or catastrophe. In fact, even without any other medical problems our health is extremely vulnerable.

Knowing what it implies, being told you have a high frailty score is not an easy thing to hear – from anyone – and it is not an easy thing to say, which is why many doctors won't discuss this directly with their patients.

But for me, knowledge is power. I want to find out my level of frailty and what it would mean to me, so I can discuss it with my doctors and family.

If we can be brave enough to ask for information about reading our frailty score before we fall into the 'frail' category, that is, when we are fit and well, this will help us manage the emotional impact of interpreting what this means as the consequences accumulate for us. I don't know how good I'm going to be at this, but my plan is to engage with it early, so I can pick up insights that will help me either face certain realities or work on overcoming the frailties as much as possible while I have the opportunity to do so. But mainly, I'm hoping it will help me to be aware of my options and the reality of my situation and that this will have a practical bearing on the advance care directive I make and how I respond to major medical events.

You might be one of those people who doesn't want to know this information. On the other hand, and quite paradoxically, you might also be among those who believes that by developing a knowledge of your frailty score, your capacity to make choices about all sorts of details relating to your body is improved, giving you more control, more power over your circumstances and more dignity.

I believe it will make a positive change to the way you think about your hospital admissions and the conversation you will have with others about them.

Note that the frailty index doesn't ask you to state your diseases, which are not as relevant as the state they leave you in. Having said that, your diseases will ultimately be an important part of the discussion, so we'll come to those next.

At the very least, if you know your frailty score you can read your hospital and doctors' notes differently to the way you might have in the past – and more accurately. If those notes say 'fit, very elderly,' they mean you are over 80 and that the diseases you have are progressive but not life-threatening. (Don't be insulted if you are an 82-year-old who has just competed in a Masters Games in tennis and you are described as being in 'very old age'. This is a medical term used for anyone over 80.)

But if those notes say: 'frail, elderly', this means you are over the age of 65 and dependent on others for the activities of daily living.

Now that you know what a frailty score is and how to work with it, why not take this insight a step further? Why don't you be the one to tell your doctor what your frailty score is, rather than the other way around? This will help empower you and put you in the driver's seat as you evaluate your risks. It will signal to your doctor that you want to be part of a very important and realistic conversation, even if this is ultimately one about dying.

Now there's a note of caution that needs to be issued here: no one is a number. If someone has a high score, that doesn't mean they should be dismissed because they are so frail they could die.

Knowing these things is about giving you more information, so you can make a better contribution to the discussion about your health, your prospects and your future.

For example, compare the following two people. One is a man who is over 90 years old. Despite having chronic lung disease, which leaves him feeling breathless at times, he manages long walks and has a strong heart. The other is a woman in her mid-70s. Because she is very overweight she finds it difficult to exercise, so over time she has gradually become quite sedentary and slow in her movements. She also has diabetes, which has left her with poor circulation and numbness in her feet. This means she is not confident about walking very far and this in turn discourages her from moving much. Looked at in terms of their age, you'd think he is the most vulnerable. But looked at in terms of their frailty, she actually is. At the very least, she is definitely more likely than he is to fall over and break a limb, which could shoot her up the frailty index in an instant, much faster than his slowly progressing lung disease will.

Both have the right to say they want to live for many, many more years. But their advance care directives are likely to look quite different and will be informed by their very different medical histories.

If your score is higher than you'd like it to be, then fight that, and if you don't like being defined by it, fight that definition. After all, thinking in terms of your frailty rather than your age is about fighting being defined by a number. If you end up in the hands of a medical team that gives you a rating and you feel that as a result they treat you like a number, not a person, and you want to leave and never come back, then do that.

Your diseases checklist

Now let's go to the next step and look at the causes of your frailty: your diseases. These will inform what treatments and hospitalisations you will have, or the point where you say, 'No more, I don't want any more treatment.'

This is a 'diseases' checklist, not a 'disease' checklist because when we die there are usually several diseases in play. For example, someone who died from ischaemic stroke – that is, clots in the blood vessels feeding the brain – might also have had slowly developing renal failure, progressing heart failure and a cancer. Someone who died of a heart attack might also have been suffering from a cancer, high blood pressure and damaged blood vessels in the brain. Someone who has gone into hospital to have a large non-cancerous growth removed from their abdomen, might develop shock and die of a heart attack.

These all interact to give us that state of immobility, cognitive impairment and dependency that gives us a high frailty score. But this doesn't happen overnight. Early disease patterns will lead us up that path quite slowly. And that slow walk gives us the opportunity for some realistic planning. Most of the diseases that are troubling us in the last year of life have been around for some time; they have not just suddenly developed. They are chronic, long-term diseases. When they were diagnosed, the doctor knew that they would never go away. It is surprising the number of people with long-term, chronic conditions that could eventually kill them – if something else doesn't – who aren't aware of this. Maybe they don't know because the doctor didn't tell them. However, it is also likely that they were told but didn't realise the significance of what they were being told.

When you are diagnosed with any disease, ask if it is chronic and long term. Ask the doctor to explain its impact on you as time passes. If you want to be in control of and understand the medical events that will surround you leading up to your death, do not be afraid to ask this question. If you are too afraid to ask it now, write it down and store it for a later time, when you are ready, remembering to work on your emotional resilience until you are. Not being able to face the implications of your chronic diseases is a little bit like wishing you were 21 again. It's a way to live, but not a very practical one.

Every disease is different and each will behave uniquely in each individual who experiences it.

However, a large number of older dying patients will have chronic illnesses that follow predictable patterns of hospital admission, so your doctor can give practical advice about likely disease progression and what this will entail for you.

Most people have several chronic diseases as they age, compounding the problems. Knowing a bit more about the features and impacts these diseases have in common will reveal something of how they'll affect you towards the end of your life. Knowing this will help you better understand and therefore have more control over what will happen to you when you die, and in the years beforehand.

Take an active approach. Take control.

At the time of writing, the latest figures for leading causes of death in Australia were for 2017. These figures won't change much from affluent country to affluent country and nor much from year to year. But you can keep updating causes of death and where you fit in, by jumping on the internet. You could even bookmark the figures, so you can watch and think about any changes.

The 2017 Australian leading causes of death were:

- ischaemic heart disease – diseases of blocked arteries to the heart (18,590)

- dementia, including Alzheimer's disease (13,729)

- cerebrovascular diseases – disease of the blood vessels of the brain (10,186)

- chronic lower respiratory diseases (8357)

- cancer of the trachea, bronchus and lung (8262)

We have to add something else to this, which will make us see it in a different way. If we combine all the cancers, they go to the top of the list. So cancer is an important part of the discussion. However, the death from cancer follows a slightly different course to other deaths, so I'll consider it separately.

Combining all cancers, not just taking them in isolation, like the cluster of trachea, bronchus and lung cancers, these account for about 30 per cent of all death, not just in Australia but just about everywhere. (In 2014, there were 44,171 deaths from cancer in Australia out of 153,580 deaths, so 28.7 per cent. In 2013 in New Zealand there were 9063 deaths from cancer out of 29,568 deaths, so 30 per cent. Cancer Research UK says the proportion of deaths from cancer in 2016 in the UK was 28 per cent.)

These figures are gloomy. But there's a few good things to remember. 69 per cent of Australians diagnosed with cancer will live for at least five years. Many of these people will live a lot longer than that, and this statistic continues to improve every year.

If cancer treatment is successful – and it's getting better and better all the time – you will not need a hospital admission because you are dying of your cancer. You can live a healthy and full life and go on to die in old age from something else. In a typical year, for every one person who dies of cancer another seven will be living with it.

But for good death planning we need to consider the possibility of cancer. We can understand about visits to hospital, and what will happen if and when we die of our cancer, and how that connects with hospitals and palliative care.

CHAPTER **10**

Where will I die?

We visualise, well before we need to,
where we want to die
so that this becomes reality.

On average, about 50 per cent of people die in hospitals, another 35 per cent in aged care facilities and a further 12 per cent at home. In this chapter I look at each of these places to try to help you visualise what your needs will be.

Dying in hospital

The 50 per cent who die in hospital are usually the very frail who are admitted when very ill. If someone is fit and healthy, with a low or non-existent frailty score, and goes into hospital for elective surgery, their chances of dying are low, so those occasions don't drive these figures up.

When you walk into a busy hospital, whether as a staff member, a new patient or the relative of someone in hospital, it is immediately clear that this is an institution with protocols and ways of doing things established over many years. To challenge the wisdom and authority of such institutionalised care feels foolish. We feel small and unknowing in the face of such power. For me, it brings to mind the sense of my own insignificance when I watch water cascade down the spillway of a big dam.

In many ways this is a good thing. After all, when the question of whether we will survive or die is at stake, we don't want our care or the care of those we love managed in any other way than the best, tried and tested. We want to be managed by those who know what we don't know. In the hospital setting, that often translates into receiving the most scientific treatment. And whatever your background or education, from the academic to the truck driver, this unknown world can be intimidating.

So we have to juggle our rights and desires in this setting, something we can be unsure of, against what we don't know in this hospital experience. One of the best ways to do this is to have built up an awareness of our disease or diseases that allows us to have a meaningful discussion with healthcare professionals.

Elective surgery is planned in advance. It might be to have a gall bladder removed or even cardiac bypass surgery. Whenever a doctor suggests going to hospital for elective surgery, there's a set of questions it's good to form the habit of asking. Top of this list is: 'Given my medical history, what are the risks for me in having this surgery?'

Doctors must obtain your informed consent before surgery takes place. When having surgery planned in advance, this discussion should happen in the doctor's surgery, well before the captive moment when you've arrived at the hospital. Two questions covered in your informed consent are: What is the treatment for? What are the side effects or complications?

A responsible doctor will always give you plenty of time to think about a procedure before then. They will invite questions and encourage you to ask anything you would like, well before. But if that opportunity somehow feels as though it's been missed, you can ask these questions:

- ❧ What is the treatment? Please give me the formal name. Can you write it down for me, so I can do a Google search on it? (Don't be ashamed to admit you will look up its meaning on Google. This is the modern equivalent of a library.)

- ❧ Are there other ways to manage this problem that don't involve going to hospital?

- ❧ What would happen if I did nothing?

- ❧ What is the complication rate?

- ❧ What are your personal side effect and complication rates for this operation?

- ❧ If I get a particular complication, will I need another operation?

Complications are different to risks, which are about us and our personal history. The complication rate is about the surgeon and their success with the operation, compared to other surgeons and other hospitals.

While insurance companies, private hospitals and certain professional bodies collect this data and keep accurate figures, these are not in the public domain. As individuals we haven't been good at asking these questions and demanding answers, so even though this information is very important to know, it can be hard to pin down.

Hopefully this will change – helped along by the pressure of changed attitudes and new questions from lay people. In the meantime, ask your surgeon anyway. You might be given good answers. And if you can make this type of proactive conversation the habit of a lifetime, it will feel natural when you are older and frailer.

What about the situation when we are elderly and frail and contemplating surgery? Keep in mind the way of understanding your frailty discussed earlier. Ask your doctors, your general practitioner and your surgeon to talk about your frailty with you.

Ask what impact this will have on your operation, explaining you'd like to plan realistically.

If the surgeon dismisses your concerns without discussing them, alarm bells should ring. If you have been thoughtful and brave enough to ask the question, you deserve to be taken seriously. You might like to have a discussion with your referring general practitioner, an opportunity to ask for other forms of support beyond hospital.

And once again a reminder that if you really want to have the surgery, your doctor supports this, and you are confident about the surgeon's credentials, you have every right to be confident about the surgery, no matter how old you are.

Dying in an ambulance

What if I have a not-for-resuscitation order but an ambulance is called? Whatever age you are, if you are taken to hospital in an ambulance, you are already in the hands of a team that has an agenda to save life, no matter what. Someone has called the ambulance because they want life-saving action taken.

If you are unconscious, you are automatically assumed to have given 'implied consent' to be transported to hospital. You can't give informed consent, because as you were unconscious, you couldn't be informed. This means you cannot say 'no'. Informed consent laws do not cover emergency situations. Tattoos and tags stating you refuse emergency treatment are not legally binding in this situation; you have to be able to refuse verbally.

When a person needs cardiopulmonary resuscitation (CPR), then the legal justification is, simply, the necessity.

In some places, if you do not want to be given CPR and you have an advance care directive to that effect, this needs to have been communicated by your doctor to the ambulance service. This is done by filling in an 'authorised palliative care plan', which is then registered with the ambulance service.

In addition to covering a decision not to perform CPR, there is also a release on the plan that gives the ambulance the instruction to withhold airway management, oxygen, nasopharyngeal suctioning, and insertion of an intravenous line to administer drugs. The plan also notes that ambulance paramedics will administer life-saving drugs unless there is written documentation to do otherwise.

However, one palliative care specialist made the point that we need to be aware of what attempts at resuscitation can achieve: 'In television programs, 70 per cent of patients survive an attempt to resuscitate them. In real life, the figure is closer to 5 per cent.'

Dying in hospital from cancer

As I mentioned before, when you are admitted to hospital with terminal cancer, it is managed in a slightly different way to other hospital admissions.

Living with cancer

Let's talk about going to hospital because of cancer. In the list of leading causes of death in Australia mentioned before, a predictable pattern occurs. A person's health gradually worsens with a series of hospital admissions that come closer together until death.

In contrast, cancer will involve treatments to kill the disease altogether (if possible), maintain your health and keep you out of the terminal stage. Hospitalisation is not seen as inevitable. You will have a period of frailty, but this will only be relatively short, compared to that of the aged person entering hospital for repeat admissions.

The way your cancer is treated, and therefore your pattern of hospital admissions, will depend on which of the more than 250 different types of cancer that you have. Admissions will be for surgery, chemotherapy, radiotherapy and other treatments aimed at stopping or managing the cancer.

Some can be treated very aggressively with high success rates. For others, we are not quite so lucky. For example, currently, 80–90 per cent of women diagnosed in the early stages of breast cancer will still be alive after five years. In contrast, only 44 per cent of women diagnosed with ovarian cancer will survive for five years.

Early detection has a huge impact on cancer outcomes. Breast cancer can be detected when it is a small lump, and screening has been developed for it. By contrast, ovarian cancer, with symptoms that mimic ordinary bowel bubblings and gurglings, tends to be detected much later than breast cancer, and there is currently no early screening test for it.

This difference in whether a cancer is detected earlier or later is significant because the longer the cancer is present, the more time it has to spread. In layman's terms, cancer develops because the aberrant cells and their growth slip under the radar of our immune systems. The body does not recognise the growing cells as different, so it mounts no defence against them. As the cancer cells multiply, the chances increase for tiny cells to replicate and expand into a new area of the body. Our lymphatic systems work with our blood systems, weaving their way around and through our bodies transporting a clear fluid called lymph in vessels in the same way that the blood circulatory system does. The lymphatic system is like a vacuum cleaner, clearing out debris and detritus left when our immune system has conquered infections, disease and any other threats. The trouble is, apart from not detecting the difference in the cancer cells, the lymphatic system can carry them throughout the body, towards the heart, giving them a free ride to a new and faraway destination.

Doctors use a staging system for all cancers. With a few exceptions, this system means the same thing across a range of cancers. Stage I is early, and if caught at this stage, for example in the case of prostate cancer, you can be lucky enough that the cancer is held in a small, sealed capsule. It is growing but has not spread. Surgery to remove it at this point is highly successful because it is like picking out seeds encapsulated in their own pod.

In the next stage, Stage II, the cancer has spread outside its contained capsule and is roving and settling in other tissues. If this cancer is removed, then other tissue has to be removed too. Mapping this tissue is the purpose of a lot of investigative cancer management and treatment today. Specialists working with your cancer will have a long-standing and highly developed knowledge of the most likely pattern of spread for that cancer. So, for example, when removing a melanoma that has reached this stage, they know to look for a cancer growth shaped like a tap root on a plant and to remove this and all the margins of flesh around it.

The take-home message in your death planning is that if you want to be proactive in minimising your chances of dying from a cancer death, currently the best and simplest thing to do is engage with early detection. This means taking advantage of screening programs for some of the most common cancers – prostate, cervical, skin, bowel and breast cancer – that are easily accessible now. Such are today's data collection systems that you don't need to remember to have your regular tests; you can register to be contacted every time your tests are due.

You could take one further step: prevention, where this is possible. Researchers continue to work on immunisation or vaccine-style blocks to cancer. Cervical cancer is now on the decrease because of the development of the human papilloma virus vaccine, and there is now new hope for preventing melanoma from spreading through the body after the first surgery, by managing it with treatments called 'vaccines' (they are not true vaccines but act like them).

But these will not have the same impact on lowering your cancer risk as not smoking, limiting your alcohol consumption and keeping your weight down. Without suggesting that there are any guarantees, for each successive year that you can keep these three under control, you are, statistically, likely to buy more time cancer free. And doing so will also have a significant impact on lowering your chances of having heart and blood vessel diseases, which, as noted before, are big killers.

At the next stage of cancer, Stage III, the cancer has moved into the lymphatic system, and lymph nodes are involved. Lymph nodes are nestled at various sites in the body, such as the groin and under the arms. If the lymphatic system is a waterway used to transport debris, then the lymph nodes are high-powered cleaning and sluicing centres, which transport cleared and cleaned lymphatic fluids back to the blood. Cancer cells tend to collect in them before dispersing to other parts of the body. If your surgeon is removing lymph nodes, it is with the goal of stopping that diffuse spread.

Now the cancer takes a free ride through the lymphatic or blood system and is spreading, even just in patterns of one or two cells at a time. In Stage IV, the cancer has spread throughout the body, or metastasised. Each cancer behaves differently and some will throw tumours to different sites within the body.

Removing cancer tumours at these sites can be a very powerful strategy. Doing so will not eliminate the cancer from the body entirely, but it will protect individual organs to buy more time. The extent to which surgery buys more time will vary from cancer to cancer and from individual to individual. But I know of a woman with ovarian cancer at this stage, Stage IV, who with successive surgical procedures has now lived ten years from diagnosis and is determined to get more time. She is not free of cancer, but she is living while she has her cancer – and not just passing the time. She travels and enjoys life.

It is this set of nuanced variations, stretching short-term survival into long-term survival within the prognosis of cancer, that has been one of the major prompts and inspirations for the redefinition of palliative care.

In its early days, palliative care was seen as a treatment offered at the very end of life. But as cancer treatment pushed and punched out longer and longer survival times, palliation in cancer expanded its scope. This continuous challenging of the disease boundary redefined palliative care to mean giving a patient the fullest quality of life possible, while working to eliminate the disease. People with all sorts of diseases have benefited from this change. The downside of this, though, is that many people associate palliative care with cancer only, not realising it applies to all diseases.

Some cancers respond well to chemotherapy and radiotherapy, even to ease symptoms, although not cure, in the palliative stage. Others will not. Cancer specialists will offer care and advice based on the type of cancer and your fitness. They will take into account your age, but once again it will be your fitness and strength that will be most significant in the treatments you are offered. This underlines the importance of keeping yourself low on the frailty scale.

If you are a patient who is physically fit, then you will be able to tolerate chemotherapy well. If you are extremely frail, that is, you are bed-bound and weak, quite possibly because of other diseases you suffer from, then your doctors are likely to say you won't tolerate chemotherapy, because the side effects will kill you. The more frail your doctors observe you to be, whether they've done a formal frailty scale evaluation or not, the more reservations they will have about offering you treatments that are so extreme that you might not survive them.

When you're dying from your cancer

The point may come where, even after many years of life, some cancers become terminal and it has to be conceded that the patient will die from it and not another disease. When someone has terminal cancer, typically there's a relatively short period of time between the point where the patient's physical and mental abilities start to decline, and death.

The effort now switches from trying to cure you to focusing on eliminating your pain and managing any psycho-spiritual symptoms that come to the fore.

Each cancer has a different potential for treatment. If you are diagnosed with a cancer that is unlikely to be treatable, for example a rapidly growing lung cancer, you will be well supported emotionally if you say, 'All I want is to be looked after. I don't want any treatment at all. I don't want any chemotherapy, radio-therapy, surgery, I just want to be kept comfortable.'

However, even in lung cancer, which tends to have a bleak outcome, chemotherapy can make a big difference. For example, if you have extensive small-cell lung cancer, chemotherapy won't be offered with the goal of curing you but to improve your symptoms, and your quality of life.

Without this you could die in, let's say, six weeks. But with the chemotherapy and other supports you might live two or three more years and live relatively well for the majority of that time, until the disease comes back again.

In contrast, chemotherapy and/or radiotherapy for metastatic, Stage IV colon cancer – meaning that the cancer has spread extensively throughout your body – might give you only three more months, rather than three more years.

So for different cancers the ability of chemotherapy and radiotherapy to extend life will be very much dependent on the type of cancer, how aggressive the cancer is and whereabouts in your body it is located.

Judging all these different possibilities is where treatment becomes an art, not just a science. The ideal treatment for me will be different to what is an ideal treatment for you.

But knowing what questions to ask, and what length of time your treatment will give you, is crucial in your decision about whether you will have that treatment at all.

At this late point, cancer pain can be caused by fractures, the tumour invading new areas of the body, or the surgery, radiation and chemotherapy that are used to fight the cancer itself.

Bone pain is a leading specific cause of pain. Up to 85 per cent of patients with bony tumours or metastases experience severe pain at some time in the course of their disease. This is in contrast to patients with lymphomas or certain leukaemias. Less than 10 per cent of these patients will experience the severe pain of the type that those involving the bones will.

Anaesthetists are starting to play an important role in alleviating the pain of cancer, using pain relief methods such as nerve block therapy, in which a medication is injected around the nerve that's causing pain. This is a small subspecialty in medicine today, but the role is growing.

Hope

The good news is that rigorous treatments offering a lot of hope are available for cancer. You can be like my friend Holly, diagnosed with lung cancer and brain secondaries, which were removed. The primary was in her lung, and the surgeon wouldn't remove it until she was clear of those secondaries. 'After several rounds of very strong chemo,' said Holly, 'he rang to say, "We couldn't have asked for a better result." Music to my ears.

'He removed the top lobe of my left lung, and four months later I led a group to Bhutan, where we all climbed up to the tiger's nest.' That was seven years ago.

Equally, you are well within your legal rights to decide to do the exact opposite, saying to your doctors that you want no treatment at all, that you just want to go home and spend time with your family, and then you want the best pain relief possible, so that you become completely unaware as you begin the active phase of dying.

Each of the different cancers has its own course of treatment. Cancer research is constantly evolving, and we are learning more about what works and what doesn't. Enormous investments are being made in this. The diseases that are most researched are those that capture our imaginations the most, something that drives public awareness campaigns around each cancer type. That means there are other cancers that haven't been as well researched because they are not in the public eye, or are so rare that too few cases come forward for study. Our understanding of these cancers inches along painfully slowly, with few breakthroughs.

'Breakthrough' is a word that causes heart-sink for doctors. When their patients read about 'breakthroughs' they can be bombarded by requests for the treatment, even if it's a complete mismatch with the cancer the patient suffers from. But there are real breakthroughs and developments that do happen and can give a lot of hope.

So part of your death planning can include tracking and observing the developments that are likely to cause improvements in your disease. This is about locking in a 'hope' strategy to inspire your death planning to be about life. Hope can be a difficult thing to retain when you're faced with a bad prognosis. But we can be facing the bleakest reality and be hopeful at the same time. This capacity to carry opposing and complex threads of thought and emotion is one of the gifts of being human.

An area offering particular hope in cancer research at the moment is immunotherapy. This treatment strategy involves activating and enhancing the immune system so that it detects and eliminates cancer cells that it would not otherwise respond to. Cancers grow because our immune system doesn't detect them as foreign and therefore doesn't mount a fight against them.

Immunotherapies for treating cancer have been developing over the last twenty years, but recent developments suggest a revolution in their use may be just around the corner. Immunotherapy for cancer is having its 'penicillin moment'. These new immunotherapies involve using specific antibodies that boost the body's anti-tumour responses. Their use has led to longer survival times and even the possibility of cure in an increasing proportion of patients.

People have survived with advanced and metastatic cancers because of these treatments, which was previously unimaginable. In 2018, scientists reported that a patient with metastatic breast cancer – that is, the disease had advanced throughout her whole body – was now cancer-free after immunotherapy treatment.

To give you an idea of how recent these developments are, the drugs nivolumab and pembrolizumab were approved by the US Food and Drug Administration in 2014. Pembrolizumab became accessible in Australia to treat melanoma in 2015. Nivolumab became available in 2017 on the Australian Pharmaceutical Benefits Scheme for treating advanced and metastatic non-small cell lung cancer.

There are now close to 400 clinical trials being conducted around the world to see how effective these drugs will be in a range of other cancers.

So this takes us back to the beginning of the cancer discussion – with a reminder of what I said before: while cancer causes around a third of all deaths each year, an enormous number of cancers develop, are cured and are eradicated each year too, so the patient goes on to live a happy and full life and then die of something else.

And in addition, so many new treatments are offering reasons for hope. And that's not what the newspapers are saying – that's what the researchers themselves are saying.

Elderly and frail –
in hospital again

When going to hospital becomes a regular feature of your chronic disease management, that's a realistic, even if confronting moment, to start talking with your family and healthcare professionals about what you want at the end of your life. Why not see the second hospital admission in the same year as a turning point, the moment to not only think but to talk about how you want to plan for a good death? Don't rely on your family to initiate this conversation. For all sorts of cultural reasons, most will be waiting for you to raise it with them.

In most families, when Nana is admitted to hospital having suffered a stroke and a broken hip, or she goes into hospital with a broken hip and tests reveal she has lung cancer, people in her family will turn to someone over a coffee and explain that they are afraid Nana will die some time soon – or that they hope she will die some time soon, so she doesn't linger in pain and suffering. But very few will actually talk to Nana about it. (Palliative Care Australia notes that: '82 per cent of Australians think it is important to talk to their family about how they would want to be cared for at the end of their life. Only 28 per cent have done so.')

And of course, it's a conversation that will be easier if Nana has talked about it before.

In New South Wales, seven conditions were considered by the Bureau of Health Information's *Exploring Clinical Variation in Mortality 2017* report and this exposes quite bluntly the reasons people who'd been in hospital that year died. It's a study that's not massaged for public consumption.

Here is that table.

Condition	Numbers of people who died within 30 days of being admitted to hospital	Number of deaths per 100 hospital admissions	Average age at death	Number of people hospitalised	Number of other diseases they also had in the year before they died	Percentage who died within 30 days after leaving hospital
Haemorrhagic stroke (brain blood vessel bursts)	1855	33	74	5659	5.8	24%
Congestive chronic heart failure	3793	14	80	27,484	6.0	41%
Ischaemic stroke (blocked blood vessel in brain)	1861	12	74	15,475	7.0	43%
Pneumonia	5037	11	71	47,133	4.8	38%
Chronic obstructive pulmonary disease	3160	10	74	30,525	4.3	43%
Acute myocardial infarction (heart attack)	2108	7	70	30,488	4.8	32%
Hip fracture surgery	1093	7	83	16,193	9.4	53%

These conditions were the most likely causes of hospital admissions, in the elderly, outside of accidents. Because such large numbers of deaths were evaluated, they can tell you a lot about mortality in not just New South Wales, but pretty much anywhere else in the world that has the same lifestyle factors.

It was sobering to see just how many people died within 30 days of leaving hospital or close to it.

Uncomfortable as it is to read, the report shows a few important things:

- Only a third of people who have strokes that involve the sudden rupturing of a brain blood vessel (haemorrhagic stroke) survive them.

- Damage to the heart and blood vessels is still a big killer, despite fewer heart attacks.

- Pneumonia is the biggest reason for entering hospital (in the old days it was called 'the old man's friend'. Death from pneumonia would most likely come on the top of other incapacitating, serious diseases. The patient would die in a fever, unconscious and pain free).

- Those with hip fractures have at least nine other medical conditions. A frail, elderly person who enters hospital with a hip fracture has a 53 per cent chance of dying within 30 days.

Except for the hip fracture, all those who died in that 30-day period were in hospital because of chronic diseases with accumulating effects.

The good news is that over the last fifteen years, the rates of death within the 30-day period of leaving hospital have dropped dramatically. Death within 30 days from burst blood vessel strokes dropped by 15 per cent and death from heart attack by 41 per cent. This tells you the chances of surviving going to hospital if you have any of these conditions are getting better and better.

Yet I was still shocked by the sheer numbers of those deaths, even today. I've heard all the public education talks before, but it wasn't the same as reading the numbers in a table. But the biggest lesson I learnt from the statistics was, of course, a very personal one.

Yes, cancer could sweep in and change the picture completely and quickly. But I have a tendency towards high cholesterol, and my mother had a triple bypass operation after a heart attack in her late 70s. She ate a healthier diet than I do and had lower cholesterol than mine. (Her palate was shaped before the rich gourmet foods that I'm a sucker for became readily available.) So I have to do everything I can to keep my heart fit. That includes exercise and managing my diet.

But much more importantly, I now know to think about the consequences of heart and blood vessel disease in my end-of-life planning. Since the average age of the deaths from blood vessel and heart diseases is between 70 and 74, I also now know that even though I'd like to follow in my father's footsteps and get to 94 with no heart disease, blood vessel disease or dementia, and that my mother died at 88 from cancer, I have to plan as though heart and blood vessel disease could happen up to 24 years earlier.

But it's troubling to know that one hospital physician describes the 30-day period as artificial.

'Why do we look at 30 days? That's a number chosen by academics. If we looked at 60 days out from hospital discharge, the figures would really be much bleaker,' he said.

There's a lot to think about.

Are you elderly and frequently being admitted to hospital because a condition such as lung or heart disease is deteriorating? This is very different to admissions for elective surgery. You're relying more frequently on hospital to ease symptoms.

In these circumstances, you and your family need to convey your desires and expectations to the medical staff. Let's take the example of a woman who's had several hospital admissions for congestive lung or heart failure. As she gets older, admissions will get closer together, and the time between stints in hospital will shorten. The hospital admissions will be about relieving her symptoms and pain, but there will be no cure. She doesn't want to die in hospital, so her challenge is to explain this in such a way that she can help the doctors and medical team working with her to sort out alternatives.

Switching from being a patient with a disease who is frequently admitted to someone who is dying doesn't happen in an instant. It's an evolving process. And it might sound strange, but active medical treatments and palliative care can both be administered at the same time.

Offering a hip replacement to a very elderly person is a good example. A hip replacement is offered routinely to the elderly who fall and break their hip. Even though they might have (according to NSW figures) a 7 per cent chance of dying while in hospital and a 53 per cent chance of dying within 30 days of being hospitalised, they are not expected to live with the agonising pain of a broken hip.

Another example is chemotherapy for small-cell lung cancer. Treatment will not cure the disease, but it can give the patient more time free of pain.

Moving to palliative care

In an ideal world, the shift from the care of your disease specialist to a palliative care team will be seamless. Unfortunately, this is not always the case, since there is still a wide variation in attitudes by other teams in hospitals to palliative care, and some members of the medical team may resist 'handing you over'.

In addition, particularly in much of rural Australia, there may not be a full palliative care team available to treat you, although there may be a palliative care nurse.

Hopefully, this is a problem that will be addressed following recommendations by the Australian Royal Commission into Aged Care Quality and Safety, announced in October 2018, since incidents of substandard levels of end-of-life care are to be examined by the commission.

Here are some questions you or your family might want to ask the staff, as your condition and circumstances start to change:

- I'm experiencing changes, what do these changes mean?

- Will my pain get worse from now on?

    ▶ Who will see me on a regular basis from now on? I'm frightened of losing the care I'm getting from the people who are supporting me now.

    ▶ What is the role of my GP from now on?

    ▶ Who will help me control my pain from now on?

    ▶ Do you think I need palliative care now?

If you meet resistance to the idea of palliative care from the team caring for you, you can speak to the hospital's palliative care team yourself or you can talk to the social work team involved in your unit. If these groups appear to be floundering with your request, ask to speak to the hospital's Patient Liaison Officer.

If you are not comfortable doing this, or you are too sick to do it yourself, discuss the situation with your family members, making sure to include the person you have assigned as your substitute decision-maker. If they are not available when you need them, talk to your general practitioner.

When your illness becomes terminal, it will become clearer to the doctors that a number of treatments won't give you any benefit. In fact, they will cause you discomfort and become a burden, for no good reason. This process is often gradual, where success is followed by success, then less success, and so on until treatment has no success at all.

The point will come when the doctors managing you will evaluate whether your treatment has become 'non-beneficial'. (This used to be called 'futile' treatment.)

Non-beneficial treatment is a term that means something to your medical team. It can include observations, even minor ones, such as taking a temperature or checking blood pressure, surgery, investigations such as x-rays and ultrasound tests, and the administration of medications. It can include giving you food and liquids through nasogastric tubes.

Family might start questioning the benefits of treatment before or about the time the medical team does. A 2005 US study showed when patients are on artificial respiration and treatment is futile, only 24 per cent of families wanted treatment to continue, but

76 per cent of staff wanted it to continue. Ironically, sometimes this is because the staff thought the family wanted it. Of course, there are situations where the family does want 'heroic' intervention, even in circumstances where there is little likelihood the person will survive – a situation doctors often find hard to deal with.

This presents a very contemporary challenge.

Hospitals can now keep people alive in circumstances that in the past would not have been possible. As a consequence, we tend to think what can be done must be done in all situations. As Dr Bernadette Tobin points out, this is sometimes called 'the technological imperative'.

'What follows is the misunderstanding in our culture that every opportunity should be taken to extend life, and a sense of guilt if this is not taken,' she said.

Over the years, many studies have revealed just how hard it is for doctors to communicate that treatment has no benefit and therefore might as well be stopped. A 2016 Queensland study, reported in *The Journal of Medical Ethics,* looked at this issue. It involved interviewing 96 doctors from emergency, intensive care, palliative care, oncology, renal medicine, internal medicine, respiratory medicine, surgery, cardiology, geriatric medicine and medical administration departments. These doctors were asked why they thought 'futile' treatments were offered at the end of a patient's life. They said they do so because they:

- want to cure

- were uncomfortable talking about death – often because of their youth and lack of experience

- were worried about the legal consequences of not offering the treatment

- had difficulty communicating

- responded to pressure from families for further treatment

- were uncertain of the medical outcome themselves

- lacked information about the patient's wishes.

Other reasons related directly to the hospital. High levels of specialisation in the hospital meant more routine tests and interventions could be offered. Also, within the hospital, there were barriers to diverting patients from curative to palliative care.

The two major reasons noted by the researchers were pressure from families and the doctors feeling locked into the curative role.

Maybe this suggests that doctors need to be given confidence by families that they are not expecting miracles. Again, this comes back to how we communicate with our doctors – and our family, who are likely to be taking responsibility if we are unable to communicate.

Even if you are still fully alert and there is no doubt about your capacity to make decisions, to ensure your end-of-life wishes will be taken seriously it's a good idea to have your ideas clearly thought through and written down before you're admitted to hospital.

Not for resuscitation

Are not-for-resuscitation orders to be followed? If they are, they need to be explained in your advance care directive (this is a circumstance where you need a directive, not just a plan). Be aware that the traditional understanding has always been that not-for-resuscitation orders are *not* followed during or immediately after surgery.

Ideally, we would discuss our desire not to be resuscitated very clearly with both our anaesthetist and surgeon before surgery. But anaesthetists are still not involved much in these discussions. We need to have untangled our own thinking very clearly – being able to both explain that we want the operation but don't want to be revived if something goes wrong.

This will lead to another question: Will your not-for-resuscitation decision be considered justifiable if it's possible that you'll have a really good quality of life if you are revived? You may well find your not-for-resuscitation order is ignored if doctors think resuscitation will lead to a good outcome. Their clinical responsibilities will outweigh their questions about what they think you might want. Doctors are not obliged to adhere to a directive if they strongly believe it falls outside of 'best practice'. In such a situation the matter must be discussed beforehand and a consensus reached.

It's worthwhile thinking about another situation, too. If your not-for-resuscitation order was written some time ago and you don't now actually want it to be followed literally, in this circumstance, with this particular operation, make this clear to your doctors and your family.

Usually, 'Not for resuscitation' (NFR) and 'Do not attempt resuscitation' (DNAR) orders relate solely to a decision not to perform cardiopulmonary resuscitation, that is heart resuscitation, if the patient has a cardiac or respiratory arrest. But there are other actions that are taken to keep a person alive in an intensive care ward or an emergency situation. For example, they can be placed on a ventilator to help them breathe. A tube can be placed down their windpipe (intubation) to protect their lungs, or they might be fed through a feeding tube.

Make sure that you have thought this through very clearly, and that all your treating doctors and children understand your position on this. As your adult children grow and lead different lives, subtle and sometimes not-so-subtle variations will develop in their attitudes to this, in line with the gradual shifts in their values, as they shape their own lives. So make sure your position is unambiguous and not open to misinterpretation.

If discussing your death – or even your health – is taboo, then you'll simply not know about or understand possible family tensions. It is your right not to talk to family about every new development in your disease, but if you have had occasional benchmark conversations about this important topic, your family will not be left in a position of having to guess – and then argue with each other about what you might want.

Discord over this subject is common, and it can also ignite conflict between siblings that has lain dormant since they were little children living in your home and doing the human business of struggling to assert themselves in a family. This conflict occurs because the subject is so important.

If you have your documentation in place, then your family is only giving effect to a decision that you have already made.

Dying at home

Julie F has no doubt that taking her father Norman home to die was the right thing to do, even though she had to 'fight' his major public hospital to get him away from it. She explained how many people die in big public hospitals because it's too hard to get out, once you get in.

Julie's story illustrates goals you can achieve at home, with the support of palliative care teams.

All the decisions were up to Julie because her elderly mother had dementia. Norman felt belittled at the public hospital, and told Julie he wanted to go home.

'I used the words, "We want palliative care at home" as much as I could,' Julie told me. 'The young doctors didn't take any notice or kept telling me that the hospital could do more for him.

'"We can care for him better in the hospital than you can at home because of all the facilities we have here." But I just kept saying, "He wants to die at home." I started using the words die, death. They didn't like me very much but I kept at it.'

After a delay Julie didn't think was reasonable, the palliative care team was eventually contacted. Once Norman was out of hospital, the team threw its support behind the family. Norman was cared for in Julie's lounge room, in the middle of the family home, with people coming and going.

'The palliative care team had said, "If you put him in a bedroom, they're usually at the end of the house and he'll be away from others and he still needs to be around people."'

Norman was incontinent of urine and faeces.

'We did the washing. The family are all adults, so whoever was here; my brother, my sons, my nieces, anyone who was here would wash him.'

Norman was lucid and talked often during the ten days at home before he died.

'He'd say, "Can I have a lemonade ice-block?" And as he finished it we'd just sit there and talk, usually with him saying he wanted me to look after Mum.'

The lemonade ice-blocks became such a fixture that at Norman's wake, held at the house, the family served them as a way of remembering him. Towards the end, Julie administered morphine, which the community nursing staff had taught her to do. Norman slept more and more.

'But when he was awake, he was really awake.'

'He started saying, "I want to die", and I said, "It's okay. If you want to die, it's okay. We're all okay with that and I've got Mum organised." Because he was mentally still there, right to the very end, I believed he would choose, he would decide the time of his dying. I said to my brother that he'll decide when it's best, he'll know.'

In the early hours of one morning Julie and her brother were, unusually, both awake. They sat for a couple of hours at their father's bedside. At five o'clock, Julie's mother came and joined them – also unusual, as she normally slept through the night and had little awareness of what was happening.

'We said, "Come and sit down." So I was sitting on the chair, Mum was in the middle and my brother was on the other side. I jokingly said, "Well Dad, the three of us are all here and no one's having a fight." And he smiled.

'About half an hour later we were talking and my brother and I looked across and Dad just stopped breathing. We both recognised that split second – Mum didn't – between breath and no breath. Mum didn't understand but we all got up and kissed him. We touched him and said goodbye. I knew he would choose. We were all together and that's what he wanted. We were all sitting there in the dark with our pyjamas on and a blanket over us.'

About a month later Julie had a dream. Norman came back and he said: 'You've done the right thing, you're on the right road. I'm off now.'

And she woke up saying: 'Off you go then, Dad.'

The drive to 'go home' at death is very powerful. The first Australian data to suggest 70 per cent of Australians wanted to die at home, in their own bed, was based on figures collected by a South Australian study in 2000–02. A similar statistic is quoted extensively for other countries too. But in Australia, only about 12 per cent actually die at home.

In Australia until recently, public hospital palliative care teams going out into the community to work in people's homes couldn't spend large periods of time at the bedsides of the dying. At the time of writing, with more funding from federal and state governments, it is hoped this situation will improve.

Anyone can ask for a referral to a palliative care team. However, hospital inpatients cannot be seen by the palliative care team unless referred by the treating specialist. In the community, a GP referral is required in all but exceptional circumstances.

Dying 'better' in an aged care facility

Aged care facilities offer levels of care that range from personal care assistants who help you with the normal activities of daily living through to 24-hour nursing.

Some residential facilities focus on independent living. They have separate units for private living, a common dining room, and staff to help with maintenance and housekeeping. The great advantage of the independent living facility is that someone is keeping an eye on you. Apart from not having to worry about shopping, maintenance and cleaning, you know you would be missed if something went awry. If you got sick and didn't turn up for dinner one night, this would be noticed and acted upon.

While staff will keep an eye on residents, they are not nurses. It is usually a condition of buying into this style of facility that if a resident develops the need for nursing care, or cannot move independently to the dining room for their meals, then the terms of the leasing contract are void. The resident then has to find an aged care facility with a higher level of care. Some institutions have both levels, but this should not be assumed.

The next stage of aged care facility is one where your nursing needs are met. These are places people go to when they can no longer care for themselves. There are problems in this setting, when it comes to dying, right now in Australia – problems that I suspect don't occur in quite the same way in the United Kingdom and New Zealand, even though a 2011 study revealed that the number of New Zealand residents who die in long-term residential care is quite high – up to 48 per cent.

Once again, many advocates hope the issues relating to end-of-life care will be addressed through the recommendations which will follow the Royal Commission into Aged Care Quality and Safety.

End-of-life problem areas in aged care facilities

A number of aged care facilities, where 35 per cent of Australians do their dying at the time of writing, have a blind spot when it comes to palliative care.

I'm not pointing the finger here at the mostly devoted people who work in them, although there are a few exceptions. But I will single out a lack of our collective imagination combined with arguments between state and federal bodies about who should do what, and lack of consistent government-led negotiation with the businesses who run them to make the improvements needed. This is something we as a society are all responsible for.

Lucy, whose mother died of dementia in an aged care facility in 2018, described an all-too-familiar scenario.

Her mother, Angela, was dying. She was in the late stages of severe dementia and had lost the capacity to communicate, had been in a very distressed state for a week, crying out, self-harming, frightened and possibly in pain. This was despite her being on several medications to control symptoms of agitation at the end of life.

'Mum had crossed a line very obviously where she had become incredibly distressed – crying, pinching, punching and scratching herself.'

Angela's Sydney aged care facility was new and swish, with very glamorous accoutrements. But it was understaffed.

Angela had an advance care directive, but her wishes were overruled by her husband, Lucy's father, who was very distressed himself. This deference to the living partner, despite the wishes of the patient themselves, is common.

'Dad couldn't really see what needed to be done. The rest of us knew Angela wouldn't have wanted to be in that state, but he was frozen by his own grief and indecision, even though he was a doctor himself,' Lucy said.

'We have to do something for Mum,' the adult children kept telling him.

'I don't know what can be done for her,' their father kept saying in response.

'You don't need to be the one who knows what can be done, Dad. You don't need to be the one who has the answers,' they replied.

Eventually the GP who attended the nursing home came to see Angela, but nothing in her care plan changed.

'He made a very short, perfunctory visit and didn't even examine her.'

'Mum continued in this terrible state. So my sister and I decided we'd ring the palliative care team from the major teaching hospital, which had a relationship with the nursing home. But they said they couldn't do anything, couldn't come to the hospital, without a referral from the GP. But by now we'd lost faith in him. We took matters into our own hands and that night rang the geriatrician who Mum had been seeing before she entered the nursing home. She hadn't seen him for three months.

'We told his secretary that Mum really needed to see him urgently and he came the next day.'

When the geriatrician arrived, he did an immediate assessment, and identified that Angela had quite likely had a stroke.

'He tested Angela's vision and could see really clearly that she was not seeing out of one eye or using that side of her body. We look back now and wonder whether some of her self-harm was because she'd lost sensation due to the stroke and was confused and frightened by it.'

The geriatrician immediately mapped out a pain management plan involving what he described as 'comfort measures' with morphine, whereby pain is controlled to keep the patient comfortable, physically and psychologically. He asked the family if they realised the implications of this and the risks associated with it and they said 'Yes'. Lucy and her sister asked if this plan could be started immediately, even though their father didn't respond. The geriatrician immediately prepared the appropriate prescriptions.

Approaches to morphine prescription in nursing homes vary widely and tend to be ad hoc. Further distress had to be endured by Lucy's mother and family because the nursing home would only work with a specific pharmacy to fill the script for morphine and that pharmacy had no supplies in stock, even though the nursing home was one of its major clients. So Angela was not given the first dose until 1 p.m. the next day.

At last, after about two doses of the morphine, Angela started to get relief from a week of pain and suffering that might have been avoided had palliative care been more rigorously applied in the nursing home.

Death came to Angela nearly four days after she was prescribed morphine. Suffering and trauma were also experienced by her adult children, their families and her husband; they still have not fully recovered from this experience.

Variations on this story have been repeated frequently to me as I've listened to people's experiences of an elderly relative dying in an aged care facility. The point will come soon when we will look back and ask why we let this happen. Those suffering from dementia are particularly vulnerable.

We'd like to think the elderly, demented and unconscious, in some cases for years – simply slip away, unaware of what is happening and, by implication, pain free. This does happen but there are others for whom it doesn't. Maybe until recently we didn't think a death like this mattered.

In 2016, the Australian Institute of Health and Welfare revealed that across Australia, only 5 per cent of permanent aged-care residents were assessed as requiring palliative care. Yet their palliative care needs must surely be the highest in the country. After all, about 96 per cent of people living in an aged care facility will die there. Nestled as they are in ordinary suburban streets, these are places where so many elderly people in our culture do the hidden business of old-aged dying.

However, palliative care specialists are increasingly gaining access to aged care facilities. One such a specialist said it needs to be remembered that 'Only a small percentage of dying patients require specialist palliative care. End-of-life care is everyone's responsibility, including general practitioners and other specialists. Along with community and hospital-based nurses, they do the bulk of the work. Depending on circumstances, palliative care specialists may or may not be consulted in such instances. Palliative care specialists would drown in work if they were to care for all of the dying.'

And we don't want more experts involved in what is natural. But we need to make the distinction better between those cases where less intervention is needed and those where more is needed.

It's predicted that the number of Australians aged over 85 years will increase from 400,000 in 2016 to 1.8 million in 2050. By then, an estimated 3.5 million Australians will be accessing aged care services, such as residential aged care, each year.

Too many Australian aged care facilities mistime the need for palliative care, delivering it very late: this in an age when it is now recognised the earlier palliative care is introduced the better. Yes, there are cases where the extremely elderly will die peacefully and quickly, rather than in pain because of their disease, with no need for this special care. But we should question whether enough is invested in ensuring we understand the needs of these two quite different groups, when they live in nursing homes.

This disconnect is disturbing. Some improvements are being made. In recent years, some facilities have started employing palliative care teams with clinical nurse consultants. But too few do this. Many rely on palliative care services that come in from teaching hospitals on an as-needed basis. But the need is defined, and therefore the access controlled, by the aged care facility and not the hospital.

Because of an accident of history, aged care facilities fall under the control of the federal government, rather than state governments. So the innovations that are occurring in palliative care in state-run public hospitals are therefore not occurring across the board in aged care facilities. Palliative care teams don't get automatic access to aged care facilities. If they do, it's because the organisation running them has made a commitment to do so, for which it is unlikely to be remunerated. Palliative care teams can reach out from hospitals into homes in the community and offer nuanced support immediately or when needed, but they typically cannot extend their care into aged care facilities. At the time of writing, palliative care units and aged care policy-makers are trying to rectify this situation, but the problem is not going to be solved any time soon.

Another problem in Australia, which compounds the experience of so many, is that as mentioned before, federal laws don't require residential aged care facilities to have registered nurses on duty at night.

Karen Hitchcock, a general physician at Melbourne's Alfred Hospital who writes passionately about the elderly and end-of-life care, is responsible for the care of the elderly in Melbourne's Alfred Hospital. Often, her patients have been transferred from an aged care facility. They have gone to live in aged care facilities because they are too frail to live at home but then end up in hospital.

'There's a lot of problems with patients coming to hospital because there's no registered nurse in aged-care facilities overnight. If we had mobile medical teams with adequate education and adequate staffing in nursing homes, then probably some of those admissions could be prevented.'

It's been estimated that of all Australian deaths that occur in hospitals, about 13 per cent involved long-term residential care patients who'd been transferred there.

In New South Wales, when personal care assistants who are not trained to intervene and make medical assessments see a problem with a patient, they have to alert the rare and over-worked registered nurse in charge to ring a general practitioner, who is not on-site.

As personal care assistants communicate up the chain of command to registered nurses, who then communicate with doctors who can prescribe pain relief, pain relief comes too slowly.

One hospital physician explained that the simplest solution for everyone, particularly if the institution is short-staffed, is to ring for an ambulance to deliver the dying person to a hospital.

'Very few involved will let these elderly, unwell patients die in their aged care facility any more, even if that's where they have lived for some time,' he said.

Sometimes the opposite happens and personal care assistants hesitate about disturbing their busy superiors.

If a teaching hospital's out-reach palliative care team is called, advice is given only if the patient is registered with that palliative care service. This often creates clunky, awkward situations with too many steps to be negotiated between the patient's first surge of pain and its effective treatment. This has enormous implications for patients' pain management.

The federal government's policy on end-of-life care states that in aged care facilities, systems should be in place to provide access to essential palliative medications 24 hours a day, seven days a week. And doctors should be able to get the specialist palliative care advice they need through telephone and video-conferencing. But the stories shared by relatives in Australia reveal this is not happening enough.

What to consider

If you are considering entering an aged care facility, research its approach to palliative care before committing yourself. By the time you are considering an aged care facility, you are too frail to care for yourself at home. By extension, you are likely to be too frail to be able to carry on these discussions in an effective and robust way. So make it clear to your family or other advocates that there are questions you want answers to. You should flag the need for these questions to be asked before your need to enter an aged care facility arises.

Here are some suggestions for the questions you might want to raise:

- How is palliative care in this institution managed?

- What palliative care training do staff receive?

- Can I discuss my advance care plan with the staff?

- ❧ Is the doctor who attends familiar with palliative care and elderly dying patients?

- ❧ Who do my family contact if I need special equipment, for example an undulating mattress for bed sores, or oxygen?

- ❧ Is there a clinical nurse consultant in palliative who can be contacted if I'm dying and the doctor is not available?

- ❧ What is the system used to contact the nearest specialist palliative care team and how speedily will they be able to respond if I'm in pain?

- ❧ How will my family be supported and will they be encouraged to be with me when I die if they want to, even if this is at night?

- ❧ Who can I talk with about my religion and culture?

- ❧ Can I have answers to these questions in writing?

- ❧ What literature do you have addressing these questions that has been produced by the board of governance of the aged care facility?

Where does all of this leave you?

One of the striking characteristics that comes out of research conducted by palliative care academic Peta McVey is that when nursing home residents were asked why they were there they said, 'Because the doctor said this is where I should be.' Often, this was explained to them at their last hospital admission. (They didn't say 'Because I have unstable diabetes or a worsening heart condition'.)

The trouble with that answer is that it gives control over your circumstances to someone else, and leaves you in a state of cultivated ignorance. It also invites the medical teams involved to talk with someone else – not with you. That attitude may have been socially acceptable in the past, but why should you accept this now? So again, the key to maintaining control over how you will die is to maintain your literacy about what your body is doing, and what it is telling you.

Another matter relates to the period immediately after death. The family is entitled to gather to say goodbye to the newly dead. In one case in Sydney, an elderly woman died at 1.30 a.m. The family were contacted and told her body needed to be removed within three hours for occupational health and safety reasons. This is not true. Families should be given the opportunity to gather at the person's bedside after the death, according to the Australian Commission on Safety and Quality in Health Care. If a nursing home cannot accommodate the body until the family have done this most important and basic of human activities, something is very wrong.

Dying in hospices and palliative care units

The explosion of medical knowledge after World War II led to the growth of the large, sophisticated, modern, scientifically based teaching hospitals of today, where miracle cures are expected and extraordinary feats of healing are trumpeted by the hospital's public relations staff. Hospices and palliative care units represent a small fork in this technological healthcare road. They lack the dazzling array of machines such as CT scans and scientific laboratories searching for cures to enigmatic diseases. (Around the world, the term 'palliative care unit' or 'palliative care hospital' is sometimes replacing the word 'hospice', so the language used to describe this institution can vary.)

In Australia, hospices and palliative care units vary from state to state in their approaches to planning and delivering services, and operate according to a variety of local service delivery practices and healthcare systems. But the goals of palliative care are widely understood and gaining momentum.

As palliative care expands, so too does the range of skills within the support team. There's a shift to a different way of thinking also. Instead of a hierarchical structure, with the person who knows the most science directing the care team, the care roles become much 'flatter', since it is not the science that's going to make the only contribution to the comfort of the dying. 'Shared decision-making' is a big feature of palliative care, and its guiding philosophy says that the quality improves when strong networks operate between everyone involved – including the community.

Palliative care planning involves tuning in to the physical, psycho-social, emotional, cultural and spiritual needs of the patient. Distress in any one of these areas will be assessed with the goal of relieving it and managing it appropriately. Good palliative care teams will be as concerned about the family as the dying patient. Family members will be considered. This is not just better for the dying patient, but lowers the risk of psychological or other health problems for family members further down the track.

Palliative care was once strictly defined as care at the end of life, but the definition has grown to include supporting the person to live better. Sensitive and aware doctors will involve, as early as possible after the diagnosis, a palliative care specialist, whose role becomes increasingly important as the condition progresses. For example, as an oncologist is able to do less for their patient, the palliative care team can do more.

Talking about death with hospital staff

When wanting to communicate your wishes about your impending death, your written words will speak loudest.

The phenomenon of doctors finding it difficult to talk honestly with their patients about their end of life and the reality of their prospects is discussed a lot in the medical literature. Many intensive care specialists find themselves discussing end of life issues with their patients, even though that is not what their patients expected would happen at that time. Some of the most vocal advocates for a holistic approach to care are intensive care specialists. So it's not the intensive care unit staff who don't want to talk frankly, it's often family. Hospital staff have to make decisions in your best interests, and to do this they are committed to receiving your input. But they need to feel absolutely confident that what you are telling them now is well thought through and not based on fleeting reactions to experiences you are having that are only temporary.

All specialists in all areas of care have seen patients in the doldrums, wondering why they undertook a particular care or surgery, only for that same person to walk through the door cheerily in a few months time to give them a hug and thank them for helping them to get back to a normal life.

In the case of a patient with a terminal illness, the same scenario can happen, except that the patient is grateful for being given either a little or considerably more extra time. Heart bypass surgery used to be in the same category for the elderly. Until relatively recently, doctors were reluctant to do coronary bypass surgery on anyone over the age of 80. Now it is done routinely on people much older. A heart surgeon explained recently that he did coronary bypass surgery on a 93-year-old patient who got four more years of healthy life, for which she was very grateful. The surgeon had believed in her enthusiasm for those extra years. He was confident she would survive the surgery well and that she would have a high quality of life.

So if you do not want to be revived or do not want heroic medical treatment, you will need to be able to show that this is a well thought-through decision, made before you became ill and while your judgement was sound. This is when written documents and the involvement of those who you've nominated to speak for you become very important.

The role of End of Life Directions for Aged Care (ELDAC) coordinator was first introduced in hospitals in 2018. Some palliative care nurses made the point that the ELDAC coordinator in their hospital was attached to the palliative care department, when really the information this person can offer is needed much earlier in the disease trajectory, when the patient is still in the care of other specialist hospital units.

'By the time it gets to the point where people are entering palliative care, it's really too late for them to be thinking about working on their end-of-life planning. Ideally, the coordinator will work with people from all the hospital's other departments,' one palliative care nurse said.

The good news is that six months later, such a coordinator explained that she *is* working with the other teams, gathering data to develop better ways to document patients' pain, to improve liaison with palliative care nurses, to detect signs of agitation early.

Do you need an independent advocate?

People often realise they'll feel overwhelmed just by the medical setting, the equipment, the well-trained staff, the technical processes, let alone their concerns over their own health issues. Whatever they feel about these things, in addition they care about wanting to respect the earnest best efforts of those working with them, trying to repair their ill bodies. So they don't like to interfere or say anything.

Even if you've made an advance care directive earlier in life, as you confront a disease, particularly at its later stages, you might want the help of an independent advocate who specialises in this work.

This is a relatively new concept in Australia. Healthcare advocates independent from the treating hospital are only now developing their professional role.

While most hospital staff are well intentioned, and highly professional, some people feel more secure working with someone who has got to know them and their situation before they entered a particular hospital setting.

The autonomy of advocates suggests an independence that can help people trust them if they feel uncertain about the hospital staff. Such advocates can play a key role in helping people as soon as they are diagnosed, before any decisions about surgery and long-term care are made.

Dorothy Kamaker built her advocacy practice after years working as a nurse. Through this experience she became aware of a need in the community. She describes two patients who came to see her with completely different goals.

Betty wanted her 93-year-old mother Elaine to be allowed to die. Elaine had been three weeks in hospital with a terminal illness and was receiving treatments that were non-beneficial because there was no hope of recovery. Betty believed she was letting her mother down because she couldn't prevent her unnecessary suffering.

'Together we were able to negotiate the realignment of the treatment regime from curative to palliative care, and the relief for Betty was incredible to see. She had orchestrated the best outcome: a peaceful death. She was proud even if she was sad,' said Dorothy.

Another of Dorothy's patients, Anna, received a completely unexpected diagnosis of terminal cancer.

'Anna went literally from a session at the gym to receiving a death sentence at a doctor's surgery. Her apparent good health made her completely unprepared for her grim prognosis and she became overwhelmed with grief and loss. For Anna, chemotherapy and immunotherapy were unacceptable further assaults.

'Her view was that it was futile trying to delay the inevitable. My role has been to understand Anna's goals and treatment options and become the independent expert supporter she can rely on to keep those goals at the forefront of her management. To cut a long story short, her house goes to auction in a month, her successful immunotherapy has her telling me, "If I didn't have those scan results I would not believe I had a problem", and "the single most unexpected piece of advice you have given me has been to use palliative care as a way to go on living well rather than as a last resort option". The incredible sadness and negativity have disappeared.'

Dorothy says that for many people, the time of greatest medical need will coincide with a time of their least capacity to cope, to assess and to decide what course of action reflects their best interests and wishes.

'It is not a time to go it alone.'

Recently, she worked with a woman whose family did not think her nursing home was working out. They didn't have the expertise to evaluate it themselves, so they consulted Dorothy.

'This last week I've had two client "deaths": one (dementia) where the wife/family saw the process for what it was, listened to the advice about what would happen and how to cope and have created the most wonderful experience.

'In the second family (a 78-year-old approaching the end of eight years of declining health), there is struggle, conflict, bullying, legal orders to force the hospital to continue the treatment, anger, expense and misery. Not to mention, questionable moral choices.

'It's been two poles of an issue. Like textbook "how to" and "how not to". My take home has been that there is a strong responsibility on every person to establish their wishes, well in advance of the crisis or the sadness. We need community forums and TV shows about this,' Dorothy said.

Louise Mace offers a similar service, New Way to Stay, inspired by the difficulties she faced when her father was dying. (I recount their story below.)

'Nearly all people feel completely overwhelmed by the ageing journey, especially when a health crisis happens,' Louise said. 'As a direct legacy of my late father, and my own personal experience, I have now become the person families turn to, and I help them manage their own later life plan,' she said.

'We start by drawing up a plan with goals and then, if requested, we can also stay to support the whole process to help them realise those goals. We have a whole raft of well-researched providers and we connect our clients quickly and effectively with solutions, such as legal, medical, financial, palliative care, home modification services and many more. By doing this we can improve our client's chances of staying at home right up until the end of their lives, if that is their preference. Each situation we find is totally different, so the personalised plan we create is essential to ensuring they are empowered to live where and how they choose to. This helps not just the person in their later stages of life but also the whole extended family. It means they get to have a much better focus on "quality" time versus "working" time,' said Louise.

A significant feature of these advocacy services is that they pull together groups of professionals such as financial advisers, doctors and the healthcare professionals who have the same objectives and values as their clients. This has the potential to save you and your family a lot of time at a stressful part of your life.

If you think you might need an advocate, let your family know, even writing this down with your other advance planning notes. You can do the research to find the person you would like to represent you. But if you've run out of oomph to find this person yourself, you have set your family in the right direction. They will have work to do, but they can start with a Google search, punching in the words 'patient advocate'. When doing this research, aim to have a conversation with the family member of someone who has worked with the advocate, in much the same way you would when looking for a carer to work with your toddler.

Looking towards the future

Unfortunately, there are still plenty of examples today of situations where the palliative care team is not called in early enough. This can be because of the resistance of the family and carers or because of the medical professionals involved.

Louise Mace supported her father, aged 81, as he died in a Sydney hospital in 2015. Her father had several conditions that were potentially going to kill him, among them cancer. When he entered hospital he was very frail and Louise's intuition told her he did not have very long to live. She asked a hospital-appointed social worker about getting palliative care involved.

'She reprimanded me, saying it was way too early,' said Louise. 'It was terrible, because I was left feeling as though I was pushing for Dad's death, which wasn't how I felt at all. Some time passed and, despite the social worker's refusal to help connect us to palliative care, as Dad's suffering worsened each day, I decided to approach the hospital's palliative care team directly. They were wonderful and immediately referred a specialist to meet with us.

'This new doctor quickly confirmed that Dad was dying and close to the end. As hard as it was to hear, it was an enormous relief to know that someone within the hospital system might help to do something about Dad's suffering.

'The palliative care doctor spoke frankly to us both about Dad's options. He explained that there would be no option for Dad to relocate to rehabilitation, as he was beyond it. Dad and I had both been hoping for this for weeks.

'That left two choices, the first, moving him from the hospital bed to a nursing home to wait for his imminent death, or the second, to go off all medication while still in hospital and let death happen naturally, sooner rather than "potentially" later. It didn't even occur to us at this time that there may have been a way to bring him home, nor did anyone mention, suggest or even counsel us on this.

'Dad chose the second option and within days of stopping just one of those many medications his body started finally completely shutting down. It felt like his body had been trying to die for such a long time and the fight for survival of each failing organ was exasperated by a whole raft of specialists, focused on correcting one problem, only to create another.

'One afternoon the social worker, for only the second time in weeks, revisited us at the door of Dad's hospital room and asked why a plan was not yet in place to move him out of the hospital bed and into a nursing home bed. I explained that Dad had chosen the support of palliative care. Incredibly, once again, I was challenged – on both the involvement of palliative care and whether the hospital's administration would even "allow" Dad to die in the hospital bed.

'Right up until his final hours, despite the fact he was dying and frail, Dad was still of sound mind and his hearing impeccable. I have no doubt that he heard that conversation. He died three hours later. The whole experience left me utterly raw and disillusioned.'

It's an example of something many healthcare professionals acknowledge: that despite the best intentions of major teaching hospitals to involve palliative care teams, it's often those within the hospital's system, even doctors, who can, even though well meaning, put obstacles in the way. Louise's disillusionment led her to form her business to support people in just this situation, New Way to Stay.

But attitudes are changing. Palliative care teams also recognise that providing the best medical support is not the same thing as simply being present to the dying person. So their care goals also involve engaging empathic listeners, such as volunteers and chaplains, in the work of 'being there' with the patient.

June was the primary carer for her husband, who she looked after at home as he died, until his hospitalisation at the very end.

She said it was a relief to be able to talk to the non-medical supporters in her husband's palliative care team because she could vent and say anything, without it becoming a documented action point for the team.

We come full circle and talk again about quality of life and the 'good death'

Today's palliative care environment, whether it's a hospice, a ward or just a room set aside in a small hospital, is ideally a place where traditional hospital rules are relaxed. Pets can visit, visiting hours are not restricted and people can have as many visitors in their room with them as they like. These are places where the dying can come and go on a short-term basis for palliative treatment of their terminal illness and then come in again when it is time to die. The overall aim is to manage the patient's symptoms to ensure good quality of life.

A comprehensive palliative care team will include:

- nurses

- palliative care specialists

- and/or general practitioners with a special interest in palliative care (particularly in remote areas where specialists are scarce)

- loss, grief and bereavement services

- volunteers

- allied health workers

- chaplains and pastoral care workers

- hospital staff

- community members

- oncology doctors

- complementary therapists.

If laid out as an illustration, this set-up would be a circle, with the patient, the family and the carer at its centre, and the team members arranged around them. Palliative care leaders believe a holistic and non-hierarchical approach works best. Palliative Care Victoria has the slogan, 'There is no super person who can meet all the person's needs'.

And a reminder, one thing we have to be careful about when we consider 'the good death', is that we don't turn the 'good' death into the 'normal' death. We have to be careful that a good death isn't redefined as a death outside a hospital, just as a way of cutting hospital costs. We also have to be careful about assuming that if more people want more pain relief, sedation, and sleep until they die, that this does not become the narrow interpretation of a 'good' death.

'A "good death" is not a term I like,' one palliative care specialist told me. 'Who decides what is a good death? It is more about a person dying the way they choose to die – dying their own death.'

Hospices and palliative care wards involve a wide range of care – medical assessments, then nursing assessments, then psycho-social and finally 'functional' assessments. Your nursing needs may be minimal with the initial diagnosis, but then they grow at a later stage of the illness. A psycho-social assessment asks: What are your emotional needs, your spiritual needs, your welfare needs and your family's needs?

Functional assessments are where occupational therapists become involved. Who would have imagined, only a short while ago, that occupational therapy would be an arm of palliative care? In fact, it is becoming an increasingly important one. Occupational therapy is a profession that aims to help people to do the everyday things that are important to them, as well as enabling them to do the things that they need to and want to do.

As the goal of providing better palliative care widens, hospitals everywhere have realised the best thing they can do is to help people live better while they die. Occupational therapists who work in the palliative care team will go out to homes and assess the person's environment so that they can live longer at home, to fulfil their goal of dying there.

For example, an extra handrail might be placed in a bathroom beside a toilet, so that when someone is frail, they've got something to grab when they want extra support, or they might change the way someone does something, such as the way they cook, so that they can keep doing it on their own for as long as possible. So far, that's not all that different to what occupational therapists do when they modify the home of someone who is frail and elderly for an aged care assessment.

But the palliative care occupational therapist makes sure that the required equipment, such as a hospital bed, is borrowed from the local hospital's pool of community resources and delivered to the home, and that the person and the caregiver know how to use it. This means that those caring for the patient at home will find it easier and the person who is dying is more comfortable. But a palliative care occupational therapist can also, for example, help them to complete activities one last time, or help them to gather the resources and energy to write reflections for those they love.

Most importantly, they will sit down with the palliative care patient and do an assessment of what their goals are and how they can keep achieving them.

Dr Kathrine Hammill, of Western Sydney University, who researches occupational therapy practice in palliative care, explained how occupational therapists help people to keep on living and participating in valued activities.

'While most people value spending time with friends and family, what is important to them can differ from person to person,' she said.

She went on to give the example of how one person might really want to be able to go for their regular cup of coffee at the local coffee shop with friends.

'The occupational therapist will help them organise their schedule and daily activities, so that they have enough energy to be able to do this, have identified if the coffee shop is accessible and make sure they have a wheelchair if needed. As the person declines physically and is no longer able to go to the coffee shop, the occupational therapist would look at alternative way for them to continue to have their coffee and friend fix.

'However, another person might have no interest in regular coffee dates at all. To them, the greatest goal is to be able to cook and have their family around for a regular family meal. Again, the occupational therapist will help them work out how to work with the limited energy they have left to keep doing this. For example, rather than shopping, and preparing, and cooking the whole meal, the occupational therapist might help the person to plan the recipes the family are going to eat, teach them how to shop online, or they might suggest different ways to prepare meals than what they are currently doing.'

Dr Hammill said: 'While some of the scheduling we do, and restructuring of activities might seem like common sense, our clients often don't feel like they can stop doing what they used to do – even if it is making them feel tired or sicker. In this way, our clients appreciate being taught new strategies and routines, as it helps them to stay active and involved, but in a new and different way. They also tend to feel less guilty when they can no longer continue doing something that isn't as meaningful, if we have had discussions around their participation and goals. This is really important as it enables them to both live their lives, and face death simultaneously.'

It's worthwhile getting rid of the notion that when you're admitted to the palliative care unit or hospital, this means death is near. You can be admitted to a palliative care hospital for a short time to get your symptoms under control or to give your family a break and then go home again. Of course, being in palliative care can be a powerful support close to death, but you can still go home.

Janine, with end-stage renal disease, was determined to die at home. By late in her disease progression, Janine had not defecated for two weeks and the palliative care team who visited regularly explained to Janine's chief carer, her daughter Janet, that Janine's impacted faeces was causing her a lot of her pain and discomfort and this could be avoided. But Janine kept refusing to have her impacted faeces cleared away.

Janet had promised Janine that nothing would be done to prolong her life unnecessarily. But Janet realised that Janine, who by now was experiencing confusion because of the toxins in her blood stream, was frightened that she would be given a treatment that would extend her life.

Many years before, Janine's grandmother had died quickly when her bowels became blocked at the end of a terminal illness. Janine had shared her memories about this with Janet, who realised this was the idea that was driving Janine's refusal to have treatment.

Janet explained this to the palliative care team. When something like this happens, team members have to balance what they believe is best for the patient against wishes that are clearly based on a misunderstanding. Their obligation is to protect the patient from errors of judgement that will interfere with their care, while at the same time respecting the patient's autonomy.

The team decided to admit Janine to a palliative care ward to have the treatment. Although this was against Janine's wishes, they realised she was refusing treatment because she misunderstood their intentions. They also recognised there was a level of cognitive impairment specific to her illness, which was affecting her judgement. The procedure was conducted, and Janine later said she was glad it had been carried out.

Janine's story illustrates something else: that you need to understand what your treatment involves if your decision not to accept it is to be acted upon. So it is valuable to go through the process of planning what you will be treated for and what you don't want to be treated for in advance – and accepting that to be able to do this, you will need good advice.

When accessing palliative care, think about these three questions:

- Palliative care is now common. But has it reached your community? You may find that palliative care is not well developed or easily accessible where you live – for example, in a remote area. Or that being fit and well, and not needing doctors until now, can mean you are off the healthcare service's radar, so you haven't been offered palliative care.

- What is the attitude of the team treating your medical condition to palliative care? At what point in the illness progression do they involve the palliative care teams from their own hospital? Do they bristle when palliative care is mentioned? Are they engaged with and positive about the service available, two floors down from them?

  ⪽ What is the palliative team like? Are they cranky and over-worked? Have they made you feel as though you belong? Do they accept your gender orientation, your clothing choices, your religious beliefs? Do enough people who are part of the service make enough effort to 'get' you, or if not you personally, your tribe?

Sometimes a lot of our anxieties about these things can be dispelled once we talk to people for the first time. A nurse might initially seem severe and old-fashioned enough to disapprove of your sexual orientation, until you discover that she threw a party for her beloved gay son when he got married recently. A Sri Lankan person may look Sinhalese, but turn out to be Tamil, just like you, or to be unaware of ancestral tensions between your peoples because their grandparents emigrated from Sri Lanka and vowed never to talk to their family about that country's ethnic strife.

Most professional palliative care workers will have had training in managing diversity. But as an empowered individual, entering any palliative care system or entrusting someone you love to it, you are entitled to ask questions about the standard of care. To be listened to and respected, you will need to be able to discuss the problem as objectively as your sadness and distress allows.

CHAPTER 11

The journey ends: we say the word 'die'

We learn to talk about how we will die, because
using words will both show others what we want
and dispel fear – ours and that of others.

After intensely planning we can sit back and reflect. We do not want to die but now we are less afraid. Life begins and life ends.

Newcastle journalist Jill Emberson has a terminal illness, having been diagnosed with ovarian cancer two years ago, when she was 58. Her oncology team predicted she is likely to live only between two and five more years. She is open about her terminal condition but she is also open about the fact that the way she is dealing with this is to refuse to believe she will die.

'My oncology psychologist told me it's a coping mechanism and its called "functional denial". It's a thing. I know I'm in denial but I know that if I wasn't, I wouldn't be able to get out of bed in the morning.

'Functional denial is a really useful coping mechanism where we know the reality of the situation: it's really unlikely you will live for lots of years. Functional denial allows us to go, "Okay, I know that that's going to happen but for now I can actually not be in that place. I can think about what I'm going to do and I can even have hopes and dreams for ten years time and twenty years time."'

These are words Jill has used in a podcast she has created called *Still Jill*. Jill's purpose in preparing the podcast is both to snub the disease by refusing to let it define her (her journalism–social justice agenda does that) and to raise awareness of ovarian cancer.

'The reason ovarian cancer research doesn't get the attention that it deserves is that most ovarian cancer patients don't live long enough to fight for public awareness the way, for example, breast cancer patients do,' she explained.

Jill's got her financial affairs in order, actively campaigns for ovarian cancer research, has had a beautiful big wedding to her partner Ken and has travelled through Spain with her beloved daughter, Malia. She has put herself, as best she can, in charge of one of the most challenging scenarios anybody could be asked to endure: getting the best out of each day, knowing you will die very soon.

'When you know your days are limited, you don't have time to have a bad day,' she explained in a passionate speech to the crowd gathered for her wedding recently.

Jill focuses on hope: the hope that she will live long enough to be placed on a clinical trial for a drug that can control her cancer. This is not as unrealistic as it sounds, since a number of recent clinical trials have shown strong promise in launching a successful cellular level attack on advanced cancers, just like hers.

Hope is important and it should never be taken away, even towards the end of someone's life.

A graphic being shared through end-of-life networks at the moment says: 'Rather than "We are withdrawing care", try: "We are switching the focus of care to concentrate on comfort." Rather than "There is nothing more we can do", try: "There is no treatment that will stop the progression of your disease."'

It goes on to say: 'Our words make a difference. Do we stop caring when someone is approaching the end of their life? Is there really nothing more we can offer them when a treatment is no longer working?

'We never stop caring. There is always more we can do. But if that's what we say, that's what people will hear.'

Dr Charlie Teo, an Australian brain surgeon, often does brain surgery in those cases where many of his colleagues wouldn't. He argues he is driven by hope – even though his critics accuse him of offering false hope. He says that while he encounters failures, his decision to do surgery when others would not has relieved suffering. His wider definition of hope than his peers has drawn much criticism, but his position is to respect the hope of his patients.

He once told a patient she would not have much quality of life if he operated on her brain tumour, since she would still be a quadriplegic afterwards, she still wouldn't be able to go for a walk along the beach, still wouldn't even be able to scratch her nose. She challenged him on this, arguing that for her, quality of life was to be able to impart wisdom to her growing teenage daughters. He operated and she lived on, retaining a quality of life by her definition.

Hope takes other forms too. Drop-in centres called 'Maggie's Centres' can now be found all over the United Kingdom. An important feature of these centres is their use of beautiful architecture to express hope. Set up by landscape designer Charles Jenks, they provide respite care in a beautiful environment.

Why talking about your death is important for you

Talking about your death makes it easier to deal with, in much the same way as anything else in life. If you want to change the colour your house is painted, even if you don't want to talk to your family about it or involve an interior designer, you are still likely to discuss options with the store that sells you the paint. But of course talking about death is very different to any other discussion you will ever have.

William had lung cancer and was dying at home. His wife of many years, Belinda, agreed to his wish to die at home and was determined to be at his side. They had talked this through with their general practitioner and all the relevant specialists, such as William's oncologist. His oncologist registered William for palliative care through the major teaching hospital in their local area and each fortnight the community palliative care nurses visited.

After a while it became clear to the nurses that Belinda was afraid. She explained to them how frightened she was to be in the house with William as he died, and apprehensive about the time afterwards, when she had to decide what to do with his dead body.

It became clear that although they appeared to be in harmony on how events would play out, they were not.

'Have you done any end-of-life care planning?' one of the nurses asked William.

He didn't think he needed an advance care directive, but agreed to do one now. Through the process of writing a plan, the couple were able to discuss a range of different scenarios. He then developed a better, more realistic idea of what Belinda could cope with, and together they changed some of their ideas.

When treatment offers are being considered, the first person to be consulted will always be you, the patient, because medical staff have a legal obligation to inform the patient and obtain their consent when any medical intervention is to take place. But sometimes this is not always possible.

Since complex decisions often need to be made at a time of either unconsciousness or physical vulnerability so intense that communication is very difficult, it is legal for someone to be nominated to help make those decisions. In the absence of anyone else, the hospital will look to the person identified as the next of kin.

This 'someone' will be a family member unless you have written down that you want someone else. Should your situation deteriorate rapidly, this person will be expected to negotiate for you right up until death. This means the ideal companion is someone who has the time to be involved in as many bedside discussions with nurses and doctors as possible, so they are well equipped to be a strong advocate at your death.

The reason families are involved is that it's assumed that if the patient is no longer able to have the conversations needed with hospital staff, the family are the ones most likely to know what you would have wanted, what forms of treatment and care you would and wouldn't have accepted. (And it can be that, quite deliberately, just one person is asked to represent the family in this discussion.)

This means you need to talk to your family about what you think you'll want. The more detailed the conversations are, the better. Most importantly, if these chats are done regularly, your family is kept up to date with any changes in your attitudes and thinking.

The earlier you bring your ideas into family discussions the better. These conversations may be difficult to start with, but they do get easier, and eventually become normal. They shouldn't be a one-off: 'Oh, we had that talk once...'

Having conversations at an early stage helps family members to know each other's views and to shape those views. Sometimes what we thought we might want changes after we think about it, talk with other people and gather extra information.

Healthcare professionals understand that these can be really difficult conversations for families to have. They also recognise that, particularly in our culture, which tends to avoid the subject of death, it is unusual for families to have discussed the issues fully.

But they would like to see this change, not for their sake but for their patients' sake.

Conclusion

As Indigenous Australian Anne Poelina says: 'Life is about energy in many forms. My people have a generic word, *liyan* or *lian*. *Liyan* is a word which can be translated as "feeling, emotion, spirit", your moral compass which you must learn to tap in to, to "read people and situations". It is a life force which enables people to feel their environment.

'Dying is about our journey of life, when we come to that moment whereby it is time to leave our physical and transform to the spiritual energy. It is all about relationships and connectivity. Connectivity not just to human but to non-human beings. As Indigenous people we continue to be in a deep relationship with nature and the environment. Before we are born we are connected to special places, through our *rai* or spirit being, we call *jardiny* or totem. This gives us a lifelong relationship with a particular animal or plant and teaches us about values and ethics which we must tune into with our *liyan*. Most importantly, this teaches us to have empathy for human and non-human beings.

'When we come to the time to die, to pass away, to travel back to the place of our spirit birth, if we have become a "good human being", then we can return and continue to do good in the world and stay connected to those who remain alive and on the earth.

Dying requires most importantly to be brave. If we are brave then we can be grateful for the life well lived.

'We are leaving behind those most close to us and we are going somewhere we do not know, so it can create a level of anxiety and insecurity and sadness, but also a level of happiness and hope. It is the final time for self-reflection. Did we do the best we could with the gift of life granted to us? Did we act in good faith, with integrity and honesty? Did we help others to reach their full potential as human beings? Most importantly, are we ready to tell those we love that we will be there for them, not to forget us, to hold on to the memory of us? That way, they will hold on to our life force and call us back into their dreams.'

The sad news of the death of another colleague from my early work days came through recently. Cynthia was a beautiful soul, a news journalist who despite the rough and tumble of our work always managed to hit the deadline with effortless grace. Her warm smile is what we remember.

In an earlier time, people would have gone to a bleakly solemn service for her. Maybe only those from her denomination would have attended. Word of her death would have taken time to filter out.

But a large group gathered to celebrate her life at an old Sydney pub that has escaped gentrification. Her family found a way to celebrate her life that was very spiritual, very moving and a genuine expression of Cynthia. Word of her death and memorial were spread to the old networks by the new social media, and people packed out the space to pay tribute to her, in a way that blended the old and the new, a contemporary replacement for a funeral.

And then, in the final stages of preparing this guide, Jenny C rang. Her mother Margaret was dying in a Sydney nursing home. The staff could not predict when Margaret would die but she had stopped eating and drinking four days earlier. Now her face had changed, becoming more sunken, and she was comatose.

'I have a feeling it might be tonight,' Jenny C ventured, as she wrestled with leaving the nursing home for a long-organised appointment.

Her siblings had gathered, two having flown from interstate not long before. The last goodbyes had now been said to those

Margaret had been waiting for. We agreed Jenny should trust her instincts: her mother would die soon.

Margaret was in a shared room with another elderly woman, Bev, and this was awkward for everyone. Every time a new person arrived to say goodbye, Bev turned up the volume on her television. Was she trying to cope with the noise and distress the situation was causing her? Or was she signalling that she wanted the family to have its privacy?

Surely we all have the right to our own space as we die? Maybe the nursing home would agree to the suggestion that either Margaret or Bev could be moved. Jenny C and her father decided to ask if this was possible.

Jenny C rang back the next day. Her mother had died shortly before midnight. Everyone in the family was there except for Jenny, her father and one sister. Jenny was disappointed that she had not returned late that night, despite her tiredness, and having dismissed her own intuition that her mother was close to death. But she felt she had been given the gift of her mother's presence and alchemy as she had spent the previous five days with her.

The nursing home had agreed to place Margaret in her own space to die with her noisy relatives around her. Fortuitously, another resident had died that morning, so that room became available. Three of her children and seven of her grandchildren had filled the room, talking and laughing among themselves and listening to her favourite Neil Diamond songs as they took it in turns to sit with Margaret and hold her hand. The overwhelming sense of everyone in the room was that Margaret died happy – taking her last breath as Diamond's signature song 'Sweet Caroline' played; surrounded by the family who had meant so much to her. They like to think that Caroline, Margaret's mother, took that as her cue to accompany her only daughter to the other side.

Maybe one day, we will have dying rooms in residential aged care facilities, the way we have birthing rooms in maternity hospitals now. Maybe all that needs to happen to make this standard is for enough of us to ask for it.

When I spoke with Jenny she had that strange, paradoxical emotion we had experienced when Mum died. Along with sadness, there was a kind of elation in the stories Jenny and her family told about their mother's death. It had been an intensely spiritual and uplifting experience.

We need to keep asking questions, keep pressing for changes to make death better. We can ask for changes on behalf of others. We can make little differences ourselves, inching along the needed changes.

We are always learning and human beings are nudging each other forward, in the most unexpected ways. If we are open to each other and what we can learn, either new or very old, like the ideas the medieval *ars moriendi* triggered in me, we will be transformed.

A little example, Patsy Healy was the director of WN Bull Funeral Services, Sydney, until she retired a little while ago. You'd expect her to be sombre but she's not. (She recently put a photo of herself on Facebook, just in from work, sitting fully clothed on a hot day in her grandson's bath.) She is another example of someone deeply connected to the cycle of life. She worked in the funeral business for years but she was shattered when she attended her own sister-in-law's funeral.

'Tracey just died in her sleep, tragically at the age of 42, leaving behind a ten-year-old and an eight-year-old girl and boy. It was in New Zealand and we were all in the house beforehand because there the funerals leave from home.

'The funeral director brought Trace to the house and we were all there and it was immensely sad. I remember my little niece and nephew stood at her coffin and the lining was all soft and satin, so they put their hands tucked down in between the soft fabric lining the coffin.

'They just stood there, running their hands along the soft fabric and they were just so comfortable about it, because the person in it was their mum.

'I came home here and ripped out all of the linings of our coffins and made them all soft and satin as well.'

It's not a big story, just a little one. But it illustrates how we human beings can take back from convention. All we need is the confidence.

And we can also be the ones who hold the notes on the art of dying well in our very own hands.

Acknowledgements

Thank you to my husband Michael, and to my daughters Marcella, Rachel and Madeline for their patience with this project, and the journey it has taken them on – sometimes difficult, sometimes confronting and without any assurance that they'll like where it lands them – and an additional thank you to Madeline for her technical nursing and medical advice.

Thank you to the Rices – my father Ken, who at 95 still lives a full life, and my surviving siblings Elizabeth, Cecilia, Damian and Deborah – just for being there, each in your own way. A special thank you to Cecilia, my identical twin. We have shared not only the twinship journey but a long friendship which continues, despite the changes this project has brought to us.

Thank you to Julian, who died too young, for being a big inspiration and for keeping me going, especially when the going got tough.

A special thank you to two people who were there right at the start of this experience, when I decided to take time off work to spend time at my mother's bedside as she lay dying. Wendy Bloom talked to me about what this would mean and gave me a number of spiritual resources to encourage me and set me on my path. My friend Sue Pullar gave very practical support, ready with a listening ear and sound advice as I checked in with her at various times through those long, hard days.

Thank you to Helen Carmichael, who showed me how to reclaim a creative life, and Kathryn Heyman, who encouraged me not to give up when I had a manuscript but no publisher.

Thank you especially to Dr Michael Barbato, Dr Richard Chye, Dr Keith Edwards, Professor Jane Ingham, Dr Bernadette Tobin, Dr Peta McVey, Adam Whitby and Professor Kate White for taking considerable time to share their knowledge of caring for the dying. Thank you also to Angela Boyd, who helped with suggestions on legal matters.

There are a number of Susans to thank. Susan Anthony gave me early support and John Watson's saying to live by: 'Be kind, for everyone you meet is fighting a great battle.' Susan Wyndham encouraged me to write this book and gave valuable guidance along the way. Sue Blanche believed in it and provided wonderful lunches in her warm kitchen, Susan Orr gave me a wintering place to stay in Denmark, and Susan Morgan gave me a bed in London when I researched there. Sue Bishop helped me with the medieval context for the *ars moriendi*, lending me her Sydney University History notes on Festival and Faith.

My cleaning lady, who wants to remain anonymous, came in and cleaned every Thursday through some of my darkest days and then turned out to be one of the best proofreaders anyone could wish for. She has also been a valuable support, a good listener and a very funny storyteller. Most importantly, she has become a very dear friend.

Thank you to Lisa Storrs, Marilyn Harris, Katherine Delaney, Melissa Fagan and Graham Wilson for their encouragement when I was first drafting my ideas. Thank you to Diana Giese for her early editing suggestions. Thank you also to Jenny Tabakoff, who took time out from a precious holiday to review early material that led to this book and to Hannah Killen and Julia Booth for implementing her changes.

A very big, heart-felt thank you to Corinne Roberts, my publisher, who gave me the courage and support that allowed me to transform a personal story into this more instructive one, with broader appeal.

Thank you to all the others at Murdoch Books, who helped bring this project to completion, particularly Lou Johnson, Justin Wolfers, Vivien Valk, Carol Warwick and editor John Mapps.

Nearly 150 people shared their stories and ideas, were interviewed or made other contributions to this book. I started out trying to name you all but I was frightened I would forget someone, so it didn't seem wise. Your stories, experiences and reflections were all very important to this book. I can't thank you enough for sharing these sometimes difficult and painful memories.

Thank you to those palliative care patients who I met through my volunteer work at Sydney's Liverpool Hospital. I am bound by confidentiality commitments not to name you or to discuss your cases, but you have given me so much spiritual strength and wisdom and I'm very grateful for this.

Thank you to Ellie-May, who provided a summery nook at her little cafe for me to nestle in safely while I dealt with my wintery subject.

Resources

You don't have to be an expert to be an inspirational companion to someone who is dying. Here are some resources to help you along your way.

1. COMPANIONING THE DYING

Putting family at the centre

To see one in the set of eleven of the medieval *ars moriendi*, go to https://www.britishmuseum.org/research/collection_online/collection_object_details.aspx?objectId=1459656&partId=1.

For a Buddhist guide to death, go to the Amitabha Hospice service website at http://www.amitabhahospice.org, a Buddhist guide to the stages of dying.

What is 'the good death'? Not everyone's notion of the good death will be the same: Swedish philosopher and ethicist Lars Sandman discusses this in his book, *A Good Death: On the Value of Death and Dying*, Open University Press, 2005.

For another discussion on this also see: What is a good death? A Q&A with Dr B.J. Miller, MD, at: https://goop.com/wellness/health/what-is-a-good-death.

For background on Dame Cicely Saunders, go to: www.bmj.com/content/suppl/2005/07/18/331.7509.DC1.

How to be there for someone who is dying

For insights into a correspondence course on midwifing death, see Dr Michael Barbato's site: www.midwifingdeath.com.au.

Doula is a Greek word for the woman who attends to another woman who is giving birth. The death doula is a person who attends to a dying person's needs at death. Doula services tend to involve someone who is paid. Find out more about the growing Australian profession of doula services at: australiandoulacollege.com.au.

Helen Callanan has developed a resource for professional doulas: http://preparingtheway.com.au/helen-callanan.

More on the role of family and friends at the bedside

To help understand the origins of adult sibling tensions, read *My Dearest Enemy, My Dangerous Friend, Making and Breaking Sibling Bonds, by Dorothy Rowe,* Routledge, 2007.

For an article on sibling rivalry, read 'Sibling Rivalry' by Professor David Isaacs, *Journal of Paediatrics and Child Health,* 7 November 2016, https://doi.org/10.1111/jpc.13385.

How to be a more effective companion

The work of Michael Barbato is easy to read and designed to help the layperson who is companioning the dying and the person who wants to be even more actively involved.

Reflections of a Setting Sun, by Michael Barbato (published by Michael Barbato), 2009.

Caring for the Living and the Dying, by Michael Barbato (published by Michael Barbato), 2010.

Midwifing Death, Michael Barbato, e-book, 2014. To find more on this resource, go to: www.midwifingdeath.com.au.

Conflict management

To find out more about the reasons for conflict in adult sibling relationships when a parent is dying, see: 'The Impact of Late-Life Parental Death on Adult Sibling Relationships: Do Parents' Advance Directives Help or Hurt?' by Dmitry Khodyakov and Deborah Carr. Author manuscript; available in PMC 2010 Aug 3. Published in final edited form as: https://www.ncbi.nlm.nih.gov/pmc/articles/PMC2914328.

For a newspaper columnist's perspective on this, see: 'Ageing Parents: Siblings Go to War' on the late Adele Horin's blog page 'Coming of Age', 4 March 2013, http://adelehorin.com.au/2013/03/04/ageing-parents-siblings-go-to-war.

The list of strategies for dealing with sibling conflicts at the parental death bed have been adapted from a list discussed by Lee Jay Berman, in his article '13 Tools for Resolving Conflict in the Workplace, with Customers and in Life' on the website www.mediationtools.com/articles/conflictres.html.

2. SPIRITUAL EXPERIENCES AT DEATH

'Soul' pain

The expression 'soul pain' was first coined by the Irish palliative care pioneer, Dr Michael Kearney. For insights into his philosophy, see http://medhum.med.nyu.edu/view/1484.

Michael Barbato wrote a powerful essay about 'soul pain' close to death in Elizabeth MacKinlay (ed.), *Aging, Spirituality and Palliative Care,* Haworth Pastoral Press, 2006.

To find out more about Compassionate Communities and the support they give to those companioning death, see: www.thegroundswellproject.com.

The spiritual dimension to dying

While the following book's scientific basis has been challenged, it describes a Christian neurosurgeon's experience of near death and after-life experience: *Proof of Heaven: A Neurosurgeon's Journey into the Afterlife,* by Eben Alexander, *Simon & Schuster, 2012.*

See also 'Spirituality and End of Life Care,' an essay by Scott E. Shannon and Paul Tatum, that appeared in the book *Care of the Dying Patient*, David A Fleming and John C Hogan (eds), University of Missouri Press, 2010.

According to the following article by C.D. MacLean, B. Susi and others, one-third of patients wanted to be asked about their religious beliefs during a routine consultation and two-thirds felt that physicians should be aware of their religious or spiritual beliefs: 'Patient Preference for Physician Discussion and Practice of Spirituality' in the *Journal of General Internal Medicine*. See this at: J Gen Intern Med, 2003 Jan, 18(1).

Is keeping patients' beliefs, spiritual and religious needs and supports separate from their care the best approach? For a discussion on this, go to 'The Importance of Spirituality in Medicine and its Application to Clinical Practice' by R. D'Souza in the *Medical Journal of Australia*, May 21 2007, 186(10 Suppl).

Dreams and deathbed visions

For a good, non-academic overview of deathbed visions, see: www.thoughtco. com/what-we-know-about-deathbed-visions-2594507.

Carla Wills-Brandon, *One Last Hug Before I Go: The Mystery and Meaning of Deathbed Visions*, Health Communications, 2000.

For a further exploration of the wide range of experiences at death, some of them beyond our scientific understanding, read *The End: The Human Experience of Death*, by Bianca Nogrady, Vintage Books, 2013.

Unconscious awareness

To help with an appreciation of what is known – and unknown – about consciousness and unconsciousness, read:

'Philosopher David Chalmers on Consciousness, The Hard Problem and the Nature of Reality', by Daniel Keane, ABC News, 7 Jul 2017, www.abc.net. au/news/2017-07-07/david-chalmers-and-the-puzzle-of-consciousness/8679884.

The Character of Consciousness by David Chalmers, Oxford University Press, Oxford, 2010.

For more on updates in thinking on consciousness and what was once referred to as the vegetative state, read 'Unresponsive Wakefulness Syndrome: A New Name for the Vegetative State or Apallic Syndrome', by Steven Laureys and others, BMC Med. 2010 Nov 1;8:68. Published online at doi: 10.1186/1741-7015-8-68.

Science writer Jesse Bering talks about unconscious awareness in his article 'One Last Goodbye: The Strange Case of Terminal Lucidity' in *Scientific American*, 2014, recounting a personal experience: https://blogs. scientificamerican.com/bering-in-mind/one-last-goodbye-the-strange-case-of-terminal-lucidity.

Dying alone

Pioneering death worker Elisabeth Kübler-Ross was one of the first people to describe our culture as 'death denying'. Some of her more particular theories are now seen as outdated, but Kübler-Ross's first book contains a set of searingly honest – if at times depressing – interviews with people who are dying. These interviews capture the loneliness of death. They also reveal why some people chose to be alone at death. Read *On Death and Dying*, by Elisabeth Kübler-Ross, Collier Books, 1969.

A happier read is *Insights on Death and Dying*, by Joy Ufema, RN, MS, published by Lippincott Williams and Wilkins, 2007.

Saying Goodbye – Stories of Caring for the Dying, by Megan Hender, ABC Books, 2004.

What Dying People Want – Practical Wisdom for the End of Life, by David Kuhl, ABC Books, 2005.

Where am I going?

For comforting spirituality, read *Chicken Soup for the Grieving Soul*, by Jack Canfield and Mark Victor Hansen, Health Communications, 2003.

For revealing insights into the spiritual growth of death, read: *Death: The Final Stage of Growth,* by Elisabeth Kübler-Ross (ed.), Prentice-Hall, 1975.

To understand the difference between a Catholic's and a Protestant's attitude to death, read Ray Galea's book, *Nothing in My Hand I Bring*, Matthias Media, 2012.

For an exposition of Catholic spiritual humility, go to Catholic Daily Reflections, Lord, I Am Not Worthy: http://catholic-daily-reflections. com/2018/06/29/lord-i-am-not-worthy-2.

The Lien Foundation's survey on integrating death and spirituality, Life Before Death, Death Attitudes Survey, Singapore, 8 April 2014, can be found at: http://lienfoundation.org/sites/default/files/Death%20survey%20 Presser%20Final%20-%20Combined_0.pdf.

Life review

For information about patient biography writing, see: www.svhs.org.au/ support-us/volunteer/sacred-heart-community-palliative-care-biography-service.

To find out what Palliative Care Victoria has to offer, see: www.pallcarevic. asn.au/families-patients/about-palliative-care-2/quality-of-life/recording-a-biography.

Sound Memories (recorded life stories): https://soundmemories.com.au.

For a discussion of the Christian tradition of reflection at the end of life, see Lars Sandman, *A Good Death: On the Value of Death and Dying*, Open University Press, 2005.

To consider the impact of the way we live on our death, read Bronnie Ware, *The Top Five Regrets of the Dying*, Hay House, 2012. Also see her blog at: https://bronnieware.com/blog/regrets-of-the-dying.

Managing fears and anxieties

Stroke and its associated vascular diseases are the leading of death and many who've had a stroke are afraid another one is coming. To help you manage your fears about stroke go to the Stroke Foundation (Australia) at: https:// strokefoundation.org.au.

And the Stroke Foundation, New Zealand, at: www.stroke.org.nz.

For support in dealing with fears about pain and dying, read *Your Life Matters* by Petrea King, Random House, 2005. Petrea founded the Quest for Life Foundation in 1989 to help people cope with the Ds – diagnosis, divorce, death, depression and disaster. To find out more about her Quest for Life program, go to: www.questforlife.com.au.

For a review of theories about patient anger, pain and suffering by medical experts that is very readable for a lay person, go to: 'The Angry Dying Patient', by Robert E. Houston, MD, in the *Primary Care Companion to the Journal of Clinical Psychiatry*, at: www.ncbi.nlm.nih.gov/pmc/articles/PMC181044.

3. MANAGING PAIN AND OTHER PHYSICAL PROBLEMS
Agitation

To help you better understand restlessness and its more extreme terminal agitation, go to: Hospital Patients Alliance: 'Terminal Agitation: A Major Distressful Symptom in the Dying', https://hospicepatients.org/terminal-agitation.html.

Another good explanation is: 'Dealing with the Dying Patient – Treatment of Terminal Restlessness', by Sonia Chand, in *The Pharmaceutical Journal*, 1 April 2013, www.pharmaceutical-journal.com/learning/learning-article/dealing-with-the-dying-patient-treatment-of-terminal-restlessness-and-agitation/11119466.article?firstPass=false.

When breathlessness and pain start to build

It may surprise you to find that most people do not experience intense pain at the end of life. For a further insight into this, see *The Conversation*: https://theconversation.com/no-most-people-arent-in-severe-pain-when-they-die-86835.

The Australian Palliative Care Outcomes Collaboration (PCOC) shows that pain management in palliative care is consistently improving. For more on this, see: https://ahsri.uow.edu.au/pcoc/index.html.

For more on the Clinical Excellence Commission's 'Last Days of Life Toolkit', go to: www.cec.health.nsw.gov.au/quality-improvement/people-and-culture/last-days-of-life.

To find out more about 'care pathways for the dying', go to: www.caresearch.com.au/caresearch/ProfessionalGroups/NursesHubHome/Clinical/EndofLifeCare/EOLCarePathways/tabid/1469/Default.aspx.

For WHO's discussion on the right to be free of pain, see: http://apps.who.int/medicinedocs/en/d/Js18774en. For WHO's discussion on the right to palliative care, see: www.who.int/mediacentre/factsheets/fs402/en.

Morphine and other opioids

For a good explanation of the opioid drugs, go to: www.drugabuse.gov/publications/drugfacts/prescription-opioids.

For detailed information about different ways of accessing opioids, go to: 'Controlled-release of Opioids for Improved Pain Management', by C. Martin and others, https://doi.org/10.1016/j.mattod.2016.01.016; or www.sciencedirect.com/science/article/pii/S1369702116000304#!.

For a fascinating history of opium and other drugs of addiction, read *Demons: Our Changing Attitudes to Alcohol, Tobacco, and Drugs*, by Virginia Berridge, Oxford University Press, 2013.

For an equally interesting review of the history of opium use in the USA read 'The Hidden Epidemic: Opiate Addiction and Cocaine Use in the South, 1860–1920', by David T. Courtwright, History Faculty Publications (1983) 3, http://digitalcommons.unf.edu/ahis_facpub/3.

For a reflection on Venice Treacle, see *Italy Out of Hand: A Capricious Tour*, by Barbara Hodgson, Chronicle Books, 2005.

Also see: The European Monitoring Centre for Drugs and Drug Addiction at www.emcdda.europa.eu/publications/drug-profiles/heroin.

For a discussion on improving breakthrough pain read: 'Breakthrough Medication in Unresponsive Palliative Care Patients: Indications, Practice and Efficacy', by Michael Barbato, Greg Barclay, Jan Potter and Wilfred Yeo, *Journal of Pain and Symptom Management*, December, 2018.

Did that last dose cause the death?

For more information about morphine and its use, see Palliative Care Australia's 'Facts about Morphine and other Opioid Medicines in Palliative Care': https://palliativecare.org.au.

And Hammond Care's '10 Things You Should Know about Morphine': www.hammond.com.au/services/palliative-care/10-things-to-know-about-morphine.

For more on morphine's addiction mechanisms, see: The European Monitoring Centre for Drugs and Drug Addiction, 'Heroin Drug Profile', www.emcdda.europa.eu/publications/drug-profiles/heroin.

For more on the discussion about double effect and its consequences go to: 'The Rule of Double Effect – A Critique of Its Role in End-of-Life Decision Making', *The New England Journal of Medicine*, 11 December 1997, vol. 337, no. 24, by Timothy E. Quill and others, reproduced at: www.worldrtd.net/timothy-quill-rule-double-effect.

The double effect rule and its application in nursing is also described very effectively in *Home Care Nursing: Using an Accreditation Approach*, by Patsy Anderson and Deolinda Mignor, Thomas Delmar Learning, 2008.

Palliative and terminal sedation

For more on this discussion see:

- 'Terminal Sedation: Source Of A Restless Ethical Debate', by Johannes J.M. van Delden, *Journal of Medical Ethics*, April 2007, 33(4), pp. 187–8, doi: 10.1136/jme.2007.020446 PMCID: PMC2652768 PMID: 17400612.

- 'Palliative Sedation, Physician-Assisted Suicide, and Euthanasia: "Same, Same but Different"', by Bert Broeckaert, *American Journal of Bioethics*, June 2011, 11(6), pp. 62–4, doi.org/10.1080/15265161.2011.577518.

For further clarification see Dr Robert Twycross's letter 'Regarding Palliative Sedation', *Journal of Pain and Symptom Management*, June 2017, Volume 53, Issue 6, pp. e13-e15, found at: https://www.jpsmjournal.com/article/S0885-3924(17)30044-1/fulltext.

A review of 134 articles and case reports of palliative sedations showed no hastening of death in terminal sedation: 'Palliative Sedation in Nursing Anesthesia' by Michael T. Wolf, *AANA Journal*, April 2013, 81(2).

Euthanasia, or assisted death

Do Australians support euthanasia? See *The Conversation*: https://theconversation.com/factcheck-qanda-do-80-of-australians-and-up-to-70-of-catholics-and-anglicans-support-euthanasia-laws-76079.

For a pro-assisted death argument, download the Better Off Dead podcast produced by Andrew Denton and the Wheeler Centre, in 2016, at www.wheelercentre.com/broadcasts/podcasts/better-off-dead.

To find out more about why Victoria adopted assisted dying legislation, go to: *Inquiry into End of Life Choices Final Report,* June 2016, https://www.parliament.vic.gov.au/file_uploads/LSIC_pF3XBb2L.pdf.

To read about an Oregon end-of-life doctor facing his own death, read 'When I Die: An End of Life Doctor Faces His Own End', by Brooke Jarvis, *Harper's Magazine,* January 2016.

4. WHAT WILL COMPANIONS SEE WHEN SOMEONE DIES?
The definition of death

The subtle details of brain stem death, including the fact that hair and fingernails still grow, is explained by Jake White in his article 'The Death of the Brainstem: Should Each Person be Permitted to Define Death for Themselves?' in *Ex aula, Research from the Hall*, a digital journal of St Edmund Hall, Oxford. It can be found at: http://mcr.seh.ox.ac.uk/should-each-person-be-permitted-to-define-death-for-themselves.

The UK has no legal definition of death. To read about the legal consequences, see the article: 'UK Court Accepts Neurological Determination of Death', by Joe Brierley, in *The Lancet*, 6 June 2015, 385(9984): www.thelancet.com/journals/lancet/article/PIIS0140-6736(15)61064-9/fulltext.

In Australia, the question of what constitutes death was asked after innovations in heart transplants were developed: 'Debate Over the Definition of Death, Does the Law Need to Change?' by Jill Margo, *Australian Financial Review*, 27 October 2015.

5. WHAT HAPPENS AFTER SOMEONE DIES?
Between death and burial

For guidelines on the respect you can expect to be extended to someone you love when they die, read 'Care National Consensus Statement: Essential Elements for Safe and High-Quality End-Of-Life Care', Australian Commission on Safety and Quality in Health Care, www.safetyandquality.gov.au/wp-content/uploads/2015/05/National-Consensus-Statement-Essential-Elements-forsafe-high-quality-end-of-life-care.pdf.

For a set of powerful essays on the spiritual aspects of death, including reflections on the time between death and burial, read *A Matter of Life and Death: 60 Voices Share their Wisdom*, by Rosalind Bradley, Jessica Kingsley Publishers, 2016.

For a guide to Jewish rituals at death, see 'A Guide to Jewish Death and Mourning Rituals' by Elon Gilad, *Haaretz*, 27 August 2015, https://www.haaretz.com/jewish/a-guide-to-jewish-death-and-mourning-rituals-1.5391768.

Viewing

On the death awareness website When You Die, Kate Braestrup shares the story of Nina, a five-year-old who insisted to her parents that she needed to visit her dead cousin and best friend Andy, a four-year-old, at a nearby funeral parlour: https://whenyoudie.org/a-child-shows-us-how-to-mourn.

US-based Everplans explains cultural reasons for requesting a viewing at: 'Religious Perspectives On Holding A Viewing, Wake, Or Visitation', www.everplans.com/articles/religious-perspectives-on-holding-a-viewing-wake-or-visitation.

Preparing a loved one's body for burial yourself

Elizabeth Knox transformed one of the saddest experiences anyone could be expected to endure into a social movement, Crossings. When her seven-year-old daughter died, she brought her home to prepare her for burial, as unheard of in the United States then as it is in Australia today. Read her story at: www.crossings.net/story.html.

The team who make up Crossings today have carried on Elizabeth's work, continuing to evolve a set of resources to help people take back control of the after death and burial experiences of those they love. For their general information go to: www.crossings.net/resources.html. The Crossings guide to handling the dead at home can be found at: http://crossings.net/resourceguide030109.pdf.

Read *The New Natural Death Handbook* by Nicholas Albery, Josefine Speyer and Stephanie Wienrich, Random House, 2009. Josefine has been involved in the death café movement in London.

The Natural Death Centre started in London, and its website can be found at: www.naturaldeath.org.uk.

The Natural Death Care Centre is an Australian organisation doing similar work: www.naturaldeathcarecentre.org. Information by the centre on how to care for a body can be found at: www.naturaldeathcarecentre.org/wp-content/uploads/2014/06/7.-Practical-Care-of-the-Body.pdf.

For information on the legal requirements about funerals and body disposal in New South Wales, see: www.health.nsw.gov.au/environment/dotd/Documents/disposal-of-bodies-ph-reg-2012.pdf.

Tender Funerals is a Port Kembla, New South Wales, cooperative and community movement, which has the goal of returning the rituals and rites of burial back into the control of families: http://tenderfunerals.org.

When more time is needed

To read a newspaper article about CuddleCots, go to: www.independent.co.uk/life-style/health-and-families/cuddlecots-invention-parents-stillborn-children-spend-extra-days-dead-babies-a7664916.html.

For an article on the funeral and coffin business in Australia, see: www.choice.com.au/health-and-body/healthy-ageing/ageing-and-retirement/articles/diy-funerals-and-coffins.

Embalming

To find out more about what rights you have in relation to keeping a body longer than usual, go to: www1.health.nsw.gov.au/pds/ActivePDSDocuments/GL2013_015.pdf.

Myths abound about the risk of infection from human remains. To find out some of the facts, go to the UK's Health and Safety Executive: www.hse.gov.uk/pubns/web01.pdf.

And also see: 'Dead Bodies and Disease: The "Danger" That Doesn't Exist', Funeral Consumers Alliance. https://funerals.org/embalming-myths-facts.

For a captivating book on the subject of funerary work, including the history of embalming, read *Smoke Gets In Your Eyes*, by Caitlin Doughty, Canongate, 2015.

To find out more about your rights, go to: the NSW Government's *Public Health (Disposal of Bodies) Regulation 2002*, at: www.legislation.nsw.gov.au/#/view/regulation/2002/643/full.

Notifications

For more details on who you need to notify about a death in New South Wales, go to: http://www.bdm.nsw.gov.au/Pages/deaths/deaths.aspx.

The Australian Government has also produced a checklist of the people and organisations you need to notify when someone dies. Go to: www.humanservices.gov.au/sites/default/files/documents/who-to-notify-checklist.pdf.

Probate

Each of the Australian states have their own forms for probate. The various court registries are very informative. For example, for more details on probate in Western Australian, go to: www.publictrustee.wa.gov.au/W/what_is_probate.aspx?uid=8745–7100–0334–7099.

For the NSW Supreme Court's guide to probate, see: www.supremecourt.justice.nsw.gov.au/Pages/sco2_probate/sco2_probate.aspx. For information about probate in the other Australian states and territories:

- ACT: https://courts.act.gov.au/supreme/services/probate_administration_and_foreign_grants
- NT: https://nt.gov.au/law/bdm/being-an-executor/taking-control-of-the-estate
- Queensland: www.qld.gov.au/law/births-deaths-marriages-and-divorces/deaths-wills-and-probate/estates/probate-and-deceased-estates

- SA: http://www.courts.sa.gov.au/RepresentYourself/ProbateRegistry/
  Pages/Home.aspx

- Victoria: www.supremecourt.vic.gov.au/wills-and-probate

For the Australian Tax Office's deceased estate checklist, see:
www.ato.gov.au/individuals/deceased-estates/deceased-estate-checklist.

6. THE UNEXPECTED DEATH

The role of authorities when death occurs

A flowchart showing how reports of deaths are handled can be found at:
www.aph.gov.au/Parliamentary_Business/Committees/Senate/Community_
Affairs/Completed_inquiries/2008–10/suicide/report/c03#anc4.

To hear Hugh Dillon explaining how the coronial system in New South Wales
works, go to: www.abc.net.au/radio/programs/conversations/hugh-
dillon/10557522.

Murder

For a book that explores how tragedy affects us personally, even those with a
national profile – and the potential for growth from it – read: *Any Ordinary
Day* by Leigh Sales, Hamish Hamilton Publishers, 2018.

For Cover Australia statistics, see: www.coveraustralia.com.au/blog/post/
common-causes-of-death-in-australia.

The Homicide Victims' Support Group, founded by the Cobby and Simpson
families after their experience of murder, can be found at: www.hvsgnsw.org.au.

To read insights into the psychological trauma suffered by 'co-victims' of
homicide, go to: 'Murder and the Long-term Impact on Co-Victims: A
Qualitative, Longitudinal Study' by Anton van Wijk, Ilse van Leiden and
Henk Ferwerda, *International Review of Victimology*, January 2017.

Rebecca Poulson's book about her experience is *Killing Love*, Simon &
Schuster Australia, 2015. To find out about her family's foundation aiming to
reduce the murder of children, go to: www.rebeccapoulson.com.au/poulson-
family-foundation.

Angelhands (https://angelhands.org.au) helps to find answers to the many
questions people have when they experience the violent death of those they
love. Founder Ann O'Neill has herself experienced this. In 1994, her
estranged husband murdered their two children and injured her leg so badly
it had to be amputated.

To get help with domestic violence in Australia, see www.1800respect.org.au,
or www.whiteribbon.org.au/find-help/domestic-violence-hotlines.

Accidental death

For an expert view of the accidental death of a loved one love affects those
left behind, see: 'Traumatic Bereavement: Basic Research and Clinical
Implications' by N Barlé, C.B. Wortman and J.A. Latack (2017), *Journal of
Psychotherapy Integration*, 27(2), http://dx.doi.org/10.1037/int0000013.

The Victoria state government has a detailed website offering help in supporting the bereaved: www.betterhealth.vic.gov.au/health/servicesandsupport/grief-how-to-support-the-bereaved.

SIDS deaths and the death of a child

The Red Nose organisation researches and offers advice on preventing cot death: https://rednose.com.au. Its contact point for dealing with grief and loss for SIDS is: https://rednosegriefandloss.com.au.

For background on SIDS and SUDI, see the Victorian Department of Health: www.betterhealth.vic.gov.au/health/healthyliving/sudden-unexpected-death-in-infants-sudi-and-sids.

For a book with wisdom and great insight into the death of someone you love, particularly a child, read *The Intimacy of Death and Dying: Simple Guidance to Help You Through,* by Claire Leimbach, Tryphena McShane and Zenith Virago, Allen & Unwin, 2009.

When older children die

To find out more about the Clown Doctors, go to: www.humourfoundation.org.au.

The National Association of Loss and Grief (NALAG), Tel: 1800 100 023.

Grieving mother Samantha Hayward writes, 'What I Wish Every Person Knew About the Loss of a Child': www.mamamia.com.au/death-of-a-child.

The preterm death

15 October is International Pregnancy and Infant Loss Remembrance Day.

Bears of Hope provides support after a death during pregnancy: www.bearsofhope.org.au/a/290.html.

Pregnancy Loss Australia can be found at: www.pregnancylossaustralia.org.au. It provides contact points for SANDS, and Pregnancy Birth and Baby. Both specialise in counselling for those who have lost their unborn baby.

Termination

For support in this situation go to the Pregnancy Support website: www.pregnancysupport.com.au/resources/after-abortion-support.

The Queensland-based service, Children by Choice, offers support for women considering or who have had a termination: www.childrenbychoice.org.au.

Suicide

Gotcha4Life is a social initiative encouraging men to reach out to each other, to start meaningful conversations and talk openly and honestly about their emotions. To find out more, go to: www.gotcha4life.org.

See the Beyond Blue website for advice on starting a conversation about suicide risk: www.beyondblue.org.au/the-facts/suicide-prevention/worried-about-suicide/having-a-conversation-with-someone-you're-worried-about.

To understand the grief of those dealing with the suicide of someone close, see: www.beyondblue.org.au/the-facts/suicide-prevention/understanding-suicide-and-grief.

For an extensive discussion of the mental health pressures on the LGBTI community, see: https://lgbtihealth.org.au/statistics.

Wings of Hope is an Australian organisation that provides support and education to the families, including children, bereaved by suicide: https://wingsofhope.org.au.

To help support someone coping with the suicide of someone they love, Standby Support After Suicide has a set of very good resources: http://standbysupport.com.au/resources. In particular, their sheet 'Why Is Grief after Suicide Different?' can be found at: http://standbysupport.com.au/wp-content/uploads/2017/11/Why-is-Grief-Different-2-Sides.pdf.

7. SAYING GOODBYE
The traditional ways – old and cosy

To find out more about the Victorian practice of funeral photography, see: 'Taken from Life: The Unsettling Art of Death Photography' by Bethan Bell, BBC News, 5 June 2016, at www.bbc.com/news/uk-england-36389581.

To find out more about death denial, read *The Culture of Narcissism: American Life in An Age of Diminishing Expectations* by Christopher Lasch, Norton, 1991.

After a short discussion on the importance of respecting cultural and religious differences, the following paper provides a very good list of the rituals and practices at the end of life of a range of different religions and cultures: 'Cultural Religious Competence', by Diana Swihart and James Hughes, October 2018, NCBI, www.ncbi.nlm.nih.gov/books/NBK493216.

To find out more about different cultures' funerary practices:

- Buddhism: www.thebuddhistsociety.org/page/buddhist-funerals
- Hinduism: https://cremationinstitute.com/hindu-cremation-funeral
- Islam: www.mfs.asn.au.

For a good, simple and respectful insight into Jewish care for a body, see the YouTube video, *Jewish Mourning Rituals: Caring for the Body*.

For information on Muslim burial rites, see: www.everplans.com/articles/muslim-funeral-traditions.

For a guide to non-Muslims attending a Muslim funeral, see: www.mbcol.org.uk/funeral-procedure/attending-a-muslim-funeral-a-guide-for-non-muslims/#.W4eQ9pMzYdU.

To find out more about Māori funerals, go to: https://teara.govt.nz/en/tangihanga-death-customs/page-1 and https://www.youtube.com/watch?v=UePasw8GEUk.

The new ways – bright and exciting

Funeral celebrants in Australia are prepared to be adaptive in creating funeral ceremonies – as long as you don't ask them to do anything illegal. They can be found through the Funeral Celebrants Association: www.funeralcelebrants. org.au/directory.

For a very different kind of funeral home, see HofmanDujardin's Funeral Ceremony Centre: www.hofmandujardin.nl/funeral-ceremony-centre.

For inspiration in ways to reimagine the coffin, see the movie and find out how to start a coffin club at: thecoffinclubmovie.com.

For images that might inspire you to think differently about your funeral go to www.pinterest.com.au/carolinevuyadin/green-burial-or-natural-burial.

For a recent article on natural burials in Australia, see: http://palliativecare. org.au/palliative-matters/natural-burials.

For support in finding resources for a natural burial, see: https://ndan.com.au.

For burial in an urn, with the purpose of growing into a tree, see: www. urnabios.com/urn, or www.capsulamundi.it.en.

For information on coffins made of recycled newspapers, go to: www. naturalburialcompany.com/ecopod.

Let's get down to tin tacks – or nuts and bolts, or wood and wicker

For information about conducting a family-led funeral, see Palliative Care Australia's 'Preparing a Loved-one's Body for a Family-led Funeral', http:// palliativecare.org.au/how-to-prepare-a-loved-ones-body-for-burial-and-have-a-family-led-funeral.

For information about the legal requirements (in New South Wales) to be buried and the permission-seeking process to be buried without a coffin, see: 'NSW Health Policy Directive Burials – Exemptions from Public Health Regulations 2012 for Community and Religious Reasons' at www1.health. nsw.gov.au/pds/ActivePDSDocuments/PD2013_048.pdf.

For a US approach to home-led funerals, see http://beholdingthethreshold. org/?page_id=363.

Living on

Here are two books that touch on these transcendent issues: *We're All Going To Die*, by Leah Kaminsky, HarperCollins, 2016, and *The End: The Human Experience of Death*, by Bianca Nogrady, Vintage Books, 2013.

If you want to embrace death more fully and bring it into your social and everyday life, at Death Cafe 'people drink tea, eat cake and discuss death. Our aim is to increase awareness of death to help people make the most of their (finite) lives'. Go to: http://deathcafe.com.

You can follow Caitlin Doughty's Order of the Good Death on Facebook. To find out more, go to: www.orderofthegooddeath.com.

8. COPING WITH GRIEF

For a little book on grief that has become a modern classic, read *Coping with Grief*, by Mal McKissock and Dianne McKissock, ABC Books, 1985.

For an article by someone grieving, see: 'The Things Nobody Tells You about Grief', by Sarah Parmenter, 26 September 2013: www.lifehacker.com.au/2013/09/the-things-about-grief-nobody-tells-you.

For an insight into grief as a springboard for personal growth, including the ideas of Richard Tedeschi and Lawrence Calhoun, go to: http://bigthink.com/philip-perry/this-turns-tragedy-into-an-opportunity-for-personal-growth.

A website, by the funeral company Invocare, to help people cope with grief can be found at: www.mygriefassist.com.au.

For suggestions on how we can support the bereaved more effectively, read: Doris Zagdanski, *Now That the Funeral Is Over*, Wilkinson Publishing, 2018.

For more on the Springvale Cemetery's Wellness Centre, see: https://sbc.smct.org.au/CentreforCareandWellbeing.

To find more of the gentle wisdom of the Reverend Graham Long, see: www.revgrahamlong.com.

The modern theories of mindfulness can be helpful in managing grief. For an introduction to mindfulness, read: Thich Nhat Hanh, *Present Moment Wonderful Moment*, Parallax Press, 1990.

To find out more about 'mindfulness', start with the work of Dr Russ Harris: www.actmindfully.com.au. His books, *The Happiness Trap* and *ACT Made Simple: An Easy-to-read Primer on Acceptance and Commitment Therapy*, explore his user-friendly ways of applying mindfulness.

For more on the philosophy and works of Eckhart Tolle, go to www.eckharttolle.com.

Men and grief

Beyond Blue's work with men: www.beyondblue.org.au/about-us/about-our-work/our-work-with-men.

To read about the grief of men, go to: 'Taking the Measure of a Father's Grief', by Glenda L. Thompson, *Nursing*, March 2002, 32(3), and 'Ancient Grief To Modern Mourning: A Father's Voice of Loss', by Rebecca Goss, *The Lancet*, 3 September 2016, 388(10048).

To find out how to start a conversation with someone that could help them manage their mental health issues, go to: www.ruok.org.au.

When to seek help with grief

For valuable insights into new approaches to grief, read: Christopher Hall (Director) (2014) Bereavement theory: recent developments in our understanding of grief and bereavement, Bereavement Care, 33:1, 7-12. https://www.researchgate.net/publication/271943193_Bereavement_theory_recent_developments_in_our_understanding_of_grief_and_bereavement

About pills versus therapy:

- 'Are Antidepressants and Psychotherapy Equally Effective in Treating Depression? A Critical Commentary', by Michael A. Sugarman, *The Journal of Mental Health*, 2016, 25(6), https://doi.org/10.3109/09638237.2016.1139071.

- 'Would Antidepressants Help During Grieving?' by Lindsay Abrams, *The Atlantic*, 11 February 2013, www.theatlantic.com/health/archive/2013/02/would-antidepressants-help-during-grieving/272996/.

- 'Talking Therapies Are Better than Pills, But You Have to Find the Right One', by Stephanie Merritt, *The Guardian*, 28 May 2014.

How to talk to those who are grieving

For more from Sarah Parmenter, see: www.lifehacker.com.au/2013/09/the-things-about-grief-nobody-tells-you.

For Paula Stephens' blog page Crazy Good Grief, which offers further insights into why we lose friends after someone dies, see: www.crazygoodgrief.com/why-we-lose-friends-after-a-loved-one-dies.

How to talk to people who are grieving: Doris Zagdanski, *Stuck For Words: What to Say to Someone Who is Grieving*, Wilkinson Publishing, 2017.

Examples of communities developing through the internet (unrelated to grief): stitch.net.

For those who want to find others who they can share a particular activity with, see: www.meetup.com/en-AU.

The grief of a child

What's Dead Mean? by Doris Zagdanski, Hill of Content, 2001.

Also, go to: The National Centre for Childhood Grief at: https://childhoodgrief.org.au.

The grief of an adolescent

For information for grieving adolescents about their friends' reactions, see Canteen: www.canteen.org.au/young-people/bereavement/changes-in-relationships.

The Catholic organisation, MacKillop Family Services, runs a program called Good Grief that provides evidence-based education programs to support children, young people and adults who have experienced significant change and loss in their lives. Information about it can be found at: www.mackillop.org.au/programs/good-grief.

9. PLANNING FOR YOUR OWN DEATH

Organising your paperwork

The best way to reassure yourself about your individual circumstances is to talk to the right person at your local police station – the crime prevention officer. (Do not ring the emergency-only number 000 to organise this.)

Although designed for working mothers, The Balance Careers website offers a good guide to organising your paperwork: www.thebalancecareers.com/how-to-organize-your-paperwork-3544878.

Who needs to be told when you die?

The Australian Department of Human Services has developed a handy checklist of who needs to be contacted when someone dies. This could be helpful for people living in other countries too. Find it at: www.humanservices.gov.au/sites/default/files/documents/who-to-notify-checklist.pdf.

To find out more about what happens to credit card debt after you die, go to Finder at: www.finder.com.au/what-happens-to-credit-cards-after-death.

Your will and power of attorney

The legal concept of 'capacity' is a tricky one. The NSW Department of Justice has created the 'Capacity Toolkit' to help people identify whether a person has the capacity to make their own decisions: www.justice.nsw.gov.au/diversityservices/Pages/divserv/ds_capacity_tool/ds_capacity_tool.aspx.

A very good article by the Law Society of New South Wales that discusses the social and medical implications of capacity can be found at: www.lawsociety.com.au/sites/default/files/2018-03/Clients%20mental%20capacity.pdf.

To see the issue from a healthcare perspective, go to: www.ncbi.nlm.nih.gov/pmc/articles/PMC5007079.

A classic case in which capacity was tested is *Banks v Goodfellow (1870) LR 5 QB*. It is still relied upon by courts today.

Contesting a will

Contesting wills is a busy area of law, with cases increasing. For articles on this trend, go to: Downie Stewart Lawyers of NZ, reporting on their website in 2017, www.downiestewart.co.nz/legal_news/blog/increase-in-claims-on-estates.

BBC Breakfast's Graham Satchell reports on UK trends: www.bbc.com/news/av/uk-34462706/government-figures-show-number-of-contested-wills-rising.

'Can a Person Be Left Out of a Will? A Look at Some Cases on Estrangement' by Matthew Hudspeth, Diamond Conway Lawyers, 26 November 2014: www.diamondconway.com.au/wp-content/uploads/DC-Article-MH-Can-a-Person-Be-Left-Out-Of-a-Will-141126.pdf.

For a wider history of family provision laws, see: 'Looking After One Another: Family Provision Laws in South Australia', February 2017, South Australian Law Reform Institute.

Power of attorney

For answers to questions about wills and probate go to: http://legalanswers.sl.nsw.gov.au/rest-assured-legal-guide-wills-estates-and-funerals/when-someone-dies.

What you need to write in a will varies slightly from one country to another – but not much. For advice on writing a will, google 'writing a will' and restrict the search to your own country.

For information about probates and wills in New Zealand go to: www.govt.nz/browse/family-and-whanau/death-and-bereavement/probate-and-wills.

For information about power of attorney and alternatives to family in this role, go to: www.tag.nsw.gov.au/what-is-a-power-of-attorney.html.

New Zealand and all Australian states have public trustees and guardians that can be appointed when someone has no one else for these roles. For example, in New South Wales, go to: www.tag.nsw.gov.au/easy-and-flexible-planning-ahead.html.

Next of kin

South Australia's Legal Services Commission explains next of kin at https://lawhandbook.sa.gov.au/ch36s03s08.php.

For more information on 'next of kin' registration, for those who live alone go to: www.cityofsydney.nsw.gov.au/_data/assets/pdf_file/0004/103369/NSW-Police-next-of-kin-registration-form.pdf.

Social media

To find Facebook's discussion about how to manage an account after someone has died, see: www.facebook.com/help/150486848354038.

For more detail on Facebook's memorialised accounts, see: www.facebook.com/help/1506822589577997.

For an article on social media etiquette around death, see: https://mashable.com/2017/04/08/facebook-etiquette-grief.

Reduce, reuse, recycle – even in death planning

To find out more about Swedish death cleaning, see Margareta Magnusson's *Time* magazine article: http://time.com/5063275/death-cleaning.

And her book: Margareta Magnusson, *The Gentle Art of Swedish Death Cleaning*, Scribner, 2018.

Also worth reading is anti-clutterer Peter Walsh's approach to letting go: www.peterwalshdesign.com/2016/11/11/let-it-go.

Marie Kondo's *The Life-Changing Magic of Tidying Up: The Japanese Art of Decluttering and Organizing*, Penguin Random House, 2015, is an extreme example of the art of decluttering.

Why there has never been a better time to be alive – or to die

To read about an example of new technology providing a social benefit for the dying, read how Royal Trinity Hospice is completing people's bucket lists with VR: 'VR for Good Week: When Your Last Wishes Require Only the Right App', by Husain Sumra, *Wareable*, 29 November 2018, www.wareable.com/vr/bucket-list-vr-6777.

Do you believe the person you love is getting the level of care they should be? The National Consensus Statement: Essential Elements For Safe And High-Quality End-of-Life Care, Australian Commission on Safety and Quality in Health Care, Commonwealth of Australia, 2015 has recommendations on how your hospital should deliver safe and high quality end-of-life care.

Here is the clinical governance manual of the NSW Health Department: www.health.nsw.gov.au/policies/manuals/Documents/corporate-governance-compendium-section5.pdf. This helps you to understand what the hospital expects of its staff. All health departments will have similar documents.

Your substitute decision-maker

To find out about substitute decision-making in Australia, go to the End of Life Directions in Aged Care (ELDAC) website at: www.eldac.com.au/Portals/12/Documents/Factsheet/Legal/Toolkit%20-%20Substitute%20 decision-making_v3.pdf.

To find out more about substitute decision-making across Australia, go to Queensland University of Technology's End of Life Law in Australia site at: https://end-of-life.qut.edu.au/stopping-treatment.

For a good review of substitute decision-making from a medical perspective go to: www.aci.health.nsw.gov.au/networks/eci/clinical/clinical-resources/clinical-tools/aged-care/capacity-substitute-decision-makers-consent.

For more on enduring guardians in New South Wales, see: www.tag.nsw.gov.au/enduring-guardianship.html and www.localcourt.justice.nsw.gov.au/Pages/legal_problem/family_children/enduring_guardianship.aspx.

For another perspective on this go to: www.legalaid.nsw.gov.au/publications/factsheets-and-resources/speaking-for-myself/appointing-an-enduring-guardian.

For information on the role in Western Australia, go to: www.publicadvocate. wa.gov.au/_files/epg_kit.pdf.

Your advance care directive

To see statistics on the take-up of advance care directives in Australia and other countries, go to: www.parliament.nsw.gov.au/researchpapers/Documents/advance-care-directives/Advance%20Care%20Directives.pdf.

For insights into the difficulty a heroic but ill-judged request for futile treatment causes, read 'A Wife Ask for Futile Therapy for Her Husband, a "Fighter": How to Respond' by Paul Helft, MD, Cancer Network, *Journal of Oncology*, 2 March 2013, www.cancernetwork.com/ethics-oncology/wife-asks-futile-therapy-her-husband-fighter-how-respond.

'The Impact of Advance Care Planning on End-Of-Life Care in Elderly Patients: Randomised Controlled Trial', *British Medical Journal*, March 2010, 340, doi: https://doi.org/10.1136/bmj.c1345.

A good resource that lays out a very full discussion, with many helpful resources for advance care planning – and not just for the elderly – can be found at the End of Life Directions for Aged Care website: www.eldac.com.au.

Making your own directive

Read: *A Good Life to the End: Taking Control of Our Inevitable Journey through Ageing and Death*, by Professor Ken Hillman, Allen & Unwin, 2017.

Also worth reading is *Conflict Resolution in End of Life Treatment Decisions: A Rapid Review*, by Ken Hillman and Jack Chen, The Sax Institute and NSW Health, 2008.

'Reflections on Dying from an Intensive Care Physician', by Ken Hillman, *The Conversation*, 16 November 2012: http://theconversation.com/reflections-on-dying-from-an-intensive-care-physician-10082.

In Australia, to work with an advance care directive specific to your state, you can also go directly to the Advance Care Planning Australia website at: www.advancecareplanning.org.au.

For more information on New Zealand's advance directive planning, go to: www.nzma.org.nz/patients-guide/advance-directive.

Your health

For insight into the mismatch between the reality and the perception of the state of health of many elderly people today, read: *A Palliative Approach for People with Declining Health Living in Hostel Accommodation: The State of Play*, by Peta McVey, Sydney University (thesis), 2011.

For insights into the mismatch between professional perceptions and reality, read: 'Dear Life: On Caring for the Elderly' by Karen Hitchcock, *Quarterly Essay*, March 2015.

Your frailty index – a reliable guide to mortality

To understand more about the implications in the elderly, read: 'Who Are The Frail Elderly?', *Quarterly Journal of Medicine*, New Series 68, No. 255, July 1988.

To view the Clinical Frailty Scale, go to: http://camapcanada.ca/Frailtyscale.pdf.

To view the Edmonton Frail Scale, go to: www.nscphealth.co.uk/edmontonscale-pdf.

Your diseases checklist

To get a very good sense of just how many diseases people had when they died, go to: www.bhi.nsw.gov.au/__data/assets/pdf_file/0004/356530/report-insights-return-to-acute-care-following-hospitalisation-2017.pdf.

To find out more about death from each different cancer, go to the Australian government's Cancer in Australia website at: https://canceraustralia.gov.au.

The leading causes of death figures for Australia are updated every year. To find out more about the leading causes of death in Australia in 2017, read the Australian Bureau of Statistics sheet 3303.0 – Causes of death in Australia, 2017.

10. WHERE WILL I DIE?

Dying in hospital

Is your surgeon a member of the Royal Australasian College of Surgeons, the surgeons' professional body? Any surgeon who is a member of the College routinely submits him or herself to professional auditing of their surgical operations.

Is your hospital accredited with the Australian Council on Healthcare Standards (ACHS)? Hospitals with this accreditation have to be able to prove that their surgeons go through these auditing processes.

For more information on getting a second opinion in New South Wales (other territories and states will have similar documents), see: www1.health.nsw.gov.au/pds/ActivePDSDocuments/PD2011_022.pdf.

The right to a second opinion is clarified in the following NZ government document: www.health.govt.nz/our-work/hospitals-and-specialist-care/elective-services.

For insights into clinical governance and patient liaison mechanisms, go to: www.health.nsw.gov.au/policies/manuals/Documents/corporate-governance-compendium-section5.pdf.

To learn more about the auditing processes for surgeons, go to the Department of Professional Standards Royal Australasian College of Surgeons College of Surgeons: www.surgeons.org/policies-publications/publications:

- Surgical Audit and Peer Review
- Surgical Competence and Performance.

For a good explanation by Australian doctors of your right to say no to medical treatment at the end of life, published in *The Medical Journal of Australia*, go to: www.mja.com.au/journal/2014/201/8/consent-capacity-and-right-say-no.

A writer who addresses these issues from the point of view of the doctor but with a good sense of how non-medical people would see the issues is British doctor Peter Kaye. His book is *Notes From a Hospice: A Personal Summary of Palliative Care*, EPL Publication, 2015.

For discussions about dying in hospital, read 'Non-beneficial Treatments in Hospital at the End of Life: A Systematic Review on Extent of the Problem', by Melissa Cardona-Morrell and others, *International Journal for Quality in Health Care*, 27 June 2017, http://dx.doi.org/10.1093/intqhc/mzw060.

'Acute Hospital-Based Services Used by Adults during the Last Year of Life in New South Wales, Australia: A Population-based Retrospective Cohort Study,' by David E. Goldsbury, and others, BioMedCentral, 2014.

For an insight into what happens in a typical hospital emergency department, read *Emergency: Real Stories from Australia's Emergency Department Doctors,* edited by Dr Simon Judkins, Michael Joseph, 2015.

For an insight into how modern hospitals and health professionals are approaching the complex question of which patients are most at risk going into surgery, go to: 'Clinical Review: How Is Risk Defined in High-risk Surgical Patient Management?' by Owen Boyd and Neil Jackson, *Critical Care*, 9 February 2005, 9(4), doi: 10.1186/cc3057.

Dying in an ambulance

For an insight into the legal issues for paramedical staff, see https://emergencylaw.wordpress.com/2017/03/06/a-straight-forward-answer-to-a-dnr.

For an internet Q&A addressing some of the knotty questions around this, go to: www.quora.com/If-someone-calls-an-ambulance-for-you-when-youre-unconscious-are-you-responsible-for-the-bill-even-though-you-were-picked-up-against-your-will.

Living with cancer

For an update on the dramatic improvement in breast cancer treatment, go to: www.wcrf.org/int/cancer-facts-figures/data-specific-cancers/breast-cancer-statistics, World Cancer Research Fund GB.

To read about the vaccines treating cervical cancer and anal cancer, see https://en.wikipedia.org/wiki/HPV_vaccine.

To read about vaccines being used to treat melanomas go to: The Melanoma Research Alliance, www.curemelanoma.org/patient-eng/melanoma-treatment/therapies-in-development/melanoma-vaccines.

For an extensive review of early detection research, see 'Fulfilling the Potential of Cancer Prevention and Early Detection' by S. Curry and others, Institute of Medicine (US) and National Research Council (US) National Cancer Policy Board Washington (DC): National Academies Press (US), 2003, www.ncbi.nlm.nih.gov/books/NBK223925.

When you're dying from your cancer

About cancer pain management: 'Management of Pain in the Cancer Patient', by Michael Ashburn and others, *Journal of Anesthesia & Analgesia*, February 1993, 76(2).

For the role of anaesthetics in cancer pain, see 'Role of Anesthesiology in Pain Medicine and Palliative Care Treatment in German Hospitals: Survey of Department Heads of Anesthesiology on Treatment Structures', by J. Erlenwein and others, *Anaesthetist*, August 2017, 66(8), doi: 10.1007/s00101–017–0309–1.

'Palliative Medicine. Fifth Pillar of Anaesthesia Departments', by C.H. Wiese and others, *Anaesthetist*, March 2009, 58(3), doi: 10.1007/s00101–009–1543-y.

Hope

Although not for everyone, the scientifically inclined layperson can read about new developments in cancer treatment online. Go to https://academic.oup.com/annonc.

'Recent Advances in Cancer Immunotherapy', by Weijing Sun, *Journal of Hematology and Oncology*, 24 April 2017, https://doi.org/10.1186/s13045–017–0460–9.

See press releases announcing new cancer immunotherapies being offered at affordable prices at www.medianet.com.au/releases/139546.

To read about the scientific breakthroughs in breast cancer and melanoma treatment respectively, go to:

- 'Doctors Hail World First as Woman's Advanced Breast Cancer Is Eradicated', by Ian Sample and Jessica Glenza, *The Guardian*, 5 June 2018.

- Weekly Dose: 'Keytruda May Be a Miracle Cancer Drug, but Can Those Who Need it Afford it?', by Nicholas Huntington, *The Conversation*, 11 April 2018, https://theconversation.com/weekly-dose-keytruda-may-be-a-miracle-cancer-drug-but-can-those-who-need-it-afford-it-74757.

Elderly and frail – in hospital again

To read about how hospitals are expected to manage a situation where you are in decline and your illness is becoming terminal, go to: Care National Consensus Statement: Essential Elements for Safe and High-Quality End-Of-Life Care, Australian Commission on Safety and Quality in Health Care: www.safetyandquality.gov.au/wp-content/uploads/2015/05/National-Consensus-Statement-Essential-Elements-forsafe-high-quality-end-of-life-care.pdf.

For the concerns of a clinician about this period, read: 'Dear Life: On Caring for the Elderly' by Karen Hitchcock, *Quarterly Essay*, March 2015.

See also: 'Hospital and Emergency Department Use in the Last Year of Life: A Baseline for Future Modifications to End-Of-Life Care,' by Lorna Rosenwax and others, *Medical Journal of Australia*, 2011, 194(11).

Moving to palliative care

Palliative Care Australia has published a booklet of typical questions to ask your palliative care team: *Asking Questions Can Help: An Aid for People Seeing the Palliative Care Team*, http://palliativecare.org.au/wp-content/uploads/2015/05/PCA002_Asking-Questions-Can-Help_FA.pdf.

For a discussion on futile care – a delicate issue internationally – see: 'Postoperative Futile Care: Stopping the Train When the Family Says "Keep Going",' K. Francis Lee, Tufts University School of Medicine, Springfield, https://doi.org/10.1016/j.thorsurg.2005.06.005.

To see an Australian study on the reasons for continuing treatment doctors know it will make no difference, read: 'End of Life Care in Queensland Admission to Acute Hospitals Near the End of Life' by Taku Endo and others, *StatBite*, 61, August 2014, at: www.health.qld.gov.au/__data/assets/pdf_file/0019/144712/statbite61.pdf.

And for an international paper dealing with the same issue, go to: 'Reasons Doctors Provide Futile Treatment at the End of Life: A Qualitative Study', by Lindy Willmott and others, *Journal of Medical Ethics*, August 2016, 42(8).

Also read:

- 'Dying Well', by Hal Swerissen, and Stephen Duckett, Grattan Institute, September 2014.

- 'What Can We Do to Help Australians Die the Way they Want to?' by Hal Swerissen and Stephen Duckett, *Medical Journal of Australia*, 2015, 202(1).

Not for resuscitation

For a good explanation by Australian doctors of your right to say no to medical treatment at the end of life, published in *The Medical Journal of Australia*, go to: www.mja.com.au/journal/2014/201/8/consent-capacity-and-right-say-no.

Dying at home

For research from a number of countries on the numbers of people who would like to die at home go to:

- The USA (71%): www.kff.org/report-section/views-and-experiences-with-end-of-life-medical-care-in-the-us-findings.

- The UK (66%): Age UK, 'End of Life Evidence Review', 2013, by Susan Davidson and Tom Gentry, says 66% of English people would prefer to die at home: www.ageuk.org.uk.

- Canada (75%): www.pharmacists.ca/news-events/cpha-blog/canadians-want-palliative-care-but-dont-know-how-to-get-it states that 75% of Canadians would prefer to die at home.

For more information about how to achieve palliative care at home go to: https://palliativecare.org.au. In addition, ring the switchboard of your nearest teaching hospital and ask to be put through to the palliative care team.

Dying 'better' in an aged care facility

For a definition of aged care facilities and further information on them, go to: https://agedcare.health.gov.au/programs-services/residential-care/about-residential-care.

For a discussion on people dying in aged care facilities in New Zealand, read: 'Where Do People Die? What Proportion Ever Uses Residential Aged Care?' by Joanna Broad, Michal Boyd, Martin Connolly in Freemasons' Department of Geriatric Medicine, University of Auckland, Conference for General Practice, Auckland, September 2011.

End-of-life problem areas in aged care facilities

For encouraging signs that the Australian government is thinking more about palliative care, go to: The Senate Community Affairs References Committee – Palliative Care in Australia, October 2012, www.aph.gov.au/Parliamentary_Business/Committees/Senate/Community_Affairs/Completed_inquiries/2010-13/palliativecare/report/index.

To read the government's (slightly disappointing) response, go to: Australian Government – Response to the Senate Community Affairs References Committee Report: Palliative Care in Australia, May 2016, www.health.gov.au/internet/main/publishing.nsf/Content/DFEC63B58 074ACC6CA25805600045F2E/$File/Government%20Response%20to%20 Palliative %20Care%20Senate%20Inquiry.pdf.

For information on the end-of-life problems in aged care facilities: 'Reforming Australia's Aged Care System: Are We There Yet? Social Policy' by Leah Ferris, Parliamentary Library, www.aph.gov.au/About_Parliament/Parliamentary_Departments/Parliamentary_Library/pubs/BriefingBook44p/AgedCare.

For information about palliative care in Australian aged care facilities, see: www.aihw.gov.au/palliative-care/residential-aged-care.

For nurses' perspectives of palliative care in dementia patients, see: 'Pain Relief at the End of Life: Nurses' Experiences Regarding End-of-Life Pain Relief in Patients with Dementia' by Hanna Brorson and others, *Pain Management Nursing*, March 2014, 15(1) (March), www.painmanagementnursing.org/article/S1524–9042(12)00173–7/pdf.

Dying in hospices and palliative care units

For working together to deliver the best palliative care, go to: 'Primary Health Care and End of Life' Palliative Care Australia, https://palliativecareqld.org.au/wp-content/uploads/2013/01/PCA-Primary-Health-Care-and-End-of-Life-Position-Statement.pdf.

For a discussion on family distress, go to: 'The Assessment and Management of Family Distress during Palliative Care' by Talia Zaider and David Kissane, *Current Opinion in Supportive and Palliative Care*, March 2009, 3(1), doi: 10.1097/SPC.0b013e328325a5ab PMCID: PMC5557503NIHMSID: NIHMS817421PMID: 19365164.

Talking about death with hospital staff

'Straddling the Fence: ICU Nurses Advocating for Hospice Care', by D. Borowske, *Critical Care Nursing Clinical Journal*, North America March 2012, 24(1), doi: 10.1016/j.ccell.2012.01.006.

'Extent and Determinants of Error in Doctors' Prognoses in Terminally Ill Patients: Prospective Cohort Study' by Nicholas Christakis and Elizabeth Lamont, *British Medical Journal* 320, no. 7233.

Do you need an independent advocate?

Are professional patient advocates really needed in Australia? See: http://medicalrepublic.com.au/patient-advocates-private-affair/7790.

An example of a patient advocacy service in Australia is that of Dorothy Kamaker: www.patientadvocates.com.au/index.html.

See also the Australian service New Way To Stay, founded by Louise Mace: newwaytostay.com.au.

We come full circle and talk again about quality of life and the 'good death'

This article explores the good death: 'The "Problematisation" of Palliative Care in Hospital: An Exploratory Review of International Palliative Care Policy in Five Countries' by J Robinson and others, *BMC Palliative Care*, 15(64), doi:10.1186/s12904–016–0137–0.

For information on how occupational therapists can help you, read the ebook: *Helping You To Live Until You Die – A Guide for People with a Life-limiting Illness, their Family and Friends*, by Katherine Hammill, at: http://pub.lucidpress.com/helping-you-live-until-you-die/#_0.

For more on palliative care in Australia, see the Palliative Care Australia website: http://palliativecare.org.au.

For policies that have been developed in New Zealand, see: www.health.govt. nz/our-work/life-stages/palliative-care.

11. THE JOURNEY ENDS: WE SAY THE WORD 'DIE'

The *Still Jill* podcast can be found at: www.abc.net.au/radio/programs/ still-jill.

To see Dr Charlie Teo discuss hope in terminal patients, see 'False Hope? There's No Such Thing' on YouTube: www.youtube.com/ watch?v=ZeC4dHVMCfU.

For more on Dr Charlie Teo's work and why he is so committed to 'giving hope', read *Life In His Hands,* by Susan Wyndham, Picador, 2009.

To find out more about Maggie's Centres, go to: www.maggiescentres.org.

Thich Nhat Hanh, *Present Moment Wonderful Moment*, Parallax Press, 1990.

Christopher Hitchens explains the changed meaning of his days very eloquently in his book, *Mortality*, Hachette, 2012.

Why talking about your death is important for you

If you find it difficult to talk about the way you want to die, or you believe those who you need to have the conversation with will find it difficult, Palliative Care Australia has a great document: 'Dying to Talk Discussion Starter': http://dyingtotalk.org.au/discussion-starter.

Also, we can read about what death can teach us. Read Frank Ostaseski's *The Five Invitations: Discovering What Death Can Teach Us About Living*, Pan Macmillan, 2017.

To understand more about the places where death now occurs in Australia, and its implications, particularly in relation to residential aged care facilities, see: the Australian Institute of Health and Welfare website (www.aihw.gov. au), and find the 2016 series on:

- residential aged care in Australia

- palliative care in Australia

- use of aged care services before death, data linkage series, Number19.

For the UK, this NHS guide helps you shape how to talk to your family about your end of life care: www.nhs.uk/Planners/end-of-life-care/Pages/starting-to-talk-about-your-illness.aspx.

Dying Matters is a UK organisation committed to starting these conversations: www.dyingmatters.org/overview/need-support.

Index

Note: In this index, the term 'family' follows the definition applied in the text; that is, 'Those who are closest to the patient in knowledge, care and affection. This may include the biological family, the family of acquisition – related by marriage or contract – and the family and friends of choice.'